Urban Planning

FOR

DUMMIES®

by Jordan Yin, PhD

John Wiley & Sons Canada, Ltd.

Urban Planning For Dummies®

Published by
John Wiley & Sons Canada, Ltd.
6045 Freemont Blvd.
Mississauga, ON L5R 4J3
www.wiley.com

For general information on John Wiley & Sons Canada, Ltd., including all books published by John Wiley & Sons, Inc., please call our warehouse, Tel 1-800-567-4797. For reseller information, including discounts and premium sales, please call our sales department, Tel 416-646-7992. For press review copies, author interviews, or other publicity information, please contact our marketing department, Tel 416-646-4584, Fax 416-236-4448.

For technical support, please visit www.wiley.com/techsupport.

Wiley publishes in a variety of print and electronic formats and by print-on-demand. Some material included with standard print versions of this book may not be included in e-books or in print-on-demand. If this book refers to media such as a CD or DVD that is not included in the version you purchased, you may download this material at http://booksupport.wiley.com. For more information about Wiley products, visit www.wiley.com.

Library and Archives Canada Cataloguing in Publication

Yin, Jordan, 1970–

    Urban planning for dummies / Jordan Yin.

Includes index.

Issued also in electronic formats.

ISBN 978-1-118-10023-3

    1. City planning. 2. Land use—Planning. I. Title.

HT166.Y56 2012   307.1'216   C2011-908072-9

ISBN 978-1-118-10168-1 (ebk); 978-1-118-10166-7 (ebk); 978-1-118-10167-4 (ebk)

Printed in the United States

1 2 3 4 5 RRD 15 14 13 12 11

WILEY

About the Author

Jordan Yin, PhD, AICP, is a native of Cleveland, Ohio, and his experience growing up in this great American city inspired him to pursue a career as an urban planner. He has also lived in Pittsburgh, Pennsylvania; Buffalo, New York; and Kalamazoo, Michigan. Jordan has been involved in urban planning for more than 20 years. He has worked extensively with universities, government agencies, and community organizations on a wide range of issues, including neighborhood planning, affordable housing, environmental conservation, economic development, comprehensive planning, downtown redevelopment, and poverty reduction initiatives.

Jordan is a faculty member of the Maxine Goodman Levin College of Urban Affairs at Cleveland State University, where he teaches graduate and undergraduate classes in urban and regional planning, including workshop classes that engage students in real-world community service projects related to urban planning. He received master's and doctoral degrees in City and Regional Planning from Cornell University and has been a member of the American Institute of Certified Planners since 1996. Jordan writes a blog about urban planning on his website, www.ask-a-planner.com.

Dedication

To my daughter, Evan. We'll go out for ice cream more often, I promise.

Author's Acknowledgments

The opportunity to write a *For Dummies* book about urban planning has been one of the great experiences of my career. It is also a shining example of the old adage "Be careful what you wish for, because you might just get it." Without the assistance and support of many people, this already daunting task might have become simply impossible. I thank Robert Hickey and Elizabeth Kuball of the *For Dummies* series for their invaluable assistance and encouragement on a day-to-day basis. Suggestions and comments from my technical editor, Jennifer Cowley of The Ohio State University, have been especially valuable and appreciated. I owe much of my expertise in urban planning to mentors and colleagues who have shown me the way over many years, especially Norman Krumholz and Pierre Clavel. I am also greatly appreciative of my colleagues at Cleveland State University and have particularly benefited from the support of Edward (Ned) Hill, Wendy Kellogg, W. Dennis Keating, and Sung-Gheel Jang. Joseph Grengs of the University of Michigan and Susan Hoffmann of Western Michigan University also provided valuable support. The professional assistance of Scott Shapiro and Gordon Hare is greatly appreciated. Lastly, the comfort and support of friends and family have been of tremendous importance in seeing this project to completion, including the Yin, Burness, Huston, Dowd, Kasper, Jacobs, Northeim, Henderson-Terwilliger, Holverstott-Cockrell, Wood-Provence, Wassom, May, Antisdale, Posner, Zulewski, Enos, Cross-Coleman, and Moncrief families. Thanks to all.

Publisher's Acknowledgments

We're proud of this book; please send us your comments at http://dummies.custhelp.com.
For other comments, please contact our Customer Care Department within the U.S. at 877-762-2974,
outside the U.S. at 317-572-3993, or fax 317-572-4002.

Some of the people who helped bring this book
to market include the following:

Acquisitions and Editorial

Project Editor: Elizabeth Kuball

Acquiring Editor: Robert Hickey

Copy Editor: Elizabeth Kuball

Technical Editor: Jennifer Cowley, PhD

Project Coordinator, Canada:
Elizabeth McCurdy

Editorial Assistant: Kathy Deady

Cover Photos: © iStock / John_ Woodcock

Cartoons: Rich Tennant (www.the5thwave.com)

Composition Services

Senior Project Coordinator, U.S.: Kristie Rees

Layout and Graphics: Corrie Niehausr

Proofreaders: Laura Albert, Debbye Butler,
John Greenough

Indexer: Christine Karpeles

John Wiley & Sons Canada, Ltd.

> **Deborah Barton,** Vice President and Director of Operations
>
> **Jennifer Smith,** Publisher, Professional and Trade Division
>
> **Alison Maclean,** Managing Editor, Professional & Trade Division

Publishing and Editorial for Consumer Dummies

> **Kathleen Nebenhaus,** Vice President and Executive Publisher
>
> **Kristin Ferguson-Wagstaffe,** Product Development Director
>
> **Ensley Eikenburg,** Associate Publisher, Travel
>
> **Kelly Regan,** Editorial Director, Travel

Publishing for Technology Dummies

> **Andy Cummings,** Vice President and Publisher

Composition Services

> **Debbie Stailey,** Director of Composition Services

Contents at a Glance

Foreword .... *xix*

Introduction *1*

Part I: What Is Urban Planning? *7*
Chapter 1: Making Great Cities: Why Planning Matters 9
Chapter 2: Changing Places: Planning for the 21st Century 23
Chapter 3: Who Makes Urban Plans and Why 43
Chapter 4: Making Plans: A Step-by-Step Approach 57

Part II: Putting All the Pieces Together: The Main Components of an Urban Plan *75*
Chapter 5: Land Use: A Place for Everything 77
Chapter 6: Housing: A Place to Call Home 97
Chapter 7: Moving the City: Transportation 119
Chapter 8: The City Beautiful: Urban Design 135
Chapter 9: The Great Outdoors: Natural Resources, Open Space, and More 149
Chapter 10: Infrastructure and Public Services: Something for Everyone 163

Part III: Hot Topics and Urban Planning Challenges ... *179*
Chapter 11: Greening the City: Making Sustainable Places 181
Chapter 12: Urban Revitalization: Cities on the Rebound 195
Chapter 13: Rushing to the Suburbs: Managing Sprawl 207
Chapter 14: Healing the City: Planning and Disasters 223
Chapter 15: Taking Care of Business: Jobs and Economic Development 237
Chapter 16: Global Urban Planning: Answering the
  Challenges of Growth and Development 253

Part IV: Getting Involved and Going Further *267*
Chapter 17: Getting Involved in Your Community 269
Chapter 18: Becoming a Professional Urban Planner 279

Part V: The Part of Tens 291

Chapter 19: Ten Ways to Make Your Community a Better
Place to Live, Work, and Play 293
Chapter 20: Ten Great Cities with Great Plans..............................301
Chapter 21: Ten Urban Plans You Can Find Online................................309

Appendix: Resources 317

Index 325

Table of Contents

Foreword..*xix*

Introduction 1

About This Book 1
Conventions Used in This Book...................................2
What You're Not to Read...2
Foolish Assumptions..3
How This Book Is Organized 3
Icons Used in This Book 5
Where to Go from Here..6

Part 1: What Is Urban Planning? 7

Chapter 1: Making Great Cities: Why Planning Matters............9

The Three Ps: People, Places, and Plans....................10
Planning for changing places 10
Making plans for making places.......................11
Putting people in the plan..................................12
The Way Things Work: The Components of a Plan....................12
Land use...13
Housing 13
Transportation 13
Urban design 14
Environmental issues 14
Infrastructure and services 15
Building the Future: Urban Planning Challenges and Techniques..........15
Making cities sustainable...................................16
Renewing older cities 16
Dealing with sprawling cities.............................17
Helping cities before and after disasters 18
Supporting the local economy 19
Growing globally 19
Ready for More? Next Steps and New Ideas................20
Improving your community..................................20
Considering a career in urban planning.................21

Chapter 2: Changing Places: Planning for the 21st Century 23

Some Places Are Growing and Others Are Shrinking 23
Places for People: Demographic Trends 29
Planning for all ages 29
Planning for a diverse population 30
For Richer or Poorer: Economic Trends 33
Cities that work: Where the jobs are 33
Different places, different jobs: What kind of city is yours? 35
The Shape of Things to Come: Changing Urban Geographies 38
Sprawling cities 38
Environmental concerns and changing cities 39
More People, Bigger Cities: The Global Urban Challenge 40
Going to the city: The global move to cities 40
Going big: The rise of the megacity 41

Chapter 3: Who Makes Urban Plans and Why 43

Different Kinds of Urban Plans 43
Why Communities Make Plans 44
Planning for changing communities 45
Meeting legal requirements for plans 45
Urban Plans for Different Types of Communities 47
Cities and towns 47
Metropolitan areas 48
Neighborhoods, downtowns, and districts 50
Public Participation in Urban Planning 51
Local government planners and officials 52
State, federal, and other government agencies 53
Related professions 54
Community stakeholders 55

Chapter 4: Making Plans: A Step-by-Step Approach 57

Launching a Plan 57
Planning to plan 58
Informing the community 59
Understanding the Community 60
Using information 61
Pinpointing strengths and weaknesses 62
Looking Ahead: Creating a Vision and Setting Goals 63
Seeing the future: Creating a vision statement
for the community 63
Picking priorities: Planning goals and objectives 64
Making Choices: Deciding on Planning Strategies and Actions 66
Planning strategies and actions 66
Coordinating goals and strategies 67
Describing how the plan will be implemented,
evaluated, and updated 68

Getting Busy: Carrying Out the Plan 70
 Adopting the plan 70
 Implementing the plan 70
Keeping Track: Monitoring Progress and Updating the Plan................ 71
 Making a difference? How to monitor progress............................ 71
 When and why to update the plan.. 72

Part II: Putting All the Pieces Together: The Main Components of an Urban Plan 75

Chapter 5: Land Use: A Place for Everything 77

Why Land Use Is So Important.. 78
 Land use and urban development 78
 It's all related: Land use and other plan components.................... 79
A Little Bit of Everything: Existing Land Use 81
 Examining land use classifications 81
 Classifying properties 82
 Looking at existing land use with inventories and maps............... 83
Coming Soon! Planning for Future Land Use.. 85
 How much land is available? Analyzing supply 85
 How much land will we need? Forecasting demand....................... 86
Using Zoning and Land Use Regulations 90
 Zoning laws and maps... 91
 Types of zoning classifications 92
 Zoning techniques 93
 Other land use regulations that affect site development 94
LULUs and SOBs: Dealing With Controversial Land Uses 94
 Investigating some common problem land uses 95
 Making the best of a bad situation 95

Chapter 6: Housing: A Place to Call Home 97

Gimme Shelter: The Role of Housing 98
 Housing and quality of life... 98
 Housing, land use, and the demand for public services................ 99
No Place Like Home: Kinds of Housing... 99
 Types of housing... 99
 Housing for special needs... 104
 Affordable housing 105
From Suburbs to Mixed Use: Types of Residential Areas 108
Housing and the Urban Plan: Taking Stock of Housing
 in Your Community.. 112
 Keeping up with demand: Is there enough housing? 113
 What kinds of housing are available?.. 113
 This old house: Housing maintenance 114
 Location, location, location: Is housing close to
  where people work and shop?.. 115
 Looking at costs: Is housing affordable?..................................... 116
 Going green: Environmentally friendly housing 117

Chapter 7: Moving the City: Transportation. 119

    Making Us Mobile: Why Transportation Matters 120
    The Transportation System: It's All Connected. 121
        Roadways. 121
        Public transportation systems. 123
        Pedestrians, pedals, and paths 125
        Commercial transportation 125
    Assessing Transportation Conditions 127
        Are we there yet? Assessing traffic problems. 127
        Serving the whole city: Can you get there from here? 128
        Making an impact: Transportation and the environment. 129
    Keeping Us Moving: Transportation Planning. 130
        Expanding and improving local transportation. 130
        Managing traffic: Old problems, new solutions 131
        Making it green: Reducing environmental impacts 133

Chapter 8: The City Beautiful: Urban Design. 135

    The Role of Urban Design: Making Meaningful Places. 135
    Design Elements: The Building Blocks of Cities 136
        Buildings, lots, and blocks. 137
        Streets 138
        Neighborhoods and districts 139
        Cities and regions 140
    Urban Design: Blending Form and Function 141
        Making places attractive and user-friendly 141
        Creating a sense of place 142
        Encouraging sustainability 143
    Designing the Community 144
        Participatory design methods: Engaging the community 144
        Place-making approaches: Using design techniques 146

**Chapter 9: The Great Outdoors: Natural Resources,
Open Space, and More 149**

    Saving the Future: Conserving and Protecting the Environment 150
    Identifying Elements of the Urban Environment 151
        Ecological resources 152
        Conservation areas. 155
        Open space and parks and recreation 158
    Monitoring and Managing the Environment 160
        Keeping an inventory and monitoring conditions. 161
        Coordinating the management of natural resources 162

Chapter 10: Infrastructure and Public Services: Something for Everyone 163

Keeping the City Running...164
    Providing infrastructure and services: Why they're important...164
    Coordinating infrastructure and services with changing cities...165
The Backbone of the City: Utilities and Services.........................166
    Energy...166
    Water and sewer 167
    Other utilities and related services 171
Community Facilities and Services 172
    Public safety 172
    Schools...173
    Other services and facilities...174
Are You Being Served? Evaluating Infrastructure and Services............175
    Are community needs being met? 175
    Are there adequate locations for future improvements? 176
    How much? The costs of capital improvements..........................177
    What are the environmental impacts?...................................177

Part III: Hot Topics and Urban Planning Challenges.... 179

Chapter 11: Greening the City: Making Sustainable Places 181

Examining the Pillars of Sustainability 182
Planning for Sustainable Communities.......................................182
    Tackling climate change 183
    Using local resources 184
    LEED-ing the way: Eco-friendly buildings 186
    Planning greener cities..187
    Growing the city's greenprint 190
Using New Tools to Plan for a Greener Future 192

Chapter 12: Urban Revitalization: Cities on the Rebound 195

Making Dynamic Downtowns..196
    How cities are bringing people and businesses
    back to Main Street 196
    The new wave of downtown housing: Lofts, high-rises,
    and urban villages 198
Just Add Water(fronts): Capitalizing on Proximity to Water.................199
Keeping It Cool: Arts, Culture, and Entertainment...........................199
    Creative cities: Cultural amenities that strengthen
    urban development..200
    Performance spaces: Promoting arts districts and
    cultural facilities..200
Preserving History..202
    Using historic districts to preserve the city........................203
    Restoring the past: New uses for old buildings 203

Strengthening Urban Neighborhoods 204
   Revitalizing urban neighborhoods with improved
      housing and services 204
   Expanding social services to reach distressed
      urban neighborhoods 206

Chapter 13: Rushing to the Suburbs: Managing Sprawl 207
What's Urban Sprawl? 208
Costs and Consequences: Why Urban Sprawl Matters.........................209
   Spreading too far? Environmental impacts of urban sprawl........210
   Paying more, getting less: Sprawl and government spending 210
   Growing apart: Sprawl and social issues 211
Growing Smart and Sprawling Less..212
The Big Picture: Regional Strategies 214
   Promoting regional planning 214
   Visioning regional development patterns 215
   Coordinating land use regionally..217
   Conserving open space 217
   Making smart public investments..218
Local Solutions: What Cities and Suburbs Can Do 219
   Designing communities with compact land use patterns............219
   Staying put: Building communities for the long term 221

Chapter 14: Healing the City: Planning and Disasters 223
Recognizing Risks in a Changing World..224
   Cities at risk: Types of hazards...224
   Who helps? 226
Planning for Disaster-Resistant Communities 227
   Assessing community risks 228
   Reducing potential hazards: The enemy you know 229
Recovering from Disasters: Rebuilding Cities and
   Restoring Communities..231
   Disaster preparedness and emergency response:
      Helping in a hurry 232
   Post-disaster re-planning and rebuilding......................................232

**Chapter 15: Taking Care of Business:
Jobs and Economic Development 237**
Making Places That Work 238
   Helping the local economy 238
   Looking at the local economy 239
Planning for Local Economic Development 240
   Strengthening the community's economic base............................240
   Developing major projects: Build it and they will come?.............242
   Chasing smokestacks: Attracting businesses
      to your community 243

Eds, meds, and feds: Looking at the role of
education, medicine, and government 244
Helping at home: Supporting local entrepreneurs
and businesses 245
People power: Preparing workers for good jobs 247
Economic Development Programs and Policies 248
Marketing the community 248
Using financial incentives 249
Coordinating economic development with land use 251

Chapter 16: Global Urban Planning: Answering the
Challenges of Growth and Development **253**
Finding a Place for the Next Three Billion People 254
Global urbanization trends 254
Global urban planning challenges 254
Cities of Asia: Roaring into a New Century 256
Shanghai: The "head of the dragon" 257
Mumbai: Big and getting bigger 258
Cities of Africa: Overcoming Poverty and Improving Lives 259
Johannesburg: Laying the foundation for prosperity 260
Cairo: Bringing modern changes to an ancient city 262
Cities of Latin America: Searching for Stability 263
Mexico City: Planning for growth and sustainability 264
São Paulo: The challenges of hyper-urbanization 265

Part IV: Getting Involved and Going Further **267**

Chapter 17: Getting Involved in Your Community **269**
Getting More Information on Local Planning Issues 270
Finding information about local planning 270
Getting information about development projects,
zoning decisions, permits, and other land use issues 270
Learning more about your community 271
Getting Your Point Across: Attending Public
Meetings and Hearings 271
Being a Part of the Solution: Participating in Planning 273
Taking Action! Opportunities for Volunteering, Activism, and Social
Entrepreneurship 274
Making It Official: Joining a Planning Commission 275

Chapter 18: Becoming a Professional Urban Planner **279**
What Do Urban Planners Do? 280
Preparing urban plans 280
Carrying out development projects 281
Handling day-to-day operations 281

The Skills You Need to Be an Urban Planner 282
    The ability to understand and identify patterns
       of community change 282
    The ability to manage the entire planning process.......................283
    The ability to digest lots of information 283
    Technical skills..283
    Communication skills 284
A Growing Field: Careers in Urban Planning..284
    Education and training in urban planning.....................................284
    Urban planning specialties 287
    Employment opportunities in urban planning..............................289

Part V: The Part of Tens 291

Chapter 19: Ten Ways to Make Your Community a Better Place to Live, Work, and Play 293

Make Public Places That People Will Love..293
Help People Get Where They're Going 294
Pay Attention to Design Details 295
Make Room for Nature...295
Include Different Types of Housing..296
Provide Places for Recreation..296
Build a Sense of Community 297
Revitalize Neighborhoods 297
Grow Smart..298
Make the First Move...299

Chapter 20: Ten Great Cities with Great Plans 301

Rome 301
Amsterdam 302
Savannah..302
Washington, D.C. 303
New York City 304
The Garden Cities of England..304
Canberra 305
Chandigarh 306
Vancouver 307
Celebration 307

Chapter 21: Ten Urban Plans You Can Find Online 309

A Recovery Plan for New Orleans's Lower Ninth Ward.......................310
A Regional Plan for Chicago 310
Planning for Health and Wellness in California 311

New York City: Bigger and Greener by 2030 312
Boulder's Plan for Transit-Oriented Development 313
Tulsa's Community Vision 313
Grand Rapids's Blueprint for the Future 314
Planning the Suburbs in Ohio 314
Planning for America's Megaregions 315
Designing the Future in Fayetteville 316

Appendix: Resources *317*

Professional and Educational Organizations 317
News and Blogs 318
Urban Design and Historic Preservation 319
Regional Planning and Sustainable Development 319
Community and Economic Development 320
Transportation and Infrastructure 320
U.S. Government Agencies 321
Research, Data, and Maps 322
Global Planning 324

Index *325*

Foreword

. . . .

1 have occasionally heard someone say that "urban planning isn't rocket science." My reply? "You're right — it's a lot more complex." In fact, it's also not for dummies and you're reading this book because you're not a dummy. In all likelihood, you're already involved in making your community a better place and you may even be involved in planning. If this is your first time reading about urban planning, you're taking a step in a great direction.

Urban planning, in fact, goes by many names, including *city planning, community planning, town planning,* and *regional planning.* These terms reflect the diversity of the places that we call home, and I'm proud to serve as the CEO of the American Planning Association, an educational organization whose members are making great communities happen. Urban planning works to improve the welfare of people and their communities by creating places that are more convenient, equitable, healthful, efficient, and attractive for both present and future generations. Planning creates places of lasting value where generations can prosper. Good urban planning provides civic leaders, businesses, and citizens with an opportunity to play a meaningful role in improving and enhancing their communities by envisioning the future and making choices about development, essential services, environmental protection, and innovative changes. Good planning and good governance go hand in hand — you can't have one without the other.

Urban Planning For Dummies reflects the spirit of hopefulness and commitment to progress that has driven the profession of urban planning for more than a century. Jordan Yin has been a practicing member of the American Institute of Certified Planners for more than 15 years and teaches urban planning at Cleveland State University's College of Urban Affairs, a leading program in the United States that offers accredited professional training in urban planning. Throughout this book, Jordan talks in a plainspoken manner about the challenges and opportunities facing today's communities, discusses cutting-edge techniques that are being used in urban planning, and provides numerous and valuable real-world examples of how thoughtful urban planning approaches are making a difference in communities small and large throughout the United States and around the world. This book is an excellent window into the world of urban planning, and I invite you to join myself, Jordan, thousands of professional planners, and many, many more residents and community leaders in planning a bright future for our communities.

W. Paul Farmer, FAICP

W. Paul Farmer, FAICP, is CEO of the American Planning Association (APA) and its professional institute, the American Institute of Certified Planners (AICP). He managed several departments as executive director of the Department of Planning and Development for the city of Eugene (Oregon) and served as director of the Department of City Planning for the city of Minneapolis, and deputy planning director for the city of Pittsburgh. He has taught in the graduate urban planning programs at the University of Oregon, Carnegie Mellon University, the University of Pittsburgh, the Georgia Institute of Technology, and the University of Wisconsin–Milwaukee.

Introduction

"*M*ake no little plans." So said the great urban planner Daniel Burnham, the force behind Chicago's revolutionary 1893 World's Fair and the epic 1909 *Plan of Chicago.* These plans helped transform Chicago from a gritty industrial town into an architectural palace and vibrant modern metropolis. Chicago's success also influenced the planning of other cities all over the world. Burnham believed that making great places required imaginative plans that inspired people to take bold actions.

And because you're reading this book, you probably share Burnham's enthusiasm for the future of cities and their regions — places where people can live, work, and play while treating the planet in a responsible manner and leaving a legacy for future generations. Urban planning helps make great places possible by combining an understanding of how places grow and change with a wide range of specific techniques that help communities solve problems and prepare for the future.

Whether you're looking for some background information on a specific aspect of urban planning, have ambitions to become a professional urban planner, or are looking for ways to become more involved in your community, this book can help you better understand urban planning and how to create successful communities.

About This Book

This book is a reference, which means that you don't have to read it cover to cover — instead, you can dip into it to find the information you need, and move on to the task at hand. Of course, if you *want* to read from the title page to the very last word, I think you'll enjoy the ride.

Although this book says that it's about *urban* planning, that's a bit of a lie — just a little one. Whether you live in a metropolis, city, town, suburb, village, hamlet, or something in between, you'll find all kinds of ideas for improving your community. For example, in the state of Michigan, there are plans for many different types of places, ranging from a plan for metropolitan Detroit (pop. 4,704,000) to a plan for the township of Crystal Falls (pop. 1,743). So, even though I use the term *urban planning* throughout this book, I'm talking about communities of all shapes and sizes.

I cover many different urban planning topics in this book, ranging from transportation issues to urban design techniques to disaster recovery. The field of urban planning is as diverse as communities themselves. Every urban plan addresses its community's challenges in a unique way. This book helps guide you toward ideas and strategies that can be tailored to fit you and your community.

Conventions Used in This Book

Throughout this book you'll notice some words and phrases that don't look like the rest of the text. They're a little different and here's what they mean:

- ✔ *Italics* are used when a new term is being introduced. When I introduce a new term, I define it shortly thereafter, often in parentheses.

- ✔ **Boldface** identifies keywords and important useful phrases in bulleted or numbered lists.

- ✔ Monofont is the typeface for e-mail addresses and web addresses. When this book was printed, some web addresses may have needed to break across two lines of text. If that happened, rest assured that we haven't put in any extra characters (such as hyphens) to indicate the break. So, when using one of these web addresses, just type in exactly what you see in this book, pretending as though the line break doesn't exist.

  One more note on web addresses: When a web address is so long that typing it into your web browser would be a pain in the neck, I use addresses shortened by bitly (http://bit.ly).

What You're Not to Read

Feel free to skip the sidebars (text in gray boxes). The sidebars are great to read if you have time or are interested in getting into the details, but they aren't essential to the topic at hand, so you can skip them without missing anything critical.

You also can sidestep anything marked with a Technical Stuff icon (for more on icons, see "Icons Used in This Book," later in this Introduction).

Foolish Assumptions

Good urban planning gives everyone a chance to participate in making his or her community a better place. This book is sort of the same: Everyone is welcome. So, I don't make a lot of assumptions about what you already know or why you've decided to start using this book, but here are a few things I assume about you:

- ✔ **You're at least a little bit interested in urban planning.** Maybe you've always wanted to know more about your surroundings. If you've ever asked yourself, "Why is that building over there and not over here?" then you're already thinking like an urban planner. Or maybe you have questions about a specific urban planning issue, like conserving open space or public transportation. If so, this book will help steer you in the right direction to discover more about your interests!

- ✔ **Something is probably going on in your community.** Many people start looking for more information on urban planning because they notice changes in their community or because something controversial is happening. This book points you toward good ideas on a wide range of urban planning topics and fills you in on ways to solve problems and make your community an even better place.

- ✔ **You may be a little afraid of technical details.** It's not unusual for urban planning to use lots of jargon and techniques that can seem overly complicated. Perhaps you've been to a planning commission meeting and wondered if everyone was speaking in Martian! In this book, I use everyday English and real-world examples to explain what urban planning is all about.

How This Book Is Organized

This book's 21 chapters are divided into the following five parts.

Part 1: What Is Urban Planning?

For thousands of years, people have worked tirelessly to improve the places that they call home. The earliest urban plans were made out of the necessity to simply provide clean water or survive harsh climates. Today's cities require complex plans balancing all the different elements that contribute to our quality of life and the sustainability of our environment.

This part introduces you to urban plans by looking at how urban planning helps people tackle many of the key challenges facing today's cities, suburbs, and towns. Then I take a look at who's usually involved in making urban plans, what resources are needed to make a good plan, and the step-by-step process of making one.

Part II: Putting All the Pieces Together: The Main Components of an Urban Plan

Urban plans help make cities and their regions better places by coordinating the operation and development of all the different components of a city. The chapters in this part talk about the usual components of a comprehensive urban plan, including the following:

- ✓ Land use
- ✓ Housing
- ✓ Transportation
- ✓ Urban design
- ✓ Natural resources, recreation, and open space
- ✓ Infrastructure and public services

Each chapter provides an overview of a planning topic, descriptions of urban planning techniques, and real-world examples of successful urban planning approaches, as well as explanations of how each component contributes to the overall success of a good urban plan.

Part III: Hot Topics and Urban Planning Challenges

Today's communities face a wide range of challenges that impact the quality of life in cities and towns, as well as the state of local environmental conditions. These challenges are far-ranging and include things such as pollution, rapid population growth, economic distress, and recovery from catastrophic natural disasters. Every community faces a unique set of challenges, and local urban plans work to tailor the best available solutions for the community.

Urban planners around the world are constantly developing new approaches and techniques to keep up with these challenges. The chapters in this part deal with a wide range of issues, including the following:

- ✓ Sustainable urban development
- ✓ Urban revitalization and community development
- ✓ Urban sprawl and growth management
- ✓ Planning for disasters
- ✓ Local economic development and job creation
- ✓ Global urbanization and urban planning in developing countries

Each chapter in this part examines challenges facing today's cities and looks at a wide range of problem-solving urban planning techniques and approaches.

Part IV: Getting Involved and Going Further

Ready to get some hands-on experience in urban planning? This part talks about ways to go further and get more involved. Whether you're considering a career in urban planning or you just want to take the lead in improving your community, these chapters introduce you to lots of great ways to get more involved in urban planning.

Part V: The Part of Tens

The Part of Tens gives you a quick look at some interesting, quirky, and important examples of urban planning. These lists include a checklist of ways to improve or enhance your community, a list of great places that are examples of successful urban planning, and ten urban plans you can find online.

Icons Used in This Book

Throughout this book, you see *icons* in the margins. These markers help you navigate through the book by quickly identifying material that may be of special interest to you. Here's what they all mean:

The Tip icon flags specific items in the book that will help you better understand urban planning issues, concepts, and techniques.

The Remember icon points to sections of the book worth remembering for future reference because they contain a concept or term that also appears in other parts of the book.

The Technical Stuff icon marks paragraphs that are interesting and worthwhile but not essential to understanding the main point of the chapter. Read them if you have time, but skip them guilt free.

Want to see urban planning in action? Look for this icon! It highlights interesting examples of planning trends and techniques from communities around the world.

Where to Go from Here

One way to make use of this book is to start at the beginning. But because this is a *For Dummies* book, you can use this book in a variety of ways:

- ✔ If you're looking for a general introduction to urban planning and hints on what you'll find in the rest of the book, Chapter 1 is a great place to start.

- ✔ If you already know a bit about urban planning or you have an interest in a particular issue or technique, feel free to move right along to the chapters in Part II and Part III. Each of these chapters introduces you to a different topic, including information on urban planning techniques and real-world examples.

- ✔ Looking for something specific? Maybe you're trying to find a definition of a term or an explanation of a specific issue or technique. The table of contents and index can help you find what you need.

Whether your community is a bustling metropolis or a small town, this book can help you make big plans!

Part I
What Is Urban Planning?

"At one point, they talked about adding more buses, but in the end they decided to just extend the chair lifts from the ski resorts."

In this part . . .

Urban planning helps communities steer toward their vision for a successful future. This part gets the book started by introducing the basics of urban planning and how urban planning relates to the challenges faced by today's cities and communities.

Chapter 1 is an overview of what urban planning is and how it works. Chapter 2 looks at where cities are going in the 21st century and talks about everything from population trends to environmental changes. Chapter 3 shines a light onto the reasons why communities make urban plans; it also looks at who's involved in making urban plans. Chapter 4 is a step-by-step guide to how urban plans are made from start to finish and shows how communities can turn good ideas into great results.

Chapter 1

Making Great Cities: Why Planning Matters

In This Chapter

▶ Looking at how cities make and use urban plans

▶ Identifying an urban plan's main components

▶ Planning for new challenges and great places

▶ Exploring new ideas and ways to improve your community

*A*n *urban plan* (sometimes called a *town plan, master plan,* or *comprehensive plan*) is a guide to the future of a community. Many different kinds of places — from small towns surrounded by farms and countryside to teeming metropolises that are home to millions of people — use urban planning to help sustain and improve their communities.

An urban plan shows what a place could be like in the future. Plans aren't just about what a place may *look* like in the future (the shape of its roads, the style of its buildings, or how many trees are in its parks); plans are also used to figure out how a city will *function* in the future (what kinds of jobs people will have, how much pollution will be created, or what kinds of transportation will move people from one part of the city to another).

This chapter offers an overview of how cities and towns use urban planning to come up with new solutions for their problems. I fill you in on the main components of an urban plan, such as land use, housing, and transportation. I also look at how urban plans get made and who's involved in making them, and tell you how you can get more involved in planning a great future for your community. All the topics in this chapter are discussed in greater detail in other parts of this book, so you can flip ahead when you come across something that grabs your interest.

The Three Ps: People, Places, and Plans

Urban plans help communities take stock of where they are and where they want to go. Every place is different, and different places change in different ways. Some cities have growing populations; others have declining populations. Some cities rely on subway systems to move people back and forth to work; other cities rely mostly on cars and highways for people to get around.

Urban plans look at current conditions in the community to figure out what's working well and what may need to be improved. Making a plan is also an opportunity to give members of the community a chance to express what they love about where they live and what kind of place they want it to be in the future.

Planning for changing places

Urban planning looks at what's good and bad about a community in the present, and plans ahead for how the community can maintain and improve itself in the future. A good understanding of how the community works and how it's likely to change helps make better plans for the future (see Chapter 2).

Population change

The most general type of population change is whether the size of the population is growing or declining. But the makeup of the population also can change, such as its racial or ethnic composition or changes in the number of young families in the community or the number of senior citizens.

Changing places

The geography of where people live is changing as an increasing number of people live in suburban areas rather than in centrally located urban areas. Many suburban areas are making plans to accommodate larger populations, while many existing urban areas are coping with declining populations and planning for revitalization to attract new residents and retain existing households.

Economic trends

A century ago, most cities were prosperous due to their ability to make things, from clothes and furniture to steel and sausage. In today's global economy, products can be made anywhere in the world, and successful local economies rely on lots of different types of jobs, including providing services and making products.

New technologies

Whether it's the continuing influence of the Internet or new ways of using clean energy to power our cities, a wide range of technological innovations will help shape the cities of the future.

Environmental concerns

Cities and towns are increasingly making plans that recognize a wide range of environmental concerns, such as unhealthy air quality and land contamination. Many places also are looking more closely at global environmental conditions and making plans for potential large-scale environmental problems, such as rising sea levels, which could eventually put many coastal cities literally underwater.

Making plans for making places

Most plans for cities and towns are prepared by local government agencies. An *official comprehensive plan* is the most common type of urban plan. It addresses the long-term future of the community, looks at all the different components of the community (such as housing and transportation), and is officially adopted by the community's local government.

In addition to long-range comprehensive plans, many communities also have specialized urban plans, such as a strategic revitalization plan for a specific neighborhood that aims for short-term results. A growing number of places also are making plans for metropolitan areas that help coordinate the future development of all the cities and suburbs in that metropolitan region.

In some cases, various government agencies and community organizations are involved in making informal plans for the community. For example, a nonprofit neighborhood association may develop a plan to renovate older housing in its neighborhood and work on establishing partnerships with residents, businesses, investors, and local governments to help carry out the plan (see Chapter 3).

From start to finish, the process of creating an urban plan goes through several steps (see Chapter 4):

1. **Assess the community's current conditions.**

2. **Create goals for the future.**

3. **Decide on what planning strategies and actions will be taken.**

4. **Determine how to implement, monitor, and update the plan.**

The resources needed to make an urban plan depend on the kind of plan being made. A small town may be able to produce a good comprehensive plan in a short period of time for a relatively small amount of money. But an official comprehensive plan for a large city may involve literally thousands of people, take a few years to complete, and cost millions of dollars. This may seem like a lot of effort just to plan ahead, but as the old saying goes, "An ounce of prevention is worth a pound of cure."

Putting people in the plan

Ideally, an urban plan isn't just a guide to the future *for* the community, but it's also a guide to the future *by* the community. A plan can have a big impact on the people who live in the community, as well as other community stakeholders (such as business or property owners), so getting everyone involved in making the plan is a good idea. Urban planning uses a wide range of techniques to encourage public participation in the plan-making process, from public meetings and focus groups to networking with social media and old-fashioned door knocking to meet new people (see Chapter 3).

The Way Things Work: The Components of a Plan

An urban plan is sort of a blueprint for the long-term development of a community. A plan says what the community could or should be like at some point in the future, usually between 20 and 50 years ahead. But it's a very complicated blueprint, because cities are made up of many related components, including (but not limited to) land use, housing, natural resources, public services, and transportation.

The exact components that are part of an urban plan depends on the place itself, because every place is just a little bit (or a lot) different. In some areas, economic issues may be very important to the community, whereas another place may need to make plans to protect a unique natural resource.

Urban plans take a detailed look at the current conditions of each component in the plan (such as housing or transportation) and look ahead for what the community will need in the future (such as more housing or better roads). Planning for each component also has to consider how different components are related — such as how automobile pollution can impact air quality — and figure out ways to plan ahead in a comprehensive and coordinated manner.

Land use

The land use component of an urban plan often is considered the most important part of a plan because everything that makes up a city has to be located somewhere. Different classifications are used to describe the ways in which land is used, such as for residential, commercial, and industrial uses. An urban plan looks at existing land uses by preparing an inventory of all the different types of land uses in the area and using maps that show how all the land in a city is being used, along with other important features of the city (such as roadways or rivers).

The land use component of an urban plan also illustrates the community's future land use pattern. General and specific maps show how all the land in the community will be used for different purposes in the future. One of the most important goals of planning for land use is to coordinate future land use with related planning components, such as transportation and housing, in order to make sure that these components work well together and provide enough space for future development (see Chapter 5).

Housing

The housing component of a plan looks at both the quantity and quality of housing in the community. An assessment of current housing conditions looks at a wide range of housing characteristics, including the mix of different types of housing in the community (such as single-family homes and apartment buildings), the age and physical condition of housing, and issues related to housing affordability and homeownership.

Information on how well the current housing stock is serving the community is combined with forecasts of population and economic trends to make plans for future housing improvements, including how much housing will be needed in the future and what types of housing will be needed. Plans for future housing are coordinated with other plan components, like land use and transportation, to help figure out the best locations for future housing development and to identify areas with existing housing that may require redevelopment. Chapter 6 takes a detailed look at housing.

Transportation

The transportation component of a plan looks at everything that keeps a city connected, ranging from roads and subways to rivers and sidewalks. An assessment of transportation conditions looks at how well the city is connected (can people get from here to there?) and how well people are served by the transportation system (can they get where they need to go?).

Planning for future transportation involves looking at options for improving the management of the existing transportation system, as well as making future improvements. More and more, local transportation plans are trying to come up with ways to lessen the impact of transportation on the environment, plan for alternatives to the automobile (like mass transit, bicycling, and walking), and coordinate transportation options with land use changes (see Chapter 7).

Urban design

The urban design component of a plan addresses both aesthetic and functional issues. Cities are made of up many building blocks, including individual buildings, streets, and neighborhoods. The design of each of these types of places contributes to both the beauty and usefulness of the city. For example, a well-designed street is one that is attractive to the eye, allows for car traffic to move freely, and has good sidewalks where people can stop to talk to each other. Urban design helps the city look good and work well.

The urban design component of a plan examines the design characteristics of existing areas and makes suggestions for the design of future development. Urban design plans are coordinated with other plan components in ways that improve their aesthetic appeal and functionality, such as creating design guidelines for future housing developments that provide a community with a consistent look and feel.

Planning for urban design often involves getting ideas and opinions from the community through public participation in planning exercises. A variety of approaches, including design charrettes and community visioning, help community stakeholders identify how they want the community to look and function in the future. You can find more details on urban design in Chapter 8.

Environmental issues

Urban plans look at many different types of environmental issues, including preserving a city's natural elements (such as water resources or animal habitats), providing open space and recreational areas, and preserving nearby agricultural areas. The environmental component of a plan also looks at the city's own impacts on the environment, such as how pollution from factories or automobiles contributes to environmental degradation or negatively impacts human health.

A plan's environmental component often assesses a wide range of current conditions. These can include the amount of open space in a community, an inventory of its important plant and animal species, or an assessment of the city's air quality. Future plans for preserving and protecting environmental resources are closely coordinated with related plan components, such as transportation, infrastructure, and land use. An increasing number of communities have developed plans to minimize their global impact on the environment, including efforts to reduce local levels of greenhouse gas emissions that contribute to global climate change (see Chapter 9).

Infrastructure and services

Some of a city's infrastructure, such as roadways and power lines, is obvious and easily seen. But the average person doesn't usually see a lot of what keeps the city running, such as sewage treatment plants, underground pipes, and power plants. Cities also provide lots of essential services to the community, such as schools, hospitals, and police and fire protection. All these things are addressed in urban plans, and their planning is closely coordinated with the city's land use patterns to figure out where to locate and provide needed infrastructure and services.

Planning ahead for future improvements to infrastructure and services is especially important because things like sewers, schools, and power plants are very costly and may be in service for 50 to 100 years. Careful planning for long-lasting and expensive upgrades helps ensure that cities can provide the essentials now and in the future. I cover this topic in detail in Chapter 10.

Building the Future: Urban Planning Challenges and Techniques

Today's cities and towns face unprecedented challenges, and many new approaches to urban planning are being used to help cities and towns deal with a wide range of difficult issues, including population loss, environmental degradation, industrial decline, urban sprawl, natural disaster, and even global population growth.

In some cases, cities and towns are incorporating these issues into their overall urban plans. Other places are developing strategic plans that propose short-term actions to address specific issues. Cities and towns are always changing, so no plan for the future will ever be perfect, but many communities around the world are making bold plans and taking big steps toward improving themselves and avoiding future problems.

Making cities sustainable

Communities around the world are taking steps to reduce their impact on the environment and make healthier places for people to live. By planning for sustainable development, communities are using new approaches that balance ecological concerns with the social and economic needs of communities. Planning for sustainable development also means looking at the big picture, such as how local pollution contributes to global climate change (see Chapter 11).

Here are some ways that cities and towns are planning for places that are more sustainable:

- ✔ **Protecting and preserving natural resources:** Cities and towns are making plans and taking steps to protect their important ecological resources, including land, water, air, plants, and animals. These efforts range from small-scale programs to conserve water during droughts to big plans for preserving large areas within cities as open space or nature preserves.

- ✔ **Going green:** Communities are increasingly looking at ways to reduce their environmental impact and promote new development that is more sustainable for people as well as the environment. These include efforts as simple as helping more people walk or use bicycles instead of cars, or creating complex plans for green buildings, which require less energy to operate and can significantly reduce pollution.

- ✔ **Seeing the big picture:** Many communities are looking at ways to reduce their global ecological impact, especially in how cities and towns contribute to global climate change. Many places are making plans that aim to reduce their environmental footprint in ways that make better use of local resources, consume less of the world's limited resources (especially fossil fuels), and reduce the amount of local pollutants that contribute to regional and world environmental problems.

Renewing older cities

Many major U.S. cities have fallen on hard times in recent decades. Places such as Buffalo, Cleveland, and Detroit have experienced significant population losses over the last few decades, as well as declining social and economic conditions for many of the people who still live there. And it's not just big cities that are experiencing decline. Many small towns and older suburbs also are coping with shrinking populations and other signs of distress, such as abandoned housing, increasing poverty, and rising crime rates.

Communities across the country are making plans and carrying out community development initiatives that are working to revitalize older areas, including efforts to improve specific places and build on existing strengths:

✔ **Improving downtowns, waterfronts, and other special districts:** Concentrating redevelopment efforts in existing areas can help older communities attract new businesses, create new jobs for existing residents, and attract tourists and new residents to the community.

✔ **Strengthening arts, culture, entertainment, and history:** Many communities are using their unique artistic and cultural resources — such as music festivals, museums, sporting events, and historic districts — in ways that both celebrate the heritage of existing residents and make older areas more attractive to new residents and tourists.

✔ **Supporting neighborhoods and families:** A wide range of community development initiatives are being used in places across the country. These include efforts to build new and affordable housing in urban and suburban neighborhoods, attract new businesses and stimulate job creation, and improve access to transportation to workplaces for households that don't own cars.

You can find more information on urban revitalization in Chapter 12.

Dealing with sprawling cities

Today's metropolitan areas are more spread out than ever, as cities and their suburbs continue to expand into rural and previously undeveloped areas. Roughly half of the U.S. population lives in a suburb. The U.S. population is growing, so it's natural that we need a little more space. But much of this growth is taking place at the outer edges of metropolitan areas in ways that use land less efficiently and encourage more car travel. Both of these situations have negative environmental, economic, and social impacts, and sprawling areas require increased public spending for new infrastructure and services (see Chapter 13).

Regional planning and *growth management planning* are planning approaches that help communities accommodate future growth while using their resources effectively:

✔ **Growing smart and sprawling less:** Many communities are successfully using planning approaches that aim to use existing resources more effectively and minimize the impact of development on the environment. For example, growth management planning may look at limiting new development in undeveloped areas, or planning for the redevelopment of less costly existing areas that already have access to infrastructure and services.

✓ **Encouraging cooperation and coordination:** Regional planning for metropolitan areas can be a tough sell. Most communities make plans only for themselves and don't take a broader view of the region as a whole. But curbing the trend of sprawling cities will require communities to work together on regional solutions to regional problems, and find ways for communities to make better decisions about local land use that balance local growth with the overall health of the metropolitan region.

Helping cities before and after disasters

In recent years, many places have suffered high-profile disasters, from Hurricane Katrina's devastating impact on New Orleans in 2005 to the 9/11 terrorist attacks on New York City in 2001 to the 2011 tornadoes that killed hundreds of people and destroyed major portions of Joplin, Missouri, and Tuscaloosa, Alabama. However, many other cities and towns are located in places that face natural hazards (such as hurricanes, earthquakes, and floods), as well as manmade threats (such as terrorism and oil spills).

Communities are increasingly recognizing the risks they face and taking steps to both avoid the worst consequences of disasters and make sure that they're prepared when disasters occur:

✓ **Making communities less vulnerable to disasters:** An increasing number of communities are making plans to disaster-proof themselves and reduce the risk of known hazards in the community. Plans to make communities more resistant to disasters, also known as *hazard mitigation plans,* examine potential threats to the community and help put new programs or regulations into place, such as limiting the number of new buildings in areas that are likely to flood.

✓ **Helping communities recover and rebuild after disasters:** Many communities also have adopted disaster response plans that provide a blueprint for how the community will respond in the event of a disaster. Many communities that have been impacted by disasters have adopted post-disaster recovery plans to guide their recovery and rebuilding.

Cities and towns across the United States and around the world are working to become *resilient communities,* communities that are able to both avoid potential disasters and recover from calamities more quickly with minimal losses. Chapter 14 explores cities and disasters.

Supporting the local economy

A healthy local economy is essential to the success of any community, but maintaining a strong local economy can be a difficult feat. Many communities have experienced prolonged periods of business closings, job losses, and increases in poverty and hardship. Planning for local economic development helps strengthen the local economy by looking for ways to create more good jobs in stable businesses and industries (see Chapter 15). Economic development planning uses a wide range of approaches, including the following:

- **Building on local assets:** All communities have existing resources that can be used to promote economic development, such as helping existing businesses to expand or working with local colleges and hospitals to develop new products and services. Cities and towns also can work toward a healthy economic future by preparing people to work in good jobs and through land use planning that provides good places for businesses to expand their operations.

- **Attracting new businesses:** Cities and towns also try to bolster their local economies by attracting new businesses, from supermarkets to large factories to corporate headquarters. These efforts often involve a combination of land use planning to find good places for new companies and financial or tax incentives that can make a new location more attractive to potential investors.

In some cases, economic development programs may cost tens of millions of dollars in government support and involve not just cities and towns, but also state and federal government agencies. Many cities and towns have recently adopted economic development strategic plans that deal specifically with economic development issues and are intended to stimulate the economy in the short term (usually three to five years).

Growing globally

More than half the world's population lives in cities. That's more than 3.5 billion people. And that's just the beginning. Over the next 40 years, the number of people living in cities is expected to rise to more than 6 billion. Most of this growth will happen in the world's poorer countries, and planning for the future of the world's cities faces two big challenges:

- **More people, bigger cities:** In 1950, New York City and Tokyo were the only urban areas with populations of more than 10 million people. By 2025, there will be more than two dozen cities with populations over

10 million, and several of these are likely to exceed 20 million people, including Mexico City, São Paolo (Brazil), Dhaka (Bangladesh), Delhi (India), and Mumbai (India).

✔ **Rich cities, poor cities:** By 2025, the world's population is likely to reach nine billion people, and roughly five billion people are expected to be living in cities in poor countries. In modern times, cities have been places of wealth and comfort, but this may change in the future, because most future urban development will happen in places with limited economic resources.

In a global age, the world's cities are connected through vast social, economic, electronic, and political networks. Planning for the world's growing cities is likely to be a two-way street between rich and poor places. Wealthy cities may be able to share ideas and resources with poorer cities, while poorer cities may come up with inexpensive solutions for urban problems that can be used throughout the world. With the world's urban population set to nearly double in the near future, it's clear that we've only just begun to plan for the cities of the future (see Chapter 16).

Ready for More? Next Steps and New Ideas

You can contribute to the success of urban planning in your community in many ways. Your input can help professional urban planners craft better plans for your community. You can work with your local government or community organizations to help make decisions that will lead to a brighter future. You can use urban planning techniques to improve your community. You may even be thinking about a career in urban planning. This book is filled with practical information that can help you make great plans for yourself and your community.

Improving your community

You can get involved in the planning and development of your community in many ways. In Chapter 17, I talk about how to get more information about what's happening with urban planning in your community, and how to effectively participate in public meetings and hearings so that your voice is heard when plans are being made. I also tell you how you can get directly involved in making decisions about the future of your community by serving as a community representative or joining a planning commission.

Lots of urban planning opportunities are out there for action takers, including volunteering to help carry out the implementation of a plan or being an activist to make sure that your community's plan addresses important or neglected issues.

A good plan can open new doors for social entrepreneurship by raising new issues and setting new priorities for the community. If your community is planning to go green, maybe you can lead the way by starting a green business!

Considering a career in urban planning

A career in urban planning is a great option for people who want to make cities and towns that are more livable and sustainable. It's also a career choice that's hardly ever boring, and a good fit for those who like multitasking and working in situations that are always changing. Urban planning is a growing and rewarding field that offers many different employment opportunities, from working with small cities and towns in the United States to working abroad in the world's largest cities, from London to Mumbai.

The day-to-day work of an urban planner involves many different skills. Planners use a combination of "hard" skills that rely on analysis (such as conducting detailed statistical analyses of community trends) and "soft" skills that rely on communication (such as holding small meetings with residents to discover their concerns about the community).

Becoming a professional urban planner involves a significant amount of training. In Chapter 18, I point you to universities that offer degrees in urban planning and professional associations that specialize in training urban planners.

Chapter 2

Changing Places: Planning for the 21st Century

In This Chapter

▶ Exploring how cities and metropolitan areas are changing

▶ Looking at demographic, economic, and geographic trends

▶ Planning ahead for more people and bigger cities

*U*rban planning is an inherently complicated undertaking because cities are constantly changing and no two places are exactly alike. Cities can change in many different ways, and what works in the planning of one place may not work as well in another. In this chapter, I give you a broad overview of some of the ways in which cities are changing and key trends for urban planning. You can find more detailed discussions about specific trends in later chapters of this book, particularly in Parts II and III.

Some Places Are Growing and Others Are Shrinking

The U.S. population is growing. Between 2000 and 2010, the population increased by nearly 10 percent, to more than 310 million people. And this growth trend is expected to continue for decades to come. By the year 2050, the U.S. population may reach nearly 440 million people. But not every part of the country is changing in the same way — some places are adding people much faster than the national average, while other areas are experiencing population decline.

The majority of the U.S. population lived in rural areas until the 1920s. However, the number of people living in urbanized areas has grown steadily since then, and today most of the U.S. population lives in one of the following:

- ✔ **Central cities:** A *central city* is the urban core of a metropolitan area and usually represents an area's most populous unit of local government, such as the city of Chicago or the city of Los Angeles. Central cities typically are much larger than their surrounding suburbs and towns. More than 60 million people — nearly one-fifth of the U.S. population — live in one of the 100 largest U.S. cities, ranging from New York City (pop. 8,175,133) to Birmingham, Alabama (pop. 212,237).

- ✔ **Metropolitan areas:** A *metropolitan area* typically includes many different types of communities, including its central city, other smaller cities, towns, suburbs, and nearby rural areas. Metropolitan areas usually are referred to by the name of their central cities, such as the Cleveland, Houston, or Los Angeles metropolitan area. Most of the U.S. population lives in a metropolitan area: In 2010, metropolitan areas accounted for nearly 85 percent of the national population.

Although the number of people living in the United States grew between 2000 and 2010, this growth wasn't spread out evenly. Some areas are experiencing rapid population growth, while others are coping with population losses. Here are some of the key population trends in U.S. metropolitan areas:

- ✔ **Most big metropolitan areas are getting bigger.** Table 2-1 provides a list of the 15 largest U.S. metropolitan areas. The Detroit metropolitan area was the only one that lost population. And several large metropolitan areas grew more quickly than the national average, with the Dallas, Houston, and Atlanta metropolitan areas all adding more than a million people each in just ten years.

Table 2-1	Population Trends in the 15 Largest U.S. Metropolitan Areas, 2000–2010		
Metropolitan Area	*Population, 2000*	*Population, 2010*	*Percent Change, 2000–2010*
New York–Northern New Jersey–Long Island, NY–NJ–PA	18,323,002	18,897,109	3.1%
Los Angeles–Long Beach–Santa Ana, CA	12,365,627	12,828,837	3.7%

Metropolitan Area	Population, 2000	Population, 2010	Percent Change, 2000–2010
Chicago–Joliet–Naperville, IL–IN–WI	9,098,316	9,461,105	4.0%
Dallas–Fort Worth–Arlington, TX	5,161,544	6,371,773	23.4%
Philadelphia–Camden–Wilmington, PA–NJ–DE–MD	5,687,147	5,965,343	4.9%
Houston–Sugar Land–Baytown, TX	4,715,407	5,946,800	26.1%
Washington–Arlington–Alexandria, DC–VA–MD–WV	4,796,183	5,582,170	16.4%
Miami–Fort Lauderdale–Pompano Beach, FL	5,007,564	5,564,635	11.1%
Atlanta–Sandy Springs–Marietta, GA	4,247,981	5,268,860	24.0%
Boston–Cambridge–Quincy, MA–NH	4,391,344	4,552,402	3.7%
San Francisco–Oakland–Fremont, CA	4,123,740	4,335,391	5.1%
Detroit–Warren–Livonia, MI	4,452,557	4,296,250	–3.5%
Riverside–San Bernardino–Ontario, CA	3,254,824	4,224,851	29.8%
Phoenix–Mesa–Glendale, AZ	3,251,876	4,192,887	28.9%
Seattle–Tacoma–Bellevue, WA	3,043,878	3,439,809	13.0%

Source: U.S. Census, 2000 and 2010

✔ **Some metropolitan areas are growing super-fast.** The United States has more than 360 metropolitan areas. Metropolitan New York City is the largest; Carson City, Nevada (pop. 55,000), the smallest. Some of these areas aren't just growing; they're growing much more rapidly than the national average. In fact, 65 U.S. metropolitan areas grew by more than 20 percent between 2000 and 2010 — that's more than *twice* the national average. Table 2-2 lists the five fastest-growing metropolitan areas. Notice that both the Las Vegas and Raleigh metropolitan areas, which have populations of more than a million people each, grew by more than 40 percent between 2000 and 2010.

Table 2-2	U.S. Metropolitan Areas with the Greatest Increase in Population, 2000–2010		
Metropolitan Area	*Population, 2000*	*Population, 2010*	*Percent Change, 2000–2010*
Palm Coast, FL	49,832	95,696	92.0%
St. George, UT	90,354	138,115	52.9%
Las Vegas–Paradise, NV	1,375,765	1,951,269	41.8%
Raleigh–Cary, NC	797,071	1,130,490	41.8%
Cape Coral–Fort Myers, FL	440,888	618,754	40.3%

Source: U.S. Census, 2000 and 2010

✔ **Some metropolitan areas lost population.** In some areas, the trend is downward, not upward. More than 40 U.S. metropolitan areas lost population between 2000 and 2010. Table 2-3 shows the five metropolitan areas that lost the greatest percentage of their population. The New Orleans metropolitan area suffered the most significant population loss, because many residents never returned to the area after Hurricane Katrina in 2005. Some of the other metropolitan areas showing severe population loss — including Youngstown and Johnstown — are older industrial areas that have experienced economic hardship for decades.

Table 2-3	U.S. Metropolitan Areas with the Greatest Decrease in Population, 2000–2010		
Metropolitan Area	*Population, 2000*	*Population, 2010*	*Percent Change, 2000–2010*
New Orleans–Metairie–Kenner, LA	1,316,510	1,167,764	−11.3%
Pine Bluff, AR	107,341	100,258	−6.6%
Youngstown–Warren–Boardman, OH–PA	602,964	565,773	−6.2%
Johnstown, PA	152,598	143,679	−5.8%
Steubenville–Weirton, OH–WV	132,008	124,454	−5.7%

Source: U.S. Census, 2000 and 2010

Overall, nearly 800 cities and towns in the United States have populations of more than 50,000 people, but not all these are central cities; some of these places are suburbs or large towns. And like metropolitan areas, some of these cities and towns are growing, while others are shrinking. Here's a look at some of the key trends facing U.S. cities and towns:

🗸 **The largest cities have experienced slow growth trends.** Table 2-4 lists the 15 largest cities in the United States. Only one of these, Chicago, lost population between the years 2000 and 2010, but most of the rest grew more slowly than the national average and grew more slowly than their corresponding metropolitan areas. Even the city of San Antonio, the population of which grew by an above-average 16 percent, was outpaced by a 25 percent growth rate for its overall metropolitan area.

Table 2-4	Population Trends in the 15 Largest U.S. Cities, 2000–2010		
City	*Population, 2000*	*Population, 2010*	*Percent Change, 2000–2010*
New York	8,008,278	8,175,133	2.1%
Los Angeles	3,694,820	3,792,621	2.6%
Chicago	2,896,016	2,695,588	–6.9%
Houston	1,953,631	2,099,451	7.5%
Philadelphia	1,517,550	1,526,006	0.6%
Phoenix	1,321,045	1,445,632	9.4%
San Antonio	1,114,646	1,327,407	16.0%
San Diego	1,223,400	1,307,402	6.9%
Dallas	1,188,580	1,197,816	0.8%
San Jose	894,943	945,942	5.7%
Jacksonville	735,617	821,784	11.7%
Indianapolis	781,870	820,445	4.9%
San Francisco	776,733	805,235	3.7%
Austin	656,562	790,390	20.4%
Columbus	711,470	787,033	10.6%

Source: U.S. Census, 2000 and 2010

✔ **Some cities are growing rapidly.** Table 2-5 lists the five fastest-growing U.S. cities. All these places grew nearly ten times faster than the national average. Only one, Port St. Lucie, is the central city of a metropolitan area. The other four are smaller cities or suburbs within metropolitan areas. The town of Gilbert, a suburb of Phoenix, grew by about 90 percent — ten times faster than the city of Phoenix and three times faster than the overall Phoenix metropolitan area.

Table 2-5	U.S. Cities with the Greatest Increase in Population, 2000–2010		
City	*Population, 2000*	*Population, 2010*	*Percent Change, 2000–2010*
McKinney, TX	54,369	131,117	141.2%
Gilbert, AZ	109,697	208,453	90.0%
North Las Vegas, NV	115,488	216,961	87.9%
Port St. Lucie, FL	88,769	164,603	85.4%
Renton, WA	50,052	90,927	81.7%

Source: U.S. Census, 2000 and 2010

✔ **Some cities are shrinking.** Table 2-6 lists the five U.S. cities that lost the greatest percentage of their population between 2000 and 2010. The population of the city of New Orleans declined nearly one-third in the wake of Hurricane Katrina. The other four cities on the list are older cities, including Flint and Youngstown, each of which lost more than one-fifth of its population and has been dealing with long-term economic hardships due to job losses in manufacturing.

Table 2-6	U.S. Cities with the Greatest Decrease in Population, 2000–2010		
City	*Population, 2000*	*Population, 2010*	*Percent Change, 2000–2010*
New Orleans, LA	484,674	343,829	−29.1%
Detroit, MI	951,270	713,777	−25.0%
Gary, IN	102,756	80,294	−21.9%
Youngstown, OH	82,026	66,982	−18.3%
Flint, MI	124,943	102,434	−18.0%

Source: U.S. Census, 2000 and 2010

The U.S. population is growing as a whole, but no single overall trend applies to all the cities and metropolitan areas in the United States. In some places, such as Chicago, the metropolitan area is growing while the central city is shrinking. In other places, such as Los Angeles and Houston, both the central city and the metropolitan area are growing. And in just a few metropolitan areas, such as Detroit, Cleveland, and Buffalo, there is an overall trend toward decline in both the central city and its metropolitan area.

The wide range of recent population trends means that some communities are making urban plans that deal with rapid growth — including finding more space for more people — while other places are making plans to help stop their population losses and hang on to what's great about their communities.

Places for People: Demographic Trends

In addition to the overall size of a community's population, a wide range of demographic trends also are relevant to urban planning. Two of the most important demographic trends for urban planning are the aging of the population and the changing racial/ethnic composition of the population. Knowing about a community's demographic trends helps in making plans for the different needs and lifestyles of present and future members of the community.

Planning for all ages

Not only is the U.S. population expected to increase significantly in coming decades, but the number of people in different age groups will change as well. Table 2-7 shows the projected population of the United States from 2010 to 2050 and the number of people in different age groups.

Table 2-7	Projected U.S. Population by Age, 2010–2050		
Age Bracket	*2010*	*2030*	*2050*
Under 18	75,217,000	87,815,000	101,574,000
18 to 64	194,787,000	213,597,000	248,890,000
65 to 84	34,478,000	63,347,000	69,506,000
85 and over	5,751,000	8,745,000	19,041,000
Total population	310,233,000	373,504,000	439,010,000

Source: U.S. Census Bureau, 2008 Projections of the Population

Overall, the U.S. population is expected to grow by nearly 130 million people by the year 2050. But the composition of the population won't stay the same over the coming decades — a relatively larger portion of the population will become older.

Here are some key trends that will have an impact on cities and towns in the future:

- ✔ **The number of children is increasing.** By 2050, the United States is expected to have 25 million more children than it had in 2010. This means that communities will need to expand services for children, such as building more schools and playgrounds. But although the number of children is expected to rise, children will make up only about a quarter of the total population in 2050, which is roughly the same percentage as in 2010.

- ✔ **The population is getting older.** Not only is the number of older Americans expected to more than double between 2010 and 2050, but they also will make up a larger share of the population in the future. In 2010, about 13 percent of the population was over age 65; by 2050, people over age 65 will make up 20 percent of the population. And there are likely to be more than 19 million people 85 years or older by 2050 — a record number for this age group. Communities will have to plan for the aging of the population in many ways, including providing more medical services and different types of housing for older people.

- ✔ **There will be relatively fewer working-age adults.** The number of adults between 18 and 64 will increase by about 55 million between 2010 and 2050. But this group will make up a smaller portion of the population, falling from 63 percent of the population in 2010 to 57 percent of the population in 2050. This means that there may be fewer people working and paying taxes to help pay for the services needed by growing populations of children and older people.

Planning for a diverse population

The United States is home to a population that comes from many different backgrounds and continues to change in significant ways. Table 2-8 shows the makeup of the U.S. population by race and how the population changed between the years 2000 and 2010. Although the U.S. population increased by almost 10 percent, different racial groups had higher and lower rates of change. The white population increased by about 6 percent, while all the other racial groups grew at rates faster than the national average.

Table 2-8	The U.S. Population by Race, 2000–2010		
	Population, 2000	*Population, 2010*	*Percent Change, 2000–2010*
White	211,460,626	223,553,265	5.7%
African American	34,568,190	38,929,319	12.3%
American Indian and Alaska Native	2,475,956	2,932,248	18.4%
Asian	10,242,998	14,674,252	43.3%
Native Hawaiian and other Pacific Islander	398,835	540,013	35.4%
Some other race	15,539,073	19,017,368	24.4%
Combination of two or more races	6,826,228	9,009,073	32.0%
Total population	281,421,906	308,745,538	9.7%

Source: U.S. Census, 2000 and 2010

The U.S. Census categorizes the Hispanic population independent of racial categories. That is, a person can be of Hispanic ethnicity and of any race (for example, Hispanic and white or Hispanic and African American) according to the classification method used by the U.S. Census. Between 2000 and 2010, the Hispanic population in the United States grew by 43 percent — from 35 million people in 2000 to more than 50 million people in 2010 — much more rapidly than the population as a whole.

Although the overall U.S. population is becoming more diverse, no two places are changing in exactly the same way. For example, the Boston and San Francisco metropolitan areas have about the same number of people and grew at about the same overall rate, but their racial and ethnic compositions changed in different ways. Table 2-9 shows the makeup of the population by race in the Boston and San Francisco metropolitan areas.

In both the Boston and San Francisco metropolitan areas, the white population decreased from 2000 to 2010, although the fall was sharper in the San Francisco metropolitan area. The Asian populations increased in both places, but the growth of these demographic groups was much stronger in the Boston metropolitan area. One key difference between the two places is that the African-American population fell by about 7 percent in the San Francisco area but increased by nearly a quarter in the Boston area.

Table 2-9   The Boston and San Francisco Populations by Race, 2000–2010

	Boston			San Francisco		
	Population, 2000	Population, 2010	Percent Change, 2000–2010	Population, 2000	Population, 2010	Percent Change, 2000–2010
White	3,665,535	3,587,540	–1.9%	2,334,476	2,239,519	–4.1%
African American	260,695	331,292	27.1%	390,509	363,905	–6.8%
American Indian and Alaska Native	9,810	1,138	–88.4%	21,669	24,774	14.3%
Asian	202,056	294,503	45.8%	790,066	1,005,823	27.3%
Native Hawaiian and other Pacific Islander	1,245	1,491	19.8%	25,052	31,832	27.1%
Some other race	153,514	208,307	35.5%	340,168	429,754	26.3%
Combination of two or more races	108,489	118,201	9.0%	221,800	239,784	8.1%
Total population	4,391,344	4,542,202	3.4%	423,740	4,335,391	28.0%

Source: U.S. Census, 2000 and 2010

Both areas experienced rapid growth in their Hispanic populations, with Boston's increasing by 46 percent from 2000 to 2010 (to more than 400,000 people) and San Francisco's increasing by about 28 percent from 2000 to 2010 (to 940,000 people).

So, although the overall totals may be similar, the makeup of the population and how it's changing can be very different from place to place.

For Richer or Poorer: Economic Trends

A healthy local economy is a necessary ingredient of a successful community, but different places have different local economies. Places differ in terms of how many businesses and jobs are in the community, whether the local economy is growing or shrinking, and what kinds of businesses and industries are present in the community.

Cities that work: Where the jobs are

Between 1999 and 2009, the total number of jobs in the U.S. economy grew by about 7.5 percent. But, like the growth in population, some parts of the country experienced above-average growth, while others experienced a decline in employment levels. Table 2-10 shows employment trends in the 15 largest U.S. metropolitan areas from 1999 to 2009.

Table 2-10	Employment Trends in the 15 Largest U.S. Metropolitan Areas, 1999–2009		
Metropolitan Area	*Employment, 1999*	*Employment, 2009*	*Percent Change, 1999–2009*
New York–Northern New Jersey–Long Island, NY–NJ–PA	9,793,242	10,769,920	10.0%
Los Angeles–Long Beach–Santa Ana, CA	7,124,336	7,400,886	3.9%
Chicago–Joliet–Naperville, IL–IN–WI	5,357,103	5,465,307	2.0%
Dallas–Fort Worth–Arlington, TX	3,297,116	3,887,140	17.9%

(continued)

Table 2-10 *(continued)*

Metropolitan Area	Employment, 1999	Employment, 2009	Percent Change, 1999–2009
Washington–Arlington–Alexandria, DC–VA–MD–WV	3,227,356	3,815,530	18.2%
Houston–Sugar Land–Baytown, TX	2,749,397	3,409,861	24.0%
Philadelphia–Camden–Wilmington, PA–NJ–DE–MD	3,180,220	3,389,983	6.6%
Miami–Fort Lauderdale–Pompano Beach, FL	2,665,160	3,087,468	15.8%
Boston–Cambridge–Quincy, MA–NH	2,931,053	3,063,741	4.5%
Atlanta–Sandy Springs–Marietta, GA	2,674,300	3,055,427	14.3%
San Francisco–Oakland–Fremont, CA	2,699,054	2,720,541	0.8%
Detroit–Warren–Livonia, MI	2,507,836	2,239,741	–10.7%
Phoenix–Mesa–Glendale, AZ	1,857,595	2,217,136	19.4%
Seattle–Tacoma–Bellevue, WA	1,994,341	2,188,934	9.8%
Riverside–San Bernardino–Ontario, CA	1,312,289	1,636,845	24.7%

Source: U.S. Bureau of Economic Analysis

Among the 15 U.S. metropolitan areas with the largest populations, only one — the Detroit metropolitan area — lost jobs between 1999 and 2009. Four metropolitan areas — Los Angeles, Chicago, Philadelphia, and Boston — added jobs, but at a rate slower than that of the national economy. The Atlanta, Dallas, Houston, Washington, D.C., Phoenix, and Riverside metropolitan areas all added jobs at more than twice the national rate, with job growth ranging from 16 percent to more than 24 percent.

Big differences between what's happening nationally and what's going on at the local level can exist. Some cities may be making plans to help prevent job losses and help people who are struggling economically at the same time that the national economy is growing; other areas may be making plans to keep up with the demands of businesses for more space and more workers.

Different places, different jobs: What kind of city is yours?

Not only are some places gaining jobs while other places are losing them, but different places usually also have a mix of jobs in different industries that isn't the same as the overall national pattern. An area that has an above-average number of jobs in industries that are growing nationally may fare better than an area that has lots of jobs in industries that are losing employment across the country.

Table 2-11 shows the employment trends for the 12 largest non-farm industries in the United States from 2001 to 2009. The two largest U.S. industries — government and healthcare — both grew faster than the overall economy. But the next two largest industries — retail trade and manufacturing — both lost jobs, with the manufacturing industry shedding almost 30 percent of its employment between 2001 and 2009. Overall, the national economy added jobs even though some industries gained jobs while others lost.

Table 2-11	Trends in Employment in the United States by the 12 Largest Industries, 2001–2009		
Industry	Employment, 2001	Employment, 2009	Percent Change, 2001–2009
Total non-farm employment	162,450,000	171,177,000	5%
Government and government enterprises	23,151,000	24,649,000	6%
Healthcare and social assistance	15,247,000	18,782,000	23%
Retail trade	18,256,000	17,702,000	−3%
Manufacturing	16,914,000	12,394,000	−27%
Accommodations and food services	10,807,000	12,005,000	11%
Professional, scientific, and technical services	10,273,000	11,829,000	15%
Administrative and waste services	9,605,000	9,939,000	3%
Other services, except public administration	9,075,000	9,883,000	9%
Construction	9,818,000	9,505,000	−3%

(continued)

Table 2-11 *(continued)*

Metropolitan Area	Employment, 1999	Employment, 2009	Percent Change, 1999–2009
Finance and insurance	7,806,000	9,432,000	21%
Real estate and rental and leasing	5,547,000	7,534,000	36%
Wholesale trade	6,231,000	6,162,000	–1%

Source: U.S. Bureau of Economic Analysis

But different places can have different trends. For example, among the 12 most populous U.S. metropolitan areas, the Detroit area lost the highest percentage of its employment from 2001 to 2009, while the Houston area was the strongest gainer. Table 2-12 shows employment trends by industry for the Detroit and Houston metropolitan areas.

From 2001 to 2009, Detroit lost jobs in the same industries in which the national economy lost jobs, but it also lost jobs in parts of the national economy that gained jobs. The Detroit area lost employment in 7 of the top 12 industries, with the sharpest blow coming in the manufacturing industry, where the area lost nearly half its manufacturing jobs between 2001 and 2009. But in Houston, the overall growth rate was 19 percent and only one industry lost jobs. The Houston area gained jobs in the same places as the national economy, and manufacturing was the only industry that lost jobs (and its 2 percent decline was far better than the national average).

The employment information in Tables 2-10 through 2-12 is for the years 2001 through 2009 and doesn't fully reflect the jobs that have been lost since the onset of the "great recession" in the United States, starting in 2008. It takes the government a few years to make detailed economic reports for metropolitan areas, and up-to-date information on the recession isn't yet available. But information on national industry trends through 2011 suggests that most metropolitan areas will experience job losses in key industries hurt by the recession, including manufacturing, construction, real estate, retail trade, and the financial industry.

Table 2-12   Trends in Employment in Detroit and Houston by the 12 Largest Industries, 2001–2009

	Detroit Metropolitan Area			Houston Metropolitan Area		
	Employment, 2001	Employment, 2009	Percent Change, 2001–2009	Employment, 2001	Employment, 2009	Percent Change, 2001–2009
Total non-farm employment	2,515,000	2,234,000	−11%	2,853,000	3,393,000	19%
Government and government enterprises	252,000	229,000	−9%	329,000	379,000	15%
Healthcare and social assistance	251,000	299,000	19%	203,000	293,000	44%
Retail trade	273,000	230,000	−16%	300,000	319,000	6%
Manufacturing	371,000	193,000	−48%	243,000	239,000	−2%
Accommodations and food services	151,000	155,000	3%	176,000	227,000	29%
Professional, scientific, and technical services	215,000	194,000	−10%	224,000	277,000	24%
Administrative and waste services	183,000	159,000	−13%	206,000	244,000	18%
Other services, except public administration	Data not available	120,000	Data not available	166,000	194,000	17%
Construction	127,000	90,000	−29%	242,000	270,000	11%
Finance and insurance	109,000	129,000	19%	126,000	170,000	35%
Real estate and rental and leasing	91,000	104,000	15%	109,000	146,000	35%
Wholesale trade	107,000	88,000	−18%	132,000	153,000	16%

Source: U.S. Bureau of Economic Analysis

Keeping tabs on economic trends helps cities, towns, and metropolitan areas make plans that address not only the number of jobs in their area, but also the kinds of jobs that are needed to maintain the economic health of the community. In some places, it may be necessary to keep up with rapid growth in many different industries, while other areas may struggle to maintain their employment base and replace lost jobs in declining industries.

The Shape of Things to Come: Changing Urban Geographies

As cities grow and change, their shape and impact on the environment also change. Many urban areas are rapidly growing outward in a sprawling fashion that uses more and more land that could otherwise be preserved as natural and agricultural areas. Many communities also are becoming more aware of their local environmental conditions, as well as how local environmental changes — especially increases in local greenhouse gas emissions — can impact the global environment.

Sprawling cities

Many urban areas in the United States are using an increasing amount of land as people and businesses take up locations at the outer edges of cities and metropolitan areas that used to be forests, farmland, and other undeveloped areas.

There are many definitions of *urban sprawl,* but one of the easiest ways to define a sprawling land use pattern is as one that uses land at a faster rate than population growth. For example, one report from the Brookings Institution found that, between 1982 and 1997, all the metropolitan areas in the United States collectively increased their population by 17 percent but increased their total urbanized area by about 47 percent — that's urban sprawl.

In addition to using more land, providing infrastructure and public services for sprawling urban areas can be more costly, because they have to be spread out across a larger area. Some studies show that sprawling areas can have more social problems, such as unemployment due to faraway workplaces that can't be reached by workers who can't afford to own cars.

Cities and towns are using a wide range of planning approaches to address concerns about urban sprawl that balance local population and economic growth with land use patterns that are more compact. For example, many places are looking at ways to concentrate their future growth in areas that can be easily reached by mass transportation and are already serviced by existing infrastructure, such as sewer and electrical services. (I talk more about urban sprawl and metropolitan growth issues in Chapter 13.)

Environmental concerns and changing cities

Urban planning is increasingly concerned about the relationship between cities and the environment. More and more, urban plans are dealing with environmental issues in ways that try to balance immediate needs with long-term sustainability, as well as local demands with global impacts, including several key trends:

- ✔ **Increasing land use by urban areas:** The most immediate impact of growing urban populations is that expanding cities usually need to use more land. Growing urban areas often take over forests, farmland, habitats for local plants and animals, and other environmentally sensitive areas as they grow outward.

- ✔ **Pollution and environmental degradation:** Cities and towns are increasingly taking steps to prevent pollution and reduce environmental damage to the air, water, land, and plant and animal species within urban and metropolitan areas.

- ✔ **Impacts on human health:** Poor environmental conditions often are associated with poor health for the people who live there. For example, poor air quality in some cities has been associated with higher rates of certain diseases, such as asthma.

- ✔ **Global impacts:** Cities and towns also are taking steps to reduce their local use of environmental resources that can have global environmental impacts, such as rising sea levels that could put many coastal cities underwater.

    For example, New York City recently embarked on a plan to reduce its emissions of greenhouse gases that are associated with global climate change. (You can find out more about New York's plan in Chapter 21.)

These challenges are prompting cities and towns to search for planning strategies that can help them use resources more efficiently and reduce their environmental impacts. Many cities are making plans to use new technologies and cutting-edge methods, such as eco-friendly green buildings and alternative energy sources, to keep up with growing populations while avoiding damage to the environment.

More People, Bigger Cities: The Global Urban Challenge

For the first time in human history, most of the world's population lives in a city. And the world's urban population is expected to rise sharply in the future. By mid-century, about two-thirds of the world's population will live in cities and there will be more very large cities than ever before.

Going to the city: The global move to cities

In the year 2010, the world's population stood at roughly seven billion people, almost exactly half of whom live in cities. Table 2-13 shows United Nations estimates of world population growth through the year 2050. These figures project that the world's cities will add about 700 million residents every decade. By 2050, the world's urban population is expected to grow by nearly 80 percent, and city dwellers will make up more than two-thirds of the world's population.

Table 2-13	World Population Trends, 2000–2050		
	World Population	**Urban Population**	**Percent Urban**
2000	6,100,000,000	2,800,000,000	46%
2010	6,900,000,000	3,500,000,000	51%
2020	7,700,000,000	4,200,000,000	54%
2030	8,300,000,000	4,900,000,000	59%
2040	8,800,000,000	5,600,000,000	64%
2050	9,200,000,000	6,300,000,000	69%

Source: United Nations, World Urbanization Prospects

The largest increases in urban populations will occur in Asia and Africa, especially in poorer countries. Table 2-14 lists estimates of the world's urban population by region for the years 2009 to 2050. Asia is expected to nearly double its number of urban dwellers, from about 1.7 billion in 2009 to 3.4 billion in 2050. The world's most rapid growth in urban population is expected in Africa, where the urban population is expected to more than triple to 1.2 billion people by 2050. Slower growth rates are projected for the rest of the world, and the urban population of Europe is expected to increase by less than 10 percent through the year 2050.

Table 2-14	Urban Population by World Region, 2009–2050		
Region	*2009*	*2025*	*2050*
Africa	399,000,000	661,000,000	1,231,000,000
Asia	1,719,000,000	2,382,000,000	3,382,000,000
Europe	531,000,000	561,000,000	582,000,000
Latin America and the Caribbean	462,000,000	561,000,000	648,000,000
Northern America	285,000,000	340,000,000	404,000,000
Oceania	25,000,000	30,000,000	38,000,000

Source: United Nations, World Urbanization Prospects

Going big: The rise of the megacity

Not only is the world's urban population expected to rise very rapidly, but the number and size of the world's very large cities also are expected to increase dramatically in the coming decades. The term *megacity* refers to an urban area with a population of more than 10 million people. In 1950, there were just two megacities: New York City and Tokyo. New York City was the larger of the two with a population of about 12 million people. By 2009, there were about 20 megacities, including three with populations of more than 20 million.

By the year 2025, there are likely to be 30 or more megacities, some of which will have populations over 25 million people. Table 2-15 lists the world's 12 largest megacities in 2025. Tokyo, Delhi, and Mumbai are all expected to have populations over 25 million and even the 12th largest megacity, Kinshasa, will have a population of more than 15 million people. Most of the world's megacities will also be in poorer countries — including Bangladesh, Pakistan, Nigeria, and the Democratic Republic of the Congo — where tens of millions of people manage to survive on just a few dollars a day.

Table 2-15	The World's 12 Largest Megacities in 2025	
	Population	*National Gross Domestic Product (GDP) Per Capita, 2010*
Tokyo, Japan	37,090,000	$33,649
Delhi, India	28,570,000	$3,354
Mumbai, India	25,810,000	$3,354
São Paulo, Brazil	21,650,000	$10,847
Dhaka, Bangladesh	20,940,000	$1,458
Mexico City, Mexico	20,710,000	$14,192
New York City, United States	20,640,000	$46,653
Kolkata, India	20,110,000	$3,354
Shanghai, China	20,020,000	$7,206
Karachi, Pakistan	18,730,000	$2,625
Lagos, Nigeria	15,810,000	$2,289
Kinshasa, Democratic Republic of the Congo	15,040,000	$327

Source: United Nations, World Urbanization Prospects and Human Development Indicators

Overall, the world's urban population is expected to grow very rapidly, especially in poorer countries. And there will be a larger number of even bigger megacities in the future. World urban growth trends will create lots of challenges for urban planning around the world, ranging from providing enough decent housing and clean water for billions of new urban dwellers to successfully managing the local and global environmental impacts of the planet's skyrocketing urban population.

Chapter 3

Who Makes Urban Plans and Why

In This Chapter

▶ Looking at the different kinds of urban plans

▶ Understanding why plans matter

▶ Focusing on the types of communities that make plans

▶ Seeing how different community members can play a part in the planning process

*W*e all make plans — dinner plans, wedding plans, travel plans. Making a plan for a city or town is a more complicated undertaking, but it shares many of the same underlying motivations. What should be done? Who should do it? What happens if we do this and what happens if we don't?

Urban plans are made by many different parties for many different reasons. Some plans are made by local governments representing individual cities or towns, while other plans are made by regional governments representing many cities and towns. Some plans are made by community organizations to address issues in specific neighborhoods. A city or town may make a plan in order to meet a specific legal requirement, while another place may make a plan due to the concerns of residents about changes they see happening in their community.

In this chapter, I explain who makes different kinds of plans and why plans get made. Along the way, I also describe the wide range of people and organizations that are typically involved in making plans.

Different Kinds of Urban Plans

In practice, urban planning includes different kinds of plans produced by various governmental agencies or nongovernmental organizations:

✔ **Official comprehensive plans:** An *official comprehensive plan* is a plan that is formally adopted by the local government of a city or town. These plans also are called *master plans* or *general plans.* An official comprehensive plan is broad in scope and addresses all the major components of a city or town, ranging from land use to housing to transportation, as well as other specific issues that are relevant to local conditions or community concerns.

Official comprehensive plans consider a long-range time period and typically plan ahead for 20 to 30 years (although some communities may use longer time frames, such as 50 years). The geographic scope of an official comprehensive plan usually covers an entire jurisdiction, such as a whole city or town. An official comprehensive plan is used by the government of a city or town to guide its future development and serves as the basis for developing specific laws and policies that will be consistent with the comprehensive plan.

✔ **Specialized plans:** A *specialized plan* is one that addresses a narrower range of issues, including looking at issues in a shorter time period, addressing a specific issue, or looking at a specific place, such as a neighborhood within a city or town.

✔ **Informal plans:** Some plans are *informal,* meaning that they haven't been officially adopted by the government representing a city or town. In some cases, local governments produce informal plans to complement the official comprehensive plan. Nonprofit agencies and nongovernmental organizations also make plans that address specific geographic areas, such as a neighborhood, or bring attention to specific issues, such as homelessness. Although informal plans may not have the force of government behind them, they can serve many of the same functions as official plans by helping to plot a future for the community and bring people together to work toward a common set of goals.

Your community may be represented by many different plans — official and comprehensive, informal, or specialized. For example, your local government may have an official comprehensive plan for your city or town, and your neighborhood may be addressed in an informal neighborhood plan produced by a community organization. (I talk more about different types of plans in the "Planning for Different Types of Communities" section, later in this chapter.)

Why Communities Make Plans

Communities make plans for reasons that are both pragmatic and idealistic. Urban planning helps communities address pressing issues and work toward a common vision for the future. And, in some cases, communities are legally required to prepare local plans.

Planning for changing communities

Urban planning is a way for communities to establish goals for the future of the community and to address challenges faced by the community. A good urban plan helps a community plan for change in three important ways:

- **It helps a community make long-term decisions.** Urban planning provides a process for considering important issues, especially when the long-term consequences may be very costly or even irreversible. For example, a decision to change local land use regulations to allow farmland to be used for housing development will have a permanent impact on the environment.

- **It helps a community build consensus about the future.** Urban planning is a way for a community to reach consensus on goals for the future of the community, as well as specific ways to coordinate strategies and actions that will contribute to the future development of the community. For example, many urban plans use surveys of the community to identify key issues to be addressed in the plan, such as public safety or housing affordability. Many plans incorporate input from public hearings and meetings in their planning goals, such as a goal for how much affordable housing should be available in the community within 20 years.

- **It gives a community a chance to address new issues and concerns.** Urban planning often is used by communities to address new issues comprehensively and find long-term solutions to new problems and community concerns. For example, a community may use its comprehensive planning process to address the best ways to accommodate sudden and rapid population growth. In another example, some communities have recently begun planning for the impacts of global climate change, such as rising sea levels, based on recent scientific evidence and advice (see Chapter 11).

Meeting legal requirements for plans

Many communities are legally required to have an *official comprehensive plan* (a plan that is formally adopted by the local government of a city or town; see the nearby sidebar, "Different kinds of plans," for more information). Since the 1960s, a growing number of states have enacted laws related to land use and environmental protection that require local planning by cities and towns.

The requirements vary from state to state but generally fall into five areas:

- **What planning components must be addressed in the plan?** Many state laws indicate specific areas that must be addressed in local plans.

For example, Wisconsin requires that local comprehensive plans address six specific topics:

- Housing

- Transportation

- Utilities and community facilities

- Economic development

- Land use

- Agricultural, natural, and cultural features

✔ **How long a time period must the plan cover?** Some states specify the duration of the plan and how far ahead it should plan.

For example, Michigan's statewide planning law sets a time frame of "20 or more years into the future" for plans required of its cities and towns.

✔ **Do local plans have to be consistent with state or regional planning objectives?** Some states require local plans to be consistent with broader planning goals.

In Minnesota, for example, state law requires that local plans by cities and towns in a seven-county area around Minneapolis–St. Paul be consistent with regional planning goals. The area's regional planning agency, called the Metropolitan Council, can require cities and towns to modify their local plans if the agency determines that a local plan isn't consistent with the overall goals of the regional plan.

✔ **Does the plan require coordination with other government agencies?** In some cases, cities and towns are required to coordinate their plans with those of neighboring cities and towns, as well as other agencies or organizations.

For example, Michigan's statewide planning law, called the Coordinated Planning Act, requires that local plans be reviewed by all of a city's neighboring municipalities, as well as the county government and public or private utilities servicing the community (such as railroads or electric power companies).

✔ **When does the plan have to be updated?** Some states require that local plans be updated on a regular basis.

For example, Michigan requires that local comprehensive plans be updated every five years. In California, state law mandates that the housing component of a local plan be updated every seven years.

A 2010 survey by the American Planning Association found that 16 states require local comprehensive plans and that another 7 states require cities and towns to have plans under certain circumstances.

Information on specific requirements for local plans in your community is likely to be available from your local planning department. State or regional agencies that oversee local planning in your area also should be able to provide detailed information on local planning requirements.

Urban Plans for Different Types of Communities

Although most cities and towns have official comprehensive plans, other types of community areas often prepare plans, too. Many cities and towns make specialized plans that address specific topics, such as open space conservation. Some cities and towns also produce plans for different sub-areas within their borders, such as plans for specific neighborhoods or downtown plans. Cities and towns also are included in regional plans for metropolitan areas in a growing number of places across the United States.

Cities and towns

In addition to an official comprehensive plan, many cities and towns have specialized plans, which help them address specific concerns about a variety of issues in both the short term and the long term. Specialized plans are typically prepared in coordination with the official comprehensive plan. A specialized plan addresses issues in greater detail than an official comprehensive plan does; a specialized plan also may update approaches from the most recent comprehensive plan in order to deal with changing or unexpected circumstances.

The following sections cover various types of specialized plans used by cities and towns.

Sub-area plans

A sub-area plan is for a smaller area within a city or town, such as a specific neighborhood or downtown area. These plans often are prepared by local governments, but sometimes they're made by community organizations or nongovernmental organizations.

You can find more information on sub-area plans in the "Neighborhoods, downtowns, and districts" section, later in this chapter.

Strategic plans

Cities and towns often use strategic plans to address specific issues. These plans have a shorter time frame and emphasize working toward outcomes that can be achieved quickly.

For example, the city of Portland, Oregon, recently produced its *Neighborhood Economic Development Strategy: A 5-Year Plan for Promoting Small Business Success & Neighborhood Vitality* (http://bit.ly/uRtTby), which contains a variety of short-range initiatives to address the deterioration of some of the city's commercial areas and challenges faced by the city's small businesses due to the 2008 economic recession.

Topical plans

Cities and town often prepare plans addressing specific topics that are important to the community, such as a focused plan for the preservation and improvement of parklands and open space. Some local governments also are required to produce topical plans as a requirement for receiving funding from state or federal government agencies. For example, some cities that receive funding from the U.S. Department of Housing and Urban Development are required to prepare plans that specifically address housing issues in those communities.

Metropolitan areas

A growing number of places in the United States are planning for metropolitan areas. Typically referred to as *regional plans,* these plans don't just cover a single city or town; instead, they usually address a major central city and all the surrounding suburban communities. Planning for metropolitan areas varies significantly from place to place, depending on the types of government agencies and organizations that are involved.

Regional government planning

Relatively few places in the United States have regional government authorities, but the number of such places has been increasing in recent years.

For example, the Portland, Oregon, area's Metro Regional Government and the Metropolitan Council of the Minneapolis–St. Paul area both were created by state laws that give these authorities the ability to create plans for their metropolitan areas.

County governments

Every state in the United States has some form of county governments. The specific powers of county governments vary from state to state. Most counties don't directly produce regional plans, but county governments often promote cooperation among the cities and towns in their county to help them address issues that impact multiple communities in the same county, such as planning for transportation services.

Councils of governments

A council of governments is a representative body whose members are the cities and towns of a region. This is similar to the way that the membership of the United Nations is made up of its member countries. Councils of governments sometimes produce regional plans in cooperation with their local members and also assist local governments in cooperative planning.

Metropolitan planning organizations

Since the 1970s, federal transportation funding has required that most U.S. metropolitan areas have a regional governmental agency designated as a *metropolitan planning organization* (MPO). An MPO creates transportation plans and coordinates federal transportation funding for the region. In some cases, existing regional governments and councils of governments serve as a region's MPO.

Civic organizations

Civic organizations sometimes are involved in regional planning, especially when a metropolitan area doesn't have a regional government or other agency in charge of regional planning. Regional plans by civic organizations include the Commercial Club of Chicago's *Chicago Metropolis 2020* (www. chicagometropolis2020.org), released in 2001, and the Regional Plan Association's 1996 plan for greater New York City, *A Region at Risk* (Island Press). Although these plans don't have the formal backing of a government agency, they can be very effective in helping to promote and coordinate cooperation among cities and towns in a region.

Seattle's neighborhood plans

The city of Seattle is a great example of local planning that coordinates an official comprehensive plan with specialized neighborhood plans. The city's 1994 citywide comprehensive plan established overall goals for the future development of the city in areas including land use, transportation, and the environment. The plan also identified general planning priorities for each neighborhood within the city, and these priorities were used to develop specific neighborhood plans.

Based on the comprehensive plan, the city worked closely with residents, community organizations, and other stakeholders to prepare detailed neighborhood plans. Between 1995 and 2000, specialized plans were completed for each of the city's 38 neighborhoods. By using planning to work both "top down" and "bottom up," this process allowed each neighborhood to develop its own planning approaches while still meeting the overall goals of the city's comprehensive plan. In 2008, the city began updating its neighborhood plans based on more recent versions of its citywide comprehensive plan. You can find Seattle's neighborhood plans at http://1.usa.gov/tNVRw6.

Neighborhoods, downtowns, and districts

Sub-areas within cities and towns often have their own specialized plans. These plans often are produced by local governments or other government agencies but sometimes are made by community organizations or other nongovernmental organizations. The most common small areas within cities and towns for specialized planning are neighborhoods, downtown areas, and other special districts.

Neighborhood plans

Local governments often work closely with residents and community organizations to produce specialized plans for specific neighborhoods. These plans often are comprehensive, dealing with a wide variety of issues at the neighborhood scale, and develop planning strategies that are specific to the area.

Downtown plans

Downtowns often receive specialized planning attention because of their unique nature as the heart of their cities. Plans for downtowns are usually wide ranging and deal with downtown-specific issues, such as design standards for office buildings or ways to manage commuter traffic.

Special districts

In addition to downtown areas, most cities and towns have other areas that benefit from specialized planning, such as waterfront districts or cultural districts. Like downtown plans, these specialized plans focus on issues that are specific to the characteristics of the area and may be not applicable to the rest of a city or town.

One place, five plans

The Shepard Davern district, located in the city of St. Paul, Minnesota, is home to about 5,000 residents. A combination of both residential and business areas, it occupies an area of less than half a square mile in the southwestern corner of the city, bordering the Mississippi River. The Shepard Davern district is a gateway to the city, sitting at the foot of a bridge across the river that connects the district's main thoroughfare to the nearby Minneapolis–St. Paul International Airport. This area, small as it is,

has its own district plan to guide future development and also is included in four other plans, each of which may have an impact on its future development.

The Shepard Davern Gateway Small Area Plan (http://1.usa.gov/uuUaN6), produced by the city of St. Paul in 1999, recognizes that the area is both a distinct community and an entrance to the city of St. Paul and the larger Highland Park neighborhood of which it is a part. The district plan calls for new residential and commercial development, as well as improved streets, sidewalks, and public spaces that will lend a "village" feel to the district and allow pedestrians to use the area more easily. In general, the district plan deals with small-scale transportation and physical planning issues that are likely to have immediate impacts on the residents, businesses, and other people who use the district.

The Shepard Davern district makes up one section of the larger Highland Park neighborhood, which totals about 23,000 residents. The Highland Park neighborhood plan (http://1.usa.gov/sh38i5), produced by the city of St. Paul in 2007, examines a wide variety of issues, including housing, urban design, commercial development, transportation, parks and recreation, public safety, and environmental issues. The overall plan for the Highland Park neighborhood addresses community resources not addressed in the district plan, such as access to parks and libraries for residents of the district. The neighborhood plan also identifies the Shepard Davern district as one of the neighborhood's important commercial areas and suggests improvements to the urban design guidelines for buildings in the districts.

The *City of Saint Paul Comprehensive Plan* (http://1.usa.gov/tPal8j), published in 2010, also deals with a variety of planning issues related to the Shepard Davern district. The comprehensive plan provides an overall framework for the future development of the entire city and addresses issues including housing, land use, public services, transportation, historic preservation, and the environment. In the land use elements of the city's comprehensive plan, the Shepard Davern district is identified as a neighborhood center area where the city will support increased residential and commercial development. The comprehensive plan also designates part of the district as a mixed-use corridor and recommends improvements to the district's main thoroughfare and some adjacent buildings.

Finally, the Shepard Davern district also is represented in plans by Ramsey County (http://bit.ly/s5o6u0), which includes the city of St. Paul, and the Metro Council, which plans for the seven-county Twin Cities region. Ramsey County and the Metro Council have much less direct authority over the Shepard Davern district, but both plans have recommendations for the region's transportation and infrastructure systems that will guide public investment toward the region's existing urban areas, rather than undeveloped suburban and rural areas. The Metro Council's *Regional Development Framework for 2030* (http://bit.ly/uxS3hZ) identifies the Shepard Davern district as a "developed area" and a priority for future regional investments in transportation and infrastructure that will help the region keep up with anticipated population growth.

Although it's just one place, and not a very big one at that, the future of the Shepard Davern district will be influenced not just by its own community plan, but also by other plans that address the district as part of a neighborhood, city, county, and metropolitan region.

Public Participation in Urban Planning

Many people are involved in the urban planning process, from professional urban planners working for local governments to ordinary residents who are interested in the future of their communities. Each group is important and plays a different role in contributing to a successful plan.

The exact ways in which different parts of local government are involved in the planning process vary from place to place. Your local planning department can provide detailed information on local planning issues and tell you which departments and officials are involved.

Local government planners and officials

Local governments carry out a wide range of planning activities, including preparing a city or town's official comprehensive plan, as well as working on specialized plans. Professional urban planners often are the most visible figures in local government planning, but many other parts of local government also are involved in the planning process.

Planning departments

A *planning department* is an official agency of a local government, like a police department or fire department, that reports to the local executive and legislative branches of government, such as the mayor and city council. Professional urban planners working for planning departments carry out the day-to-day tasks of preparing comprehensive and specialized plans. In some cases, planning departments also use the services of private planning consultants when there's a need to deal with specialized planning issues or to work on specific projects, such as parts of comprehensive and specialized plans.

Planning commissions

A *planning commission* (sometimes known as a *planning board*) is part of the legislative branch of a local government and is a committee that reports to a city council. The members of the planning commission are elected or appointed community residents; some planning commissions have both elected and appointed members. Members of a planning commission often work closely with the planning department as plans are being prepared. The most important function of a planning commission is to review and vote on preliminary plans before they're sent to the city council for official approval.

City councils

A *city council* is the primary legislative branch of local government that is responsible for making laws that apply to a city or town. City council members often are involved in the planning process by helping to form the goals and strategies that will be included in the plan. A city council is typically responsible for voting on the approval of official plans.

Mayors

The executive branch of local government is usually headed by a *mayor,* although some cities and towns are headed by a professional city manager. The mayor, or the mayor's staff, usually is involved in the planning process and helping to form planning goals and strategies. An official plan typically must be approved by both the city council and the mayor.

Other departments

Many other local government departments may be involved in the planning process. For example, the budget department may provide planners with detailed information related to the cost of making improvements to infrastructure, or a fire department may help planners work on building safety standards. In many cases, the implementation of a city's official comprehensive plan may delegate tasks to many different departments of a local government.

State, federal, and other government agencies

Federal and state governments often are involved in local planning, especially for larger cities and metropolitan areas. Other forms of government, such as school districts, also often are involved in local planning. These governmental partners play a wide range of roles that support local planning.

Federal government

Many federal agencies are involved in local planning, such as the Department of Transportation, the Department of Housing and Urban Development, and the Environmental Protection Agency. These agencies often participate in the local planning process by overseeing compliance with federal laws and regulations, as well as providing funding or technical expertise for local planning and development projects.

State government

Often, a variety of state agencies are involved in local planning in areas including transportation, housing, and environmental protection. A state agency may oversee local compliance with state laws and regulations. Some state agencies also are directly involved in local communities and work closely with local planners to coordinate their services with the community's plan, such as a state transportation agency that builds and maintains local roads.

Other government agencies

Most areas have a wide variety of governmental authorities that are independent of a city or town's local government but play an important role in the community. For example, in most places, school districts are separate government authorities that are independent of the general local government. Other examples of separate local government authorities include park districts, library boards, and port authorities. These agencies play important roles in the community and usually are involved in the planning process in order to coordinate the delivery of services with the overall development of the community.

Related professions

In addition to professional urban planners, people in other professions often are involved in making and carrying out urban plans. Urban plans deal with a wide range of topics and issues, involving many other kinds of professionals, ranging from specialized architects and engineers to marketing experts and attorneys:

- ✓ **Architects:** Architects frequently are involved in urban planning, especially on issues that are directly related to land use and urban design. Architects play an important role not just in developing blueprints and drawings for specific sites or buildings, but also in helping to integrate physical design issues with other planning issues. For example, many communities have adopted environmentally friendly building regulations that require local plans to coordinate architectural and environmental issues. Architects also participate in planning by working directly with the public on community design issues using innovative methods such as charrettes and visioning meetings. (You can find more information on this subject in Chapter 8.)

- ✓ **Urban planning consultants:** Local governments may use urban planning consultants to help with the planning process. In fact, some small cities and towns don't have their own planning departments and rely entirely on planning consultants; in this case, planning consultants may play a very broad role in assisting a city or town in carrying out a wide range of planning functions. In larger cities, specialized consultants sometimes are used to assist the planning department with planning tasks that they aren't able to complete themselves. Urban planning consultants sometimes also are hired by community organizations or nongovernmental organizations to help develop their plans and bring in expertise that may not be present in the organization's staff or community.

- ✓ **Civil and transportation engineers:** Civil and transportation engineers can plan and evaluate infrastructure projects.

- ✓ **Environmental scientists and engineers:** Environmental scientists and engineers can assess the environment and help understand the impacts of future development on the environment.

✔ **Real-estate development consultants:** Real-estate development consultants can help plan and execute land development and redevelopment
projects.

✔ **Tourism and marketing experts:** Tourism and marketing experts can
develop plans and programs to help manage local resources in ways
that are attractive to tourists.

✔ **Demographers and economists:** Demographers and economists can
assess social and economic conditions and help explain how the community is changing.

✔ **Lawyers:** Lawyers who specialize in land use, zoning, and public policy
can evaluate existing local laws and help develop new laws and policies
to implement plans and development projects.

Community stakeholders

Community stakeholders are people who have an interest in the community,
such as residents who live in the community or people who own property in
the community. Urban planners often are involved in extensive community outreach efforts in order to ensure that local plans reflect the needs and input of
community stakeholders who will be most directly impacted by future plans.

Residents

Residents of a community often are the most important constituency for a
local plan because they're the ones who will be most directly impacted by a
plan and its outcomes. Many residents are eager to participate in planning
for a variety of reasons, including having a financial investment in the community and an emotional attachment to it.

Residents can contribute their knowledge and experience to a plan by identifying important issues, helping to set planning goals and strategies, and providing help and support as the plan is being implemented.

Local businesses and property owners

Representatives of local businesses and property owners, some of whom may
also be residents, are important to the planning process. Local business and
property owners may have a major financial investment in the community
and contribute significantly to the community's long-term stability. Getting
local business and property owners involved in the planning process can
bring about new ideas and new solutions. For example, a specialized plan
for a neighborhood may look at approaches for improving the quality of the
neighborhood's business areas in ways that could benefit both residents and
business owners.

Community and civic organizations

Community and civic organizations can play an important role in the planning process. These organizations often can assist in reaching out to the residents of a community, helping to identify planning problems and solutions, and bringing new resources to the planning process. For example, a nonprofit organization that provides housing for developmentally disabled adults may be able to help identify appropriate sites for future housing, help urban planners coordinate their other needs (such as transportation), and even serve as a partner in carrying out policies to serve this population.

In some cases, community organizations make their own informal plans that address issues and areas that do not have an existing plan, to complement existing official plans, or to bring attention to the needs of a particular area or raise awareness of a particular issue.

Chapter 4

Making Plans: A Step-by-Step Approach

In This Chapter

▶ Getting a plan off the ground

▶ Collecting and using information

▶ Creating a vision and setting goals

▶ Deciding on planning strategies and actions

▶ Carrying out a successful plan

▶ Monitoring and updating a plan

*I*n this chapter, I take a look at how communities prepare and use their urban plans. The planning process is made up of several steps that help a community figure out where it is and move toward where it wants to be.

Although most communities develop their plans step-by-step, sometimes different steps overlap or a community may need to step backward if things aren't working out as expected. Completing the planning process for a small city or town may take several weeks or a few months; a large city may need a year or two to complete an entirely new comprehensive plan.

 The steps I discuss in this chapter are those that are typically used in making the official comprehensive plan for a city or town, but the overall process is generally compatible with making specialized plans and informal plans as well. (For more on the different kinds of plans, refer to Chapter 3.)

Launching a Plan

It may sound like something of a catch-22, but the real beginning of an urban plan starts with figuring out how the plan will be made. Urban planners and other helpers may be working behind the scenes for weeks or months to set up the planning process. Like any big project, starting with a solid foundation makes it more likely that the project will be successful in the end.

Planning to plan

Figuring out how to make an urban plan may itself require an organizational plan that lays out how the planning process is going to be managed, who will be involved, and what resources will be needed. These and other details may require a significant amount of fact finding and require some preliminary decisions to be made.

Here are some things that need to be looked into and decided on:

✓ **Plan requirements and approvals:** What are the legal or regulatory requirements for the plan? Does the plan have to address specific topics? Are there specific regulations regarding public participation; environmental review; or coordination with federal, state, or neighboring governments?

✓ **Timeline:** How long will it take to complete the plan? Will the planning process be broken up into different tasks, such as one phase for collecting information and another for setting goals? When will each phase start and finish?

✓ **Budget:** What resources need to be made available to complete the plan? How much is the plan going to cost? Who will provide the financing and other resources? Do grants, donations, or other commitments need to be secured before starting to plan?

A plan for a major city can be a very expensive undertaking, requiring both the full attention of existing planning staff and supplemental funding. For example, the city of Austin, Texas, budgeted $1.8 million, in addition to the efforts of its existing urban planning staff, for preparing the city's *Imagine Austin Comprehensive Plan* (www.imagineaustin. net), published in 2011. (See the nearby sidebar, "Getting everyone to imagine Austin," for more on Austin's plan.)

✓ **Coordination with partners:** Will official partners, such as representatives of a state or regional government agency, be involved in making the plan? Do other agencies and organizations have information or other resources that will be needed to complete the plan?

✓ **Community participation:** How will residents, local businesses, and other community stakeholders be able to participate in the plan? What events will need to be organized? What channels of communication will need to be maintained? (Check out the nearby sidebar, "Getting everyone to imagine Austin," for an example of getting the community involved in making a plan.)

✓ **Organizational structure:** How will the management of the plan be organized? Who's in charge of what? Will there be committees and subcommittees to address different parts of the plan?

Getting everyone to imagine Austin

In 2009, the city of Austin, Texas, began the process of creating a new official comprehensive plan, known as the *Imagine Austin Comprehensive Plan* (www.imagine austin.net). At the start of the planning process, the city distributed a handbook called *Making Austin: Public Participation in a New Comprehensive Plan,* which described how people could get involved in making the plan.

The handbook helped people understand what a comprehensive plan is and how the plan would be created. The handbook contained a map of the areas that would be included in the city's plan and described the topics that the plan would address, from land use and housing to health and human services. According to the handbook, the guiding philosophies of the plan were that the process be open to all, engage underrepresented groups in the community,

and be fun and generate enthusiasm for the city's future.

The handbook also identified key governmental agencies and other organizations participating in the planning process, as well as a timeline of the process. The handbook contained details on the outreach methods that would be used to get people involved in the planning process, such as community forums, focus groups, resident surveys, newsletters, and even a book club about planning. Residents and stakeholders could participate in online discussion forums and review draft sections of the plan online.

An organizational plan for public participation in the comprehensive plan helped Austin's residents and other community stakeholders know what was going on and how they could contribute.

✔ **Consulting and support services:** Are outside consultants or support services needed to complete the plan? What types of consultants are likely to be needed? Will the plan require any supporting services, such as preparing special surveys or renting buildings for public events and meetings?

Making an urban plan can be a very complicated undertaking. Plus, the planning process often runs into various detours and obstacles — including everything from unavailable data to protests by residents — that can force changes to the process. But a good organizational plan helps set the pace for the entire process and helps ensure that the resources necessary to complete the plan are available.

Informing the community

After an organizational plan is in place and it's time to start the actual planning process, the next step is to inform the community about what's happening. Ensuring that the community is involved in the planning process from the very start helps build trust and enthusiasm for the process.

Here are some key considerations when informing the community:

- **Who should be informed?** Ideally, information about the plan should be distributed as widely as possible. However, it's also a good idea to identify the plan's community stakeholders and reach out to them directly. The stakeholders may be specific people or groups of people who are likely to have a special interest in the plan, such as business owners in a particular area or representatives of community organizations.

- **How can we reach people?** The initial effort to let people know that the planning process is starting is usually a very broad one that may include issuing press releases to generate media attention, starting a dedicated website or social media group, or sending letters in mass mailings to residents.

Making personal contact with influential community stakeholders may be another important way of getting people involved, because people with a role and reputation in the community can help generate interest in the plan.

Information about the planning process should help people understand both the process that will be used to create the plan, as well as the significance of the plan itself. Including the following information will help generate interest and confidence in the planning process:

- What opportunities will there be for public participation?

- What issues and concerns will be addressed?

- How will the plan be used?

Informing the community about the plan lets everyone know that there will be an opportunity for his or her specific concerns to be addressed and can help build public support for later steps of the planning process.

A number of cities — including Portland (Oregon), Austin (Texas), and Madison (Wisconsin) — have developed specific organizational plans for public participation or handbooks that help inform the public about plans and planning process (see the "Getting everyone to imagine Austin" sidebar, earlier in this chapter).

Understanding the Community

Urban planning uses many information sources to help understand a community's past, present, and future. A small city or town may evaluate some basic measures to describe and analyze the community, such as general data about population change, household size, or income levels. A large city or metropolitan area may conduct complex and expensive studies that use detailed data and sophisticated computer models. Whether planning for a large community or a small one, effectively using information about the community helps pinpoint its strengths and weaknesses.

Although much of the technical work of collecting and analyzing community information is done by professional urban planners, there are many opportunities for public participation in this part of the process:

- ✔ **Residents and community organizations can help gather specific information about the community (for example, by helping to conduct surveys of area residents).**

- ✔ **Planners can present community information at public meetings or in briefings with key community stakeholders.** This can help people develop a more accurate understanding of the community and get people talking about goals and strategies that can be used in the plan.

- ✔ **Planners can present community information in reports or newsletters accessible by the public, especially if detailed data or documents are available online.** Making information available helps lend credibility to the process and makes it possible for anyone to become an expert about his or her community.

Using information

The type of information used in the planning process addresses a wide range of topical areas and looks at the past, present, and possible future of the community. There are three main areas in which plans collect and analyze information about the community:

- ✔ **General background information:** Many plans include general information about the community and its residents. Many plans include a historical overview discussing how the community was founded and how it has developed over the years. Surveys of residents, local businesses, and other community stakeholders identify the issues that are most important to the community.

- ✔ **Demographic and economic change:** A good understanding of a community's demographic and economic conditions is an essential element of the planning process.

  - • **Demographic change:** Urban planners use demographic data to learn about who lives in the community and how the community is growing and changing. Historical data shows how the community has been changing, and urban planners use projections about future population conditions to help identify important trends that will affect the community.

- **Economic change:** Information about the local economy and projections of future conditions help urban planners gauge the economic health of the community and help them make plans in closely related areas, such as land use and transportation. For example, a city with a growing economy may need to set aside additional land for future development and make improvements to roads used by local businesses.

Changes in the population and/or in the local economy drive changes in every other segment of the plan. For example, an increase in population will drive a further need for more public services.

✓ **Specific planning components:** Detailed information also is collected and analyzed for all the specific components of a plan, such as land use, housing, transportation, urban design, natural resources, infrastructure and public services, and other areas that are important to the community. Information on specific components is collected from a wide range of sources and analyzed in many different ways. (Part III of this book provides details on types of information that are used to look at specific planning components.)

Pinpointing strengths and weaknesses

The effective use of community information both describes the community accurately and can be used to establish priorities for the community. One common approach, known as the *SWOT approach,* looks at the strengths, weaknesses, opportunities, and threats faced by a community:

✓ **Strengths:** What are the positive features of the community?

✓ **Weaknesses:** What are the negative features of the community?

✓ **Opportunities:** What is likely to happen in the future that may have a positive impact on the community?

✓ **Threats:** What is likely to happen in the future that may have a negative impact on the community?

There are many variations on the SWOT approach, and it's worth noting that different people may feel differently about what constitutes a strength versus a weakness or an opportunity versus a threat. For example, some people in the community may view a rapidly growing population as a community strength that increases the local tax base, while others may see it as a weakness that puts a strain on existing public services.

Getting people involved in interpreting community information can be a useful step in the planning process. For example, urban planners sometimes prepare "fact sheets" about the community and ask residents to identify which things they feel are positive or negative.

The overall process of collecting and analyzing information about the community helps set the stage for future steps in the planning process. The facts and public input collected in this stage of the process can be used to help shape the plan's vision, goals, and strategies in ways that address the community and its key concerns.

Looking Ahead: Creating a Vision and Setting Goals

After taking a good look at the community and getting community input on where you are, the next step of the planning process is to start figuring out where you want to go. Looking ahead to the future of the community is a process that draws on a realistic understanding of existing conditions and trends, as well as people's hopes and dreams for the community. In this section, I talk about creating a vision statement for the community, as well as how the community works to come up with overall goals and specific objectives for the plan.

Seeing the future: Creating a vision statement for the community

In an urban plan, a *vision statement* is a description of the future of a community that provides an overall picture of what the comprehensive plan is intended to accomplish. Vision statements can be several pages in length, but here's a relatively succinct example:

> This comprehensive plan envisions a future for the city that welcomes future growth and development while maintaining the city's historic heritage, natural resources, and high quality of life for its residents. The city will have high-quality urban design and aesthetic features that are attractive and functional. The city will develop vibrant and healthy neighborhoods, offer a superb transportation system, promote a successful local economy, and maintain our downtown as the commercial center of the community. The long-term success of the city will be promoted by a responsible city government that will strive to provide the leadership and public services necessary to make this vision a reality.

Although not every urban plan contains a vision statement, vision statements are an effective way to summarize the overall purpose of the plan in a way that can be used to develop further goals and strategies for the plan. Figure 4-1 illustrates the relationship between a plan's vision statement and its goals and strategies. The goals and strategies in a plan should be consistent with the overall vision of the plan.

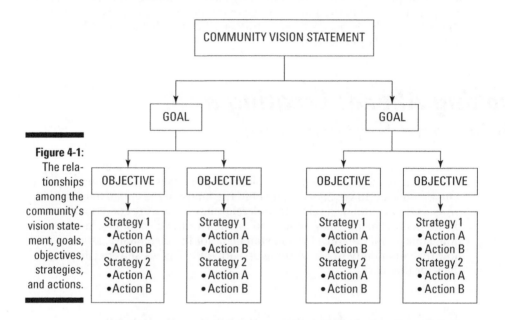

Figure 4-1: The relationships among the community's vision statement, goals, objectives, strategies, and actions.

Producing a vision statement for a plan typically involves a significant amount of public participation. Developing a vision statement often involves surveying residents and other community stakeholders, holding public meetings, and getting input from advisory committees and focus groups. Some communities refer to the overall process as *community visioning* and hold special community events dedicated to coming up with the plan's vision statement.

Picking priorities: Planning goals and objectives

Planning goals are broad statements about what a plan intends to achieve for the future of the community. These broad statements help define how a plan will address an entire topic within the plan, such as transportation or housing.

Here are some examples of planning goals:

> Promote the redevelopment of former industrial areas within the city
>
> Provide a range of transportation options to the community
>
> Preserve and enhance the city's open space and recreational areas

Planning objectives, on the other hand, are more specific than planning goals and address a specific outcome of the plan.

Here are some examples of planning objectives:

> Promote increased use of public transportation by residents
>
> Improve and enhance bicycle and pedestrian routes in the community

Each planning goal may have several planning objectives. Planning objectives help define how the plan will address subtopics within the main topics of the plan. For example, planning objectives for transportation in a plan may address specific types of transportation or different transportation problems faced by the community.

Table 4-1 is an example of how planning objectives are related to planning goals. In this table, each planning goal is followed by two specific planning objectives that help clarify how the overall goal will be met.

Table 4-1	Planning Goals and Objectives
Goal/Objective	*Statement*
Goal A	Provide a range of transportation options to the community
Objective A.1	Promote increased use of public transportation by residents
Objective A.2	Improve and enhance bicycle and pedestrian routes in the community
Goal B	Preserve and enhance the city's open space and recreational areas
Objective B.1	Encourage the preservation of existing woodlands and wetlands
Objective B.2	Promote greater use of recreational areas by residents and visitors

There are many opportunities for public participation in setting goals and objectives for the plan. Because future goals and objectives can have a tremendous impact on the future of the community, public interest in this stage of the process is usually significant. Public participation can bring the following:

✔ **New ideas:** There are many ways to solicit ideas for a plan's goals and objectives. Planners can hold public meetings or take suggestions through websites and social media. This approach not only allows new ideas to come to the surface, but also lets the planners see what goals and objectives are particularly important to the public.

✔ **Feedback:** After a preliminary set of goals and objectives has been established, planners often present them to the community and give people the opportunity to respond. This allows for unpopular or controversial goals and objectives to be reexamined before the process continues.

Making Choices: Deciding on Planning Strategies and Actions

After a plan's vision, goals, and strategies are in place, you know where the plan is going and what it hopes to accomplish. Next, you need to figure out how you're going to get there — what planning strategies and actions will be used to implement the plan and help the community achieve its vision. The final steps of making a plan involve determining how the plan's implementation will be evaluated and establishing some criteria from when the plan will be updated, such as after a certain number of years or when certain goals are met.

Planning strategies and actions

Planning strategies are broad statements about how the overall goals of the plan can be achieved.

For example, the following planning strategies make general statements about how certain outcomes can be achieved:

Provide additional land within the city to use as open space and protect environmentally sensitive areas

Develop a bicycle path system to link recreation areas

Limit the amount of development occurring along the waterfront

Whereas planning strategies identify general approaches, the *planning actions* in a plan are made up of specific tasks that will be undertaken to implement the plan.

Here are some examples of planning actions:

> Create new city parks that incorporate important natural features
>
> Provide zoning incentives to new housing subdivisions that conserve open space

Each general planning strategy may have more than one related specific action. Table 4-2 is an example of how planning objectives are related to planning actions. In this table, each planning objective is followed by two specific planning actions that help clarify how the plan will be executed.

Table 4-2	Planning Strategies and Actions
Strategy/Action	*Statement*
Strategy 1	Provide additional land within the city to use as open space and protect environmentally sensitive areas
Action 1.A	Create new city parks that incorporate important natural features
Action 1.B	Provide zoning incentives to new housing subdivisions that conserve open space
Strategy 2	Develop a bicycle path system to link recreational areas
Action 1.A	Identify street routes for new bicycle paths
Action 1.B	Pursue funding from county and state transportation agencies for bicycle-only lanes on city streets

Like the process for coming up with goals and objectives, there are many opportunities for public participation in identifying planning strategies and actions, as well as getting preliminary feedback. In some cases, communities use this step of the planning process to gain commitments from community stakeholders to the plan's goals and objectives. For example, local businesses may be asked to help identify specific goals for improving a business district and identify how they could help carry out different strategies, like improving storefronts or staying open longer hours.

Coordinating goals and strategies

A comprehensive plan may address planning goals and objectives, and planning strategies and actions, for dozens (or even hundreds) of different items. Plans often use a *plan implementation matrix* to make sure that each planning goal corresponds with a set of strategies.

Figure 4-2 is an example of a plan implementation matrix. Here's how it's organized:

✔ Planning goals and objectives are represented in the columns.

✔ Planning strategies and actions are listed in the rows.

✔ An *X* in the table cells marks the spot where a particular strategy or action fulfills a goal or objective.

	Goal: Preserve and enhance the city's open space and recreational areas	
	Objective A: Encourage the preservation of existing woodlands and wetlands	Objective B: Promote greater use of recreational areas by residents and visitors
Strategy 1: Promote land uses within the city that conserve environmentally sensitive areas	X	X
Action 1.A: Create new city parks that incorporate important natural features	X	X
Action 1.B: Provide zoning incentives to new housing subdivisions that conserve open space	X	
Strategy 2: Develop a bicycle-path system to link recreational areas		X
Action 2.A: Identify street routes for new bicycle paths		X
Action 2.B: Pursue funding from county and state transportation agencies for bicycle-only lanes		X

Figure 4-2:
A plan implementation matrix.

X - Indicates that goals and objectives are met by the corresponding strategies and actions

Describing how the plan will be implemented, evaluated, and updated

The final step in preparing a comprehensive plan is addressing how the plan will be implemented, evaluated, and updated. Later in this chapter, I talk more about how these steps are carried out when the plan is completed, but this section provides a general description of what's usually included in the plan itself.

Wiki-planning in Melbourne: A new kind of public participation

In Australia, the city of Melbourne decided to try a new way of getting people involved in its 2008 comprehensive plan, known as *Future Melbourne.* Over the course of a month, the city solicited public input on the comprehensive plan by posting a version of the plan on the Internet as a *wiki* (a kind of website that allows its users to contribute directly to the website by editing the content and contributing new material). The website carried the slogan of "the city plan that anyone can edit."

Thousands of people visited the *Future Melbourne* website and made contributions to the plan by offering comments on the plan, placing new ideas into the plan, and participating in interactive discussions about the plan. After reviewing all the input to the wiki, many of the changes to the plan were included in its final version. By using the Internet, Melbourne's wiki plan allowed for the community to collaborate more closely on making its plan.

You can find the final version of *Future Melbourne* online at www.future melbourne.com.au.

Implementing the plan

The plan usually contains detailed information about how planning strategies and actions will be carried out. It's common for each planning action to include the following details:

- ✔ **Description of the action:** For example, "Create new city parks that incorporate natural features"

- ✔ **Who's responsible for the action:** For example, "The Parks and Recreation Department"

- ✔ **The time frame for completing the action:** For example, "Five to ten years"

- ✔ **The expected outcome of the action:** For example, "Two to five additional acres of new parkland

Evaluating the plan

The plan itself sometimes includes a detailed description of how the outcomes of the plan will be evaluated. For example, a plan may establish "success criteria" or "expected outcomes" for each of its planning actions, or a plan may state the impact that it intends to have on the community, such as "providing a 10 percent increase in the amount of affordable housing in the community."

Updating the plan

A plan may be updated for a variety of reasons, including to meet legal requirements. In addition, the plan may state the reasons under which it will be updated, such as when the plan fails to achieve certain goals or if community change occurs in ways not anticipated by the plan (for example, an unexpected change in population or a major disaster).

Getting Busy: Carrying Out the Plan

There are two main steps to carrying out the plan: adopting the plan and actually implementing it. In some ways, the adoption of the plan represents the end of the planning process, because the plan itself is now complete. But local officials and community stakeholders also use the plan to carry out its recommendations.

Adopting the plan

A community's comprehensive plan is typically made official when it's formally adopted by the local government. This usually means that the city or town's city council votes to approve the plan and that the plan is approved by the city's mayor. In order for the plan to become official, it also may need to be reviewed or approved by other governmental agencies, such as a state environmental commission.

Implementing the plan

The implementation of a plan involves many more people than those involved in making the plan. For years to come, the plan will serve as official guidance to local government on the activities of all its departments. The plan also creates a blueprint for the further development of the community by its residents and other community stakeholders.

The chapters in Part IV of this book discuss how plans are carried out in order to accomplish a wide range of goals, from making cities more sustainable to revitalizing urban neighborhoods to preserving historic buildings.

Keeping Track: Monitoring Progress and Updating the Plan

Monitoring the progress of the plan's implementation and updating the plan are good ways to make sure that the plan is being used by, and is useful to, the community.

Within the actual planning documents, most urban plans include information on how the plan will be monitored and updated (see "Describing how the plan will be implemented, evaluated, and updated," earlier in this chapter).

Making a difference? How to monitor progress

In some cases, the implementation of a plan may be monitored only periodically and in very general terms. This may be especially true in smaller communities where plans don't call for many major changes. If a plan calls for lots of changes to be implemented, it may be monitored very closely, with planning staff being assigned to track specific plan implementation steps and make regular progress reports.

Monitoring the process of a plan typically addresses two key issues:

- ✔ **Is the plan being implemented?** The most basic question to be answered is whether the community is actually using the plan. For example, has a local government adopted the policies or laws recommended by the plan? Are planning initiatives identified in the plan actually being carried out?

- ✔ **Is the plan having the desired impact?** It's a good idea to determine the extent to which the plan is having the desired impact on the community. Even when planning strategies are being carried out as described in the plan, they may not be having the expected impact on the community.

Many urban plans include *community indicators,* specific measures that can be benchmarked at the beginning of the plan and then regularly monitored in order to see the before and after effects of the plan. For example, a plan recommendation to promote energy efficiency may be regularly monitored through regular reports from utilities about energy use or surveys of households to see if people are using energy conservation measures included in the plan.

A number of places have started monitoring the implementation of their plans more regularly and more carefully. For example, the state of Florida not only requires that many of its cities and towns have official comprehensive plans but also requires these communities to prepare a periodic post-plan "evaluation and appraisal report" that "evaluates how successful a community has been in addressing major community land use planning issues through implementation of its comprehensive plan."

An urban plan, no matter how well made, is truly useful only when it is used by the community and has a positive impact.

When and why to update the plan

Regularly updating a plan helps to account for changes that are taking place in the community, as well as new opportunities or constraints that may not have been present when the plan was originally prepared. Here are some of the reasons why plans are updated:

- ✔ **To meet legal or regulatory requirements:** Several states that require their cities and towns to have official comprehensive plans also require them to periodically update the plans or particular components of the plans.

  For example, Michigan requires that communities update their comprehensive plans every five years to account for changes in population and land use patterns. In California, the housing component must be revisited every seven years.

- ✔ **To respond to changing situations:** If a community is changing rapidly in ways that are not anticipated by the plan, it may be time to update the plan. For example, rapid population growth, economic problems, or a major disaster all may be reasons to reassess the community and update a plan's recommendations. In the wake of the housing crisis and economic recession in the United States that started in 2008, many communities formally or informally updated their local plans to account for changes in housing markets, local unemployment, and shrinking budgets for local governments.

- ✔ **To respond to a lack of progress or unintended consequences:** Even when an urban plan is actually being implemented, it may not be having the desired impact or it may not be making sufficient progress toward improving the community. Some urban plans contain contingency strategies that can be pursued as alternatives, but it also may make sense to update the plan in order to develop additional planning approaches.

The alternative to updating a plan is to start over and make a new plan. If conditions have changed dramatically since the plan was adopted, this may be the most beneficial option for a community. For example, the city of Austin's 1979 official comprehensive plan was updated many times before local officials moved to completely replace the plan in 2009 in order to keep up with rapid population growth (the city's population more than doubled between 1979 and 2009), as well as other major changes in the city's social, economic, and environmental conditions. (For more information on Austin, check out the "Getting everyone to imagine Austin" sidebar, earlier in this chapter.)

Part II
Putting All the Pieces Together: The Main Components of an Urban Plan

The 5th Wave   By Rich Tennant

MUNICIPAL
REFUSE-GENERATED
ELECTRICAL FACILITY

"We're running out of garbage."

In this part . . .

Cities are made up of lots of different pieces, such as transportation and housing, all of which need to fit together to make a successful city. Urban planning helps coordinate the things that make up a city, and this part looks at what's included in an urban plan.

Chapter 5 looks at land use, which is the most important element of an urban plan because urban planners have to find a place on the map for everything that goes into a city. Chapter 6 explores how an urban plan deals with housing and makes sure that everyone has a good place to live. Chapter 7 is all about transportation, which is the lifeblood of a city because it keeps all the parts connected and all the people moving. Chapter 8 deals with how urban design helps cities both look great and work better. Chapter 9 gets in touch with nature by looking at how cities incorporate natural resources into an urban plan. Chapter 10 is all about the essential infrastructure and public services that cities need to offer, ranging from clean water to good schools.

Chapter 5

Land Use: A Place for Everything

. . . .

In This Chapter
▶ Recognizing the importance of land use
▶ Making a land use inventory and map
▶ Planning for future land use
▶ Using zoning and other regulations
▶ Resolving land use controversies

. . . .

*E*verything that is part of a city has to go somewhere. Making room for people, buildings, roads, sewers, parks, and all the other things that make up a city is an essential feature of an urban plan. The land use component of a plan describes, analyzes, and proposes changes or additions to the ways that a city uses its land.

In this chapter, I take a detailed look at three items that usually make up the core of a plan's land use component:

✔ An inventory and map of current land uses

✔ A future land use plan

✔ A set of regulations to guide future development

I also discuss how land use planning relates to all the other components of an urban plan, like housing and transportation. Finally, I wrap up this chapter by looking at some of the ways that cities can put everything in a good place and resolve conflicts between different types of land use.

Unlike the virtual worlds of video games, real cities have a limited amount of space. As Mark Twain once said, "Buy land; they're not making it anymore." Cities must make room for things like factories and jails, but most residents probably wouldn't want to live next to either of these. Finding ways to fit together all the land uses that make up a city is one of the great challenges of urban planning.

Why Land Use Is So Important

Every city has a unique physical form. For example, the Dallas and Boston metropolitan areas are home to about four million people each, but they have very different land use patterns. In Dallas, people are spread out over more than 6,000 square miles, whereas Boston has roughly the same number of people living across just 2,400 square miles. This means that Boston's population density is about three times higher than Dallas's.

This difference in population density also means that people live somewhat different lives in each city. Due to the more compact land use pattern of Boston, people there are more likely to use mass transportation to get to work, live in apartment buildings or high-rise condominiums, and find shopping areas close to their homes. In Dallas, on the other hand, residents are more likely to live in low-density suburban housing and drive long distances to get to work or go shopping.

Land use is the most important component of a plan because it directly determines the amount of land used by a city and because the overall land use pattern influences what choices can be made about all the other plan components, such as where to locate new housing or deciding whether to build new roads.

A good land use plan not only establishes a city's general vision and its future development, but also focuses its specific planning and development goals. Land use planning helps communities decide how much land to use for future development, what mix of land uses will be needed by the community, where those land uses should be located, and when land should be developed. Communities that lack a land use plan are more likely to experience uncoordinated and haphazard development patterns that promote urban sprawl and negatively impact the quality of life for residents.

Land use and urban development

A land use plan guides the development of a city. As a blueprint for the future, a land use plan plays an important role in determining

  ✔ **The geographic location of all of a city's essential features:** An urban plan has to find a place for everything and put everything in its place, from schools to factories to parks. The land use component of a plan identifies locations for future development and addresses concerns about existing parts of the city, such as declining neighborhoods that may be in need of revitalization.

✔ **Relationships between the different elements of the city:** How one element of a city is related to another has a lot to do with the geographic organization of land use patterns. For example, are residential areas close to commercial areas that may provide employment for residents? If jobs are located far away from residential areas, a city will have to plan for increased transportation options to allow people to get to work, especially people who depend on mass transportation.

✔ **How much of an impact the city has on the natural environment:** At the most basic level, cities affect the environment by using land that would otherwise be undeveloped. But not all cities have the same impact on the environment. Cities with compact land use patterns and well-coordinated elements, such as transportation and housing, tend to have less of an impact. For example, if residential areas and commercial areas where people work are near each other, some people may be able to walk or bike to work instead of driving cars. (For a more detailed look at environmental issues, turn to Chapter 11.)

It's all related: Land use and other plan components

Land use is the basic building block of an urban plan. The organization of land uses establishes the framework for the physical location and functional role of all the other plan components. In the following sections, I explain how land use is related to other planning components.

Housing

The land use component of a plan is related to a plan's housing element in three important ways:

✔ It helps to determine how much land will be set aside for housing and, therefore, how much housing will be available in a community.

✔ It influences what types of housing will be considered in the plan, such as how many apartments versus single-family homes may need to be accommodated.

✔ It helps determine the best locations for housing in relation to other important elements, like transportation routes and shopping areas.

For more on housing, see Chapter 6.

Transportation

Coordinating transportation routes and services with a community's overall land use pattern is an important function of the comprehensive plan. The overall plan may intend to extend or improve transportation in areas that are designated for future development. However, a land use plan also may be responsive to the limitations of the transportation system by limiting development in areas without adequate transportation access.

Check out Chapter 7 for more about transportation.

Urban design

A plan's land use component usually designates what goes where. Then it's usually up to the urban design section of the plan to help determine the design and architectural details of future development and redevelopment. These design details not only affect the aesthetic appearance of the city, but also have an important impact on how well the city functions.

For example, a land use plan may designate an area for retail land use, and the urban design component would further address how such areas are to be developed in ways that are visually attractive and have amenities that benefit the community, such as walking paths to allow for pedestrian access.

I dig more deeply into urban design in Chapter 8.

Environmental resources

A good land use plan understands the impacts that the city will have on the natural environment and how various environmental features promote or constrain future development. For example, the land use component of a plan may designate certain areas for use as open space, and the environmental resources component of a plan may contain specific details on how such areas are to be preserved and maintained.

You can find more information on environmental conservation in Chapter 9.

Infrastructure and public services

The land use component of a plan and planning for infrastructure and public services have a back-and-forth relationship. Typically, a land use plan is used to determine the parts of the city that require services such as sewer systems or public schools. However, future land development may be limited in areas where services are difficult to provide; for example, there may be limits on the development of housing in locations that can't be reached by sewer extensions.

See Chapter 10 for more on infrastructure and public services.

A Little Bit of Everything: Existing Land Use

Ultimately, a plan's land use component will be used to develop strategies for the future development of the city, but the starting point of a land use plan is understanding what's already there. An accurate picture of a city's existing land uses shows what areas are already developed and how these areas are being used. This information enables planners to identify existing areas that may benefit from redevelopment or a change in land use, as well as to find areas that are suitable for new development.

An accurate understanding of all the currently existing land uses in a city is a fundamental part of a good urban plan. This section outlines the different classifications of land use and discusses how to assign classifications to properties. This land classification information can then be used to create an inventory and map of existing land uses that summarize current conditions.

Examining land use classifications

A land use plan typically classifies all the different land uses in a city using methods that blend local needs with various professional and technical standards. Land classification standards vary from place to place because all places are different from each other. For example, a coastal community may have several different types of waterfront areas, but an inland community may have no waterfront areas at all.

Local plans commonly use several main land use classifications, including residential, commercial, industrial, agricultural, open space, and mixed use. Land use plans also include additional classes or subclasses depending on what activities are present in the community, such as recreational areas, airports, or hospitals.

Here's an overview of land use classes and subclasses that you'll usually find in local plans:

✔ **Residential:** These areas are used for various types of housing. Subtypes of residential land uses are usually based on either the density of housing units or their physical characteristics, such as being detached single-family homes or connected town houses. Many communities sub-classify a variety of special types of housing, including mobile-home parks, college dormitories, or retirement communities.

✔ **Commercial:** These areas are used by businesses, including retailers, service businesses, and offices. Commercial land uses often include a variety of specialized subclasses, ranging from hospitals to shopping centers to theme parks.

✔ **Industrial:** This category typically includes land used for manufacturing, warehousing, wholesaling, some public or private transportation facilities, and some public or private utilities.

✔ **Agricultural areas and open space:** Many smaller communities, as well as some major cities and metropolitan areas, have significant agricultural and undeveloped lands at their outer margins. In these cases, plans classify and assess these lands for the purpose of developing conservation programs or for identifying potential sites for future development.

✔ **Mixed land use:** A single building or development site may offer a variety of uses, especially in larger cities where mixed-use developments are more common. For example, New York City's Trump Tower includes 7 floors of retail shops, 13 floors of office space, and 38 floors of residential condominiums. A land use plan may use one or more subclasses to describe mixed-use areas.

✔ **Public and institutional uses:** This group includes a wide range of land uses that are generally characterized as being either public services or government owned. Common subclasses include

- Government buildings

- Parks, public open spaces, and land preserves

- Churches

- Colleges and universities

- Transportation routes and public rights-of-way

Classifying properties

In most cases, a land use plan will assign each individual property or specific site to a particular land use classification. Most local governments have property tax or building permit records that show how a property is being used. Local governments typically use their own predetermined set of land use classes and assign each property to one of these groups when a property owner requests a building permit or applies for a deed.

However, official records sometimes become outdated or don't contain enough detail to properly classify a property. When this happens, the local government may need to send out a building inspector, civil engineer, or land surveyor to do an accurate assessment.

Satellite imagery and aerial photography are other ways to examine land uses. Sometimes called *land cover analysis,* these methods typically aren't used to classify local land uses but frequently are used by scientists to study specific geographic, geologic, and environmental conditions. Satellite images that allow anyone, anywhere to get a bird's-eye view of a city are now widely available through online services like Google Earth (http://earth.google.com). Sometimes this type of information is used in plans along with other maps and drawings to help illustrate existing land use patterns.

Looking at existing land use with inventories and maps

Organizing property-by-property information about land uses in a city can be a challenge due to the sheer amount of data that can be involved. Los Angeles County has more than two million individual property parcels spread across 4,000 square miles. Even a small city may have thousands of properties to look after.

This information can be organized or summarized for use in a plan in a couple of ways:

- ✔ **Land-use inventories:** After all the relevant areas of a city or region have been assessed and classified based on their types of land use, an inventory simply adds up total land area usage for all the categories and subcategories. This shows the overall distribution of land uses and how much land area is used by each category or subcategory. This information reveals how much land is currently being used for various purposes and is useful for understanding how much additional land may be needed to meet future demands.

    For a look at the Big Apple's land use inventory, check out the sidebar "A whole lot of stuff: New York City's land use inventory," later in this chapter.

- ✔ **Existing land use maps:** An existing land use map shows how all the land in a community is currently being used. Figure 5-1 is an example of an existing land use map. In addition to showing what usage category is associated with different areas, this type of map usually includes natural features, like water and undeveloped woodlands, and important transportation features that help demonstrate the relationship between land use and the overall resources of a city or town.

A whole lot of stuff: New York City's land use inventory

New York City has the largest concentration of urban land uses in the United States. More than eight million people live in the city's five boroughs, and the city is home to nearly 400,000 businesses, ranging from convenience stores to corporate headquarters.

The city's 2010 Primary Land Use survey (http://on.nyc.gov/AhXr0) looks at all the city's 240 square miles of land and accounts for 11 types of land use:

- One- and two-family houses (27.3 percent of total land area)
- Open space (27.0 percent)
- Multifamily residential (12.2 percent)
- Transportation/utility (7.1 percent)
- Public facilities and institutions (6.9 percent)
- Vacant land (5.8 percent)
- Commercial/office (4.0 percent)
- Industrial/manufacturing (3.6 percent)
- Mixed residential and commercial (3.0 percent)
- Miscellaneous (1.8 percent)
- Parking facilities (1.3 percent)

Commercial and office land uses make up only 4 percent of the total land area of the city, but many of these properties use their tiny footprints to stand tall. In New York City, much of the action happens hundreds of feet above ground. The Empire State Building — the tallest building in the world when it was built — sits atop less than 2 acres of land but holds the equivalent of more than 60 acres of commercial space in 102 floors of offices that rise 1,250 feet above ground.

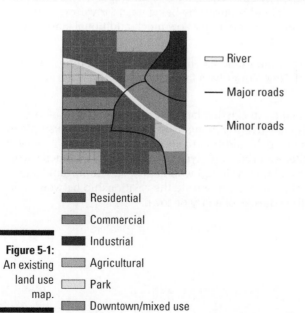

River

— Major roads

— Minor roads

Figure 5-1: An existing land use map.

Residential
Commercial
Industrial
Agricultural
Park
Downtown/mixed use

Coming Soon! Planning for Future Land Use

Planning for future land use involves understanding the relationship between the demand for future land uses and the supply of land available for development. A future land use plan forecasts these trends and develops a physical plan for future development.

How much land is available? Analyzing supply

Good land use planning helps cities develop in ways that conserve and protect undeveloped areas. Knowing how much land is available for future development involves looking at undeveloped land in or near the city, as well as developed areas that may have the capacity for additional development. Future development can occur in either developed or undeveloped areas.

Land-use planning uses various measures of *land suitability,* sometimes also called *development capacity,* to determine the supply of available land for different land uses. For example, land areas that consist of wetlands or have soils that are vulnerable to erosion may be unsuitable for development (see Chapter 9 for more on land suitability).

In order to analyze land supply, an urban planner must consult a wide variety of sources beyond the existing land use inventory and map. Other sources may include data or maps about environmental conditions, geologic features, infrastructure and transportation elements, and even archaeological surveys. These sources provide various characteristics that indicate the suitability of land areas for different land uses:

- ✔ **Site conditions:** Factors such as soil type, geologic stability, wind exposure, and other characteristics of physical geography affect what types of land use are appropriate for specific areas. For example, during the industrial revolution in the United States in the 19th century, many factories were located next to rivers and waterfalls in order to harness the energy of flowing waters to run looms and mills. In our modern times, some communities have begun identifying areas with high potential for wind or solar power that could be used by factories or new housing developments.

- ✔ **Environmental factors:** Not only is every land area affected by its surrounding environment, but it also has an impact on its environment. Determining the suitability of a site for different types of development takes these factors into consideration. For example, a site that is home to important plants and animals may be considered less suitable for development than a site without similar features.

In Seattle, local laws restrict development in designated fish and wildlife conservation areas in order to provide breeding areas and migration routes for a variety of species, including pink salmon and the spotted owl.

✔ **Proximity to existing development:** Currently undeveloped areas that are close to existing development are likely to be better candidates for future development because they may provide for a more compact overall development pattern and lower costs of extending existing infrastructure and road systems.

✔ **Existing development:** Urban plans are increasingly looking to strengthen communities by promoting development in existing areas, especially those that are adequately served by public services. For example, it may be possible to add additional floors or add extensions to existing buildings.

How much land will we need? Forecasting demand

Figuring out the need for future land uses takes a variety of factors into consideration, including likely changes in a city's population and employment levels, as well as how demographic and economic changes create a further need for supporting land uses, such as areas for schools, parks, hospitals, and transportation facilities.

Considering demographic and economic change

Cities are constantly changing, and good plans take into account what changes may lie ahead. Urban planners consider changes in the makeup of a city's population or its local economy to be the most important kinds of change because they have both direct and indirect impacts on future land use.

Demographic and economic changes directly influence how much land is likely to be needed in the future for residents and businesses. Indirectly, increases or decreases in residents or businesses have an impact on other types of land uses that are needed to support people and jobs. These demographic and economic changes help determine how much land and what kinds of land uses may be needed in the future:

✔ **Changes in the size of the population:** The overall population size of a community is driven by both *natural population change* (the difference between births and deaths) and *migration* (people moving to or leaving a city). Overall trends in the size of the population are important indicators of how much land use may be needed in the future.

✓ **Changes in demographic characteristics:** Changes in the composition of the population — including characteristics like age or income — influence the types of land uses that may be needed in the future. For example, an area that is experiencing a decrease in the average number of people per household may need to start planning ahead to use more land for smaller homes or apartments.

✓ **Economic change:** Changes in the size or function of the local economy are important indicators of future land use demand. In addition to areas used directly for businesses, an increasing number of employment opportunities in a community stimulates the demand for residential and supporting land uses.

Every city has its own unique demographic and economic features, but some national and global trends have an influence on how local areas are planning for future land use.

The Baby Boomers are the generation born between 1945 and 1964. As this generation ages, the United States will be home to an unprecedented number of older people. In 2010, about 13 percent of the U.S. population was over the age of 65; by 2030, nearly 20 percent of the population will be over 65. Experts expect the aging of the population to lead to many changes in local land use, including increasing the demand for retirement housing, medical facilities, and recreational areas.

The movement of people between states also is causing lots of changes in urban land use, as the U.S. population continues to move away from Rust Belt states, such as Ohio and Michigan, to Sun Belt states, like Florida, Texas, and Arizona. Between 2000 and 2008, the Phoenix area gained more than 500,000 state-to-state migrants at the same time that Rust Belt regions, including Buffalo, Cleveland, and Detroit, lost hundreds of thousands of residents who moved to other parts of the country. As a result of these big shifts in population, Phoenix and its surrounding suburbs are struggling to keep up with demands for housing and public services by new residents, and Buffalo, Cleveland, and Detroit are looking at ways to "right-size" their cities and address problems caused by an abundance of vacant urban land.

Estimating future land use demand

Forecasts of potential demographic and economic changes can be used to estimate future demands for specific types of land uses. A typical comprehensive plan is intended to be relevant over a span of 20 to 40 years.

For example, in Portland, Oregon, a special agency called the Metro Council is in charge of land use planning for the entire metropolitan area and is required by state law to maintain a 20-year forecast of population and employment trends to ensure that sufficient land is available for future development.

In the United States, various government agencies provide demographic and economic data on current conditions but a limited amount of data forecasting conditions for local areas. The U.S. Census Bureau provides long-range population forecasts that look ahead 20 to 30 years at the state level but not for smaller local areas. Many state government agencies produce long-range population and economic forecasts for cities, counties, and metropolitan areas. Some local planning agencies maintain their own databases and statistical models to produce demographic and economic forecasts or contract with consulting firms that produce proprietary forecasts for local areas.

Forecasts of future demographic and economic conditions can be used to estimate future land use needs. Changes in population and employment levels trigger a demand for land not only for residential and employment areas, but also for a wide range of supporting land uses.

Estimating future land use needs involves first estimating residential and employment uses, and then looking at supporting land uses.

Residential and employment uses

Urban plans typically use *ratio methods* to convert population and economic forecasts into figures for land use demand.

For example, the California city of Anaheim — home of Disneyland — estimates that the city's population will increase by nearly 70,000 residents between 2004 and 2030. Using an average of 3.3 people per household and a development pattern of 7.5 housing units per acre, Anaheim estimates that it will need to increase its urban area by more than 160,000 acres for use as future residential areas.

Supporting land uses

The amount of land needed for supporting land uses also can be estimated using ratio methods:

✔ **Assume that future land uses can be met using roughly the same proportions that already exist in the community.** For example, if an *existing land use inventory* indicates that there is 1 acre of retail land use for every 10 acres of residential land use, then a reasonable estimate may be to plan for a future residential-to-retail land use ratio of 10:1.

✔ **Follow guidelines on recommended levels for supporting land uses.** These guidelines are published by some government agencies and professional organizations.

The state of Colorado recommends that towns with less than 10,000 residents set aside 14 acres per 1,000 residents for parks and recreational facilities.

Where to grow: Making a future land use map

A future land use map is an important component of an urban plan and shows where future development is intended to take place. This includes the use of previously undeveloped land and potential changes to areas that are already developed.

By showing the geographic pattern of future development, a future land use map serves two important purposes:

- **It coordinates land use patterns with development needs.** For example, the development of new residential areas requires the development of new roads, schools, and other supporting land uses. A future land use map shows how the location of new development will be geographically coordinated.

- **It promotes an overall framework for urban development patterns.** For example, a city that is trying to prevent urban sprawl and encourage development in existing neighborhoods can use a future land use map to show a geographic pattern of future development that represents these goals. (For more about sprawl, see Chapter 13.)

Because future land use relates to both the overall development pattern of a city and the future use of specific land areas, plans often contain multiple maps. In practice, urban plans use future land use maps that are both conceptual and detailed:

- **Conceptual maps:** Some future land use maps are intended to show general geographic and functional goals for future development. This type of map emphasizes the overall development pattern of the city and how different development needs will be coordinated.

  Figure 5-2 shows an example of a conceptual future land use map. This type of map identifies the intended general character of different districts or locations in a city or town. The map in Figure 5-2 shows the general location of different types of districts in an area, such as business districts and residential districts, and identifies specific locations for possible "urban villages" that could be mixed-use areas with both housing and businesses.

- **Detailed maps:** A detailed future land use map shows intended uses for all the sites and parcels in a city. This type of map helps residents and property owners understand the types of development that are likely to occur in their community. A concept map often serves as the guiding framework for determining detailed land uses.

  Figure 5-3 is an example of a detailed future land use map of a neighborhood area that shows the proposed future land use of every property parcel in the area. This type of planning map also helps local authorities coordinate public services and other future improvements.

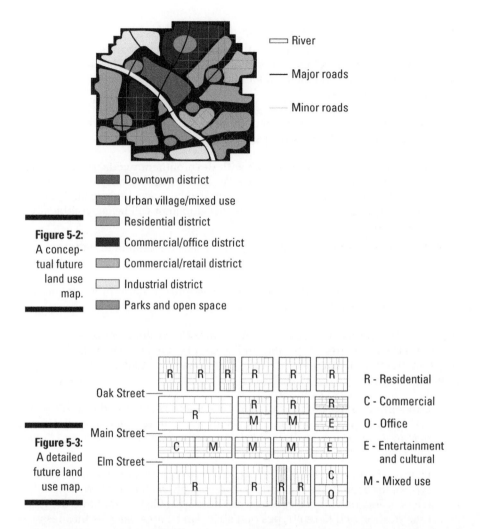

Figure 5-2: A conceptual future land use map.

Downtown district
Urban village/mixed use
Residential district
Commercial/office district
Commercial/retail district
Industrial district
Parks and open space

River
Major roads
Minor roads

Figure 5-3: A detailed future land use map.

Oak Street
Main Street
Elm Street

R - Residential
C - Commercial
O - Office
E - Entertainment and cultural
M - Mixed use

Using Zoning and Land Use Regulations

Zoning is a type of land use regulation used by local authorities to designate what types of land uses are allowable in specific locations. Zoning is the primary legal means for local authorities to shape the overall pattern of land use in a manner consistent with their urban plan. Other local regulations also help shape the pattern of local land uses by imposing specific architectural or site engineering requirements.

Zoning versus land use planning: The same, but different

Land use plans and zoning frequently are assumed to be the same thing. However, they're separate and distinct elements that serve different purposes for the planning and development of cities.

A *future land use map* shows the anticipated use of sites and properties at some point in the future. This element of a plan is considered to be *advisory* in the sense that a future land use map sets broad goals for future development that are to be encouraged through specific legal regulations and development initiatives.

Zoning is a local law that regulates how a specific site or property may be developed. In the United States, the legal authority for zoning is based on the interest of the government in protecting the health, safety, and welfare of the public.

Zoning laws and maps

Zoning laws, also known as *zoning ordinances* or *zoning codes,* usually are enacted by local governments, although in some parts of the United States, states, counties, and other jurisdictions are responsible for zoning laws. Zoning laws have two general components:

- ✔ A legal description of zoning classifications, including what type of development is allowed in each category
- ✔ A zoning map showing the zoning classification for every property

Zoning classifications legally define how a specific parcel of land may be developed and typically address three elements:

- ✔ **Permissible uses:** A zoning law uses zoning classifications and subclassifications to define a range of allowable land uses for each site. For example, zoning a property for residential use would limit the permissible use and development of the property to housing.

- ✔ **Extent of site development:** A zoning law places restrictions on the extent to which a site may be developed. These restrictions may include a limit on the height of buildings or a limit on the total number of employees in an office building.

- ✔ **Site layout and design:** Zoning laws frequently place architectural and design restrictions on properties, ranging from the distance between houses to maximum building footprint sizes to allowable colors for house paint.

A *zoning map,* which shows the zoning classification for every property in the city, is an essential element of the overall zoning law. It's considered legally binding in terms of defining which zoning classification applies to every property. An example of a zoning map is shown in Figure 5-4, which is a neighborhood area map that identifies the zoning classification for each property parcel.

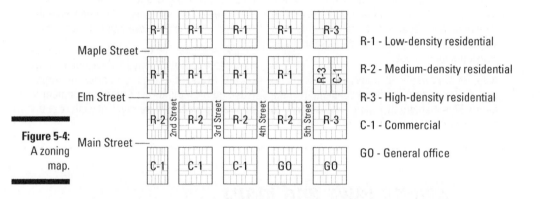

Figure 5-4: A zoning map.

R-1 - Low-density residential

R-2 - Medium-density residential

R-3 - High-density residential

C-1 - Commercial

GO - General office

Types of zoning classifications

Each zoning classification used in a zoning law must establish a specifically defined range of permissible land activities. Local authorities use as many classification and sub-classification categories as needed to regulate existing land uses and promote future development.

Zoning classifications typically fall into the following major categories:

- ✔ **Residential zones:** These zones primarily allow for housing but sometimes permit uses that are compatible with residential areas, such as schools and churches. Residential zoning often includes a variety of sub-categories, such as single-family dwelling zones, multiple-family zones, or zones for manufactured housing.

- ✔ **Commercial zones:** These areas are designated for use by businesses that sell goods or perform services, such as auto-repair shops or medical offices. This category often has a range of sub-categories with zoning criteria for specific uses ranging from office parks to sports arenas to shopping malls.

- ✔ **Industrial zones:** Industrial zones allow primarily for the production or distribution of manufactured goods. Industrial zones sometimes also include transportation and utility activities as permissible uses.

✔ **Public facilities and open spaces:** These zones permit uses by governmental or public serving establishments, such as hospitals, recreation centers, or churches. Zoning for open space typically excludes residential, commercial, or industrial development, but it often allows for low-intensity development, such as recreational areas.

✔ **Mixed-use development:** Local governments are increasingly adopting zoning classifications that legally permit the development of sites that combine a variety of land uses, such as mixed-use housing and retail developments.

Zoning techniques

Local authorities have a great deal of flexibility in how their zoning codes are used to regulate and encourage the development of land. In some instances, zoning laws are used to shape development in a very exact manner. In other instances, zoning laws allow for a broader range of outcomes.

✔ **Performance zoning:** This type of zoning ordinance has fewer specific restrictions on land use but requires development to meet a flexible set of general standards. For example, a performance zoning ordinance may simply require buildings in a commercial area to be no larger than a certain number of square feet in size but have few other restrictions as long as general standards are met.

✔ **Incentive zoning:** This form of zoning allows for greater development of a site if certain requirements are met. For example, a developer willing to set aside an area for open space conservation may be allowed to develop a taller building, which not only would be more profitable for the developer but also would create more open space for the community.

✔ **Inclusionary zoning:** This type of zoning is similar to incentive zoning but provides for a greater level of development when a proposal includes elements beneficial to the community, such as low-income housing. For example, some cities and towns have zoning ordinances that allow for developers to increase the overall amount of housing development on a particular piece of land if the development includes affordable housing for low-income residents. In some areas of New York City, developers can apply to build larger buildings with roughly one additional housing unit for every unit that is set aside for affordable housing.

For more on some other variations on zoning techniques that are being used to improve the urban design of cities and towns, turn to Chapter 8.

Other land use regulations that affect site development

A variety of other regulations used by local authorities affect the development of properties and can be used to influence development patterns in ways that are consistent with a city's planning goals. The range of land uses allowed in different areas is dictated by local zoning laws.

The types of regulation in the following list typically address specific aesthetic and site engineering concerns for individual development sites:

- **Building codes:** These are laws that a city or town uses to regulate the characteristics of buildings in order to ensure that they meet various standards or other considerations such as safety or energy efficiency. Some cities and towns also conduct official architectural reviews when there are existing architectural standards for land development.

- **Subdivision regulations:** These are official regulations that must be met in order to separate an existing property parcel into a larger number of smaller property parcels. For example, a proposal to develop an existing farm as a housing development with several separate houses would be required to meet subdivision regulations. Subdivision regulations typically consider whether land is suitable for further development and if the proposed subdivision is consistent with other regulations, such as zoning.

- **Site plan review:** Most cities and towns conduct some form of official site plan review where detailed architectural drawings and/or engineering plans for a specific development are reviewed in order to ensure that they comply with zoning and other land use regulations.

- **Environmental impact review:** A variety of states require that cities and towns conduct official environmental impact reviews (EIRs) of development proposals that are likely to have a significant impact on the environment. If a review determines that a development may have a negative impact on the environment, the project may have to be redesigned or other measures may have to be taken, such as planting new trees in a different area to make up for forest that may be lost due to development.

LULUs and SOBs: Dealing With Controversial Land Uses

Sooner or later, every community deals with public opposition to the location of a controversial land use. Although many controversial land uses may be useful (or even essential) to a portion of the community, other members of the community may cry, "NIMBY!" (not in my backyard).

Investigating some common problem land uses

Sometimes called LULUs (locally unwanted land uses), a wide variety of potential land uses often are opposed by the pubic. Here are some of the most common LULUs:

- ✔ **Sexually oriented businesses:** Sex businesses and strip clubs are frequently opposed by residents concerned about crime and morality.

- ✔ **Bars and liquor stores:** Concerns about crime and moral issues are often raised regarding locations that serve or sell liquor. In a few U.S. states, similar concerns are being raised by newly allowed medical marijuana dispensaries.

- ✔ **Big box stores:** Large retail developments often generate concerns about negative impacts on existing local businesses and traffic conditions.

- ✔ **Special-needs housing:** Housing for low-income families, homeless shelters, or transitional housing for formerly homeless or incarcerated people are often controversial due to concerns over public safety and possible negative impacts on residential property values.

- ✔ **Industrial uses:** When located in or near predominantly residential areas, industrial uses are frequently opposed due to concerns about pollution, noise, and truck traffic.

Making the best of a bad situation

A good land use plan makes room for every legitimate activity, even when some uses may be objectionable to a significant portion of the community. Here are some ways that communities can try to balance community concerns with controversial land uses:

- ✔ **Think location, location, location.** Try to find sites for controversial land uses that minimize community concerns.

Residents of Texas Township, a suburban community in Michigan, were concerned that a strip club might relocate to their area. The township passed a zoning ordinance allowing "adult establishments" in an industrial area that was unlikely to cause problems for residents (although the strip club eventually located elsewhere).

✔ **Anticipate change.** Savvy communities anticipate potential changes and put effective land use regulations in place when controversies erupt.

In 2004, California's medicinal marijuana laws began allowing the operation of dispensaries or "pot shops." The city of Oakland immediately put in place regulations that allowed for just four dispensaries citywide. The city of Los Angeles moved slowly to address the issue and as many as 1,000 unregulated dispensaries quickly opened, angering residents throughout the city.

✔ **Provide information and build consensus.** It's important to get as many people as possible to participate in finding a solution when a controversy breaks out. A compromise is not likely to please everyone, but addressing the concerns of as many people as possible is important. Planners may need to provide the public with useful information on a possibly controversial land use so that people can better weigh the pros and cons of the situation.

Chapter 6

Housing: A Place to Call Home

In This Chapter

▶ Recognizing the important role that housing plays in a community

▶ Identifying different types of housing

▶ Looking at different types of residential areas

▶ Focusing on housing in a comprehensive plan

*E*veryone needs someplace to live, and providing people with decent, affordable housing is one of the most important functions of a community. Planning for housing can be an especially complicated task, because it's intrinsically related to sometimes volatile trends (such as rapid population growth or changing financial markets) and because housing is deeply connected to other components of an urban plan (including land use, transportation, and public services).

The housing component of a comprehensive plan tries to determine how much housing will be needed by the community, what different kinds of housing will be needed, potential locations for new housing, and areas that may require housing rehabilitations. It also coordinates housing with other components of the plan. Planning goals for housing are typically supported by a wide range of policies and programs, including modifications to zoning and land use regulations, as well as recommendations for housing-specific programs and initiatives.

In this chapter, I take an in-depth look at the most important aspects of planning for housing. I discuss how housing is related to other parts of an urban plan and how housing contributes to the quality of life in local communities. I describe different types of housing and the housing needs of different segments of the population. Finally, I talk about the analysis of local housing conditions and planning for housing in ways that meet the needs of the community and its residents.

Gimme Shelter: The Role of Housing

Benjamin Franklin wrote that "A house is not a home unless it contains food and fire for the mind as well as the body." Perhaps this was his way of reminding us that housing is more than just an arrangement of stones and sticks — it's something that has a deep impact on both the people who live there and the community as a whole. Housing is an important element of the overall quality of life in a community, and planning for housing is an essential component of a comprehensive plan because of the close relationship between housing, land use, and the need for public services.

Housing and quality of life

Housing is a fundamental component of every community and plays a pivotal role in the community's overall quality of life. Housing satisfies a basic need for shelter and contributes to the social, economic, and environmental well-being of the community and its residents:

- **Housing contributes to the health and welfare of the community.** Housing fulfills a basic human need for shelter and has a direct impact on human and environmental health. For example, poorly maintained housing with lead-based paints can cause serious childhood diseases and contaminate nearby water sources.

- **Housing contributes to the aesthetic character of the community.** In many communities, housing makes up a substantial portion of the man-made environment, and the design features of a community's housing and residential areas help lend a distinctive character to the community.

- **Most communities depend on housing for tax revenue.** Revenue from property taxes of housing helps pay for essential public services, ranging from schools to streetlights. Without a stable housing market that is able to maintain (or increase) its value, a community may be unable to finance needed services and become a less attractive place to live.

Housing is a key concern of most communities, but the role of housing in local plans can vary quite a bit from place to place. For example, in so-called "bedroom suburbs," where housing is the dominant land use, urban plans may focus primarily on the quality of life in residential areas and in providing amenities desired by residents, such as parks and convenience shopping. But in communities that have a mix of land uses — including residential areas, commercial districts, and industrial areas — planning efforts may focus on balancing housing and residential concerns with the needs of nonresidential land uses.

Housing, land use, and the demand for public services

Housing is closely related to other components of the comprehensive plan, especially land use and public services.

Housing is related to land use in both direct and indirect ways. Housing uses land directly simply by virtue of the amount of land it occupies. Housing also requires a certain amount of land indirectly — it requires space for the activities of its occupants, such as schools, shops, workplaces, and parks.

Residential areas are a key driver of the public services that need to be provided to a community. An increase or decrease in the amount of housing available — as well as the types of housing that are available — can have a significant impact on the demand for public services. For example, changes in the housing stock influence how much electricity needs to be provided to power homes in the community, how many people are likely to use public transportation, and how many children will attend public schools.

Plans for housing often have a significant impact on planning for land use and public services. For example, the city of Boulder in Colorado is one of the few places in the United States that has a set limit on the number of new houses that can be built each year. By limiting the amount of new housing to a yearly quota, the city also indirectly controls how much land will be used for new housing and limits the expansion of public services that are typically required by new housing, such as water services and schools.

No Place Like Home: Kinds of Housing

Cities and towns are filled with housing of all sorts of shapes, sizes, and settings. In some places, single-family housing is located in residential neighborhoods; other places have downtown areas where high-rise apartment towers sit alongside skyscraping office buildings. In addition to different types of housing designs, urban planning also is concerned with different kinds of housing that serve important social and economic purposes, such as affordable housing and housing for people with special needs.

Types of housing

According to the most recent edition of the U.S. Department of Housing and Urban Development's American Housing Survey, nearly two-thirds of all households live in a detached single-family home. Table 6-1 shows a breakdown of the different types of housing in the United States. In addition to attached single-family homes (such as row houses) and mobile homes, nearly a quarter of the U.S. housing stock is multifamily housing. In this section, I cover these different types of housing.

Table 6-1	Types of Housing in the United States	
	Number of Housing Units	**Percent of U.S. Housing**
Single-family, detached	73,080,000	65.4%
Single-family, attached	5,970,000	5.3%
Multifamily, 2 to 4 units	8,350,000	7.5%
Multifamily, 5 to 9 units	5,270,000	4.7%
Multifamily, 10 to 19 units	4,660,000	4.2%
Multifamily, 20 to 49 units	3,630,000	3.2%
Multifamily, 50 or more units	4,000,000	3.6%
Mobile homes	6,840,000	6.1%

Source: U.S. Department of Housing and Urban Development, American Housing Survey (2009)

Detached single-family houses

The detached single-family house (see Figure 6-1) is the most popular type of housing in the United States. For many people, a stand-alone house with room for a yard and a two-car garage is a quintessential part of the American Dream. The detached single-family home can be found in almost every imaginable shape, size, and style, ranging from simple one-bedroom cottages to grandiose mansions.

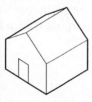

Figure 6-1:
Detached single-family houses are the most common in the United States.

The average single-family house in the United States is about 1,800 square feet, although houses built between 2005 and 2009 average about 2,300 square feet — a difference of almost 25 percent.

In addition to the size of a house, the amount of land that a house sits on helps determine whether a neighborhood is densely or sparsely populated. The average single-family house in the United States sits on a quarter-acre of land, which is equivalent to a density of four housing units per acre. An acre is 43,560 square feet, or roughly the size of an NFL football field minus the end zones. But the amount of land used per housing unit has been increasing steadily over the years. As of 2009, about 28 percent of all single-family houses in the United States were located on lots of one acre or more (although this total includes houses in rural areas where lot sizes are much larger than in urban and metropolitan areas).

Attached single-family homes

Some single-family homes are attached to adjacent homes, such as row houses and cluster houses (see Figure 6-2). These types of houses can be found in a variety of settings and styles, such as ornate multistory brownstone row houses in New York City or cluster-style condominiums surrounded by parklike settings in suburban neighborhoods. Attached single-family houses typically use less land than their detached counterparts and often are built with densities of 10 to 30 housing units per acre.

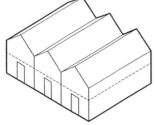

Figure 6-2:
Attached single-family houses are attached to adjacent homes.

Low-density multifamily housing

Low-density multifamily housing comes in many different variations, ranging from duplex houses to small, walk-up apartment buildings with two to four floors (see Figure 6-3). This type of housing is found in many different settings, including apartment buildings that are set side-by-side on dense street blocks, or garden apartments, which are spaced apart from other buildings and surrounded by open space. Depending on the setting, this type of housing often is constructed to yield a density of 10 to 50 housing units per acre.

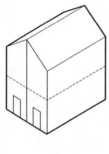
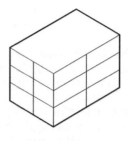

Figure 6-3:
Low-density
multifam-
ily houses
range from
duplexes
to small
apartment
buildings.

Duplex house   Small apartment building

Medium-density multifamily housing

Medium-density housing is typically apartment or condominium buildings
with 20 to 50 units and tall enough to require elevator service, usually 4 to
16 floors in height (see Figure 6-4). Some of these buildings are short and
squat (sometimes called *block-style buildings*); some are organized around
courtyards to let in light and provide open space; and others are tall and
skinny mid-rise buildings. This type of building can be set closely together
with similar buildings, especially in dense neighborhoods in larger cities, or
set more sparsely on a plot of land surrounded by open space. On average,
medium-density multifamily housing is built with a density of 40 to 80 units
per acre — that's about 10 to 20 times more dense than the typical detached
single-family house.

Figure 6-4:
Medium-
density
multifamily
houses are
typically
apartment
or condo-
minium
buildings
with 20 to 50
units and 4
to 16 floors.

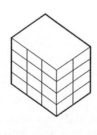

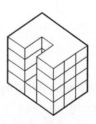
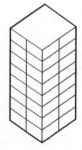

Block-style apartment building   Courtyard-style apartment building   Mid-rise apartment building

High-density multifamily housing

High-density apartment buildings (see Figure 6-5) usually are found in the downtown and mixed-use districts of large cities and suburbs, such as the North Loop section of downtown Chicago or suburban Arlington, Virginia, which is just across the Potomac River from Washington, D.C. These buildings are usually high-rises that contain 50 or more housing units. Depending on their lot setting, this type of housing usually yields a density of 80 or more housing units per acre of land.

Many cities and towns have areas where housing is located in mixed-use developments, including buildings that contain both housing and other uses (such as offices and shops) or housing structures that are located immediately adjacent to shops or office buildings. Housing in mixed-use areas can make life more convenient for residents and help businesses thrive, because residences, workplaces, and shopping areas are located in close proximity to each other.

Figure 6-5:
High-density multifamily houses usually are found in downtown and mixed-use districts of large cities and suburbs.

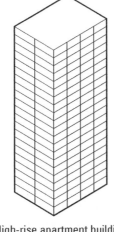

High-rise apartment building

Apartments
Offices
Retail shops

Housing in mixed-use building

Manufactured housing

About 6 percent of the entire U.S. housing inventory consists of manufacturing housing, also referred to as *mobile homes* (see Figure 6-6).

According to the technical regulations of the U.S. Department of Housing and Urban Development, the term *mobile home* refers only to certain types of manufactured housing built before 1976. The term *manufactured housing* is currently used to describe all types of housing that is preassembled in a factory and shipped to its final location, including so-called mobile homes.

Manufactured housing typically consists of one housing unit per structure and is often clustered together in developments that consist only of manufactured housing (less politely known as trailer parks). Manufactured housing is less common in dense urban areas, but often can be found in suburban and semirural sections of metropolitan areas.

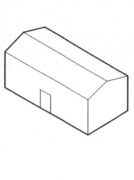

Figure 6-6:
Manu-
factured
housing
is less
common
in urban
areas but
often can
be found
in subur-
ban and
semirural
sections of
metropolitan
areas.

Housing for special needs

Every community is home to people who have special needs, ranging from people who have medical needs to people who were recently homeless. In some cases, special-needs housing is located in facilities in specific areas of the city, such as shelters for homeless people in a downtown area. However, some special-needs housing is located in regular houses and apartment buildings in residential areas.

Here's a guide to some common types of special-needs housing:

- **Adult care and group housing:** Housing for adults who have special medical needs or developmental disabilities often takes place in *group homes,* which are permanent residential facilities that are professionally supervised. In many instances, these facilities are converted or newly built houses that resemble single-family homes and are located in residential areas.

✔ **Assisted living for the elderly:** Housing for elderly people who require supportive personal care often takes place in specially built residential facilities. In some cases, these facilities are large, housing dozens of residents, and are located in commercial districts or areas with other high-density housing. In other cases, smaller facilities are located in converted houses in residential neighborhoods.

✔ **Emergency and transitional housing:** This category includes facilities that provide temporary housing for people in distress, such as runaway teenagers or women and their children fleeing abusive relationships. These housing facilities are professionally managed and sometimes located in converted houses in residential areas.

✔ **Residential medical care facilities:** Housing for people with particular medical needs, such as hospice care facilities or substance abuse treatment facilities, is sometimes located in special facilities in residential areas.

✔ **Housing shelters:** Housing shelters and other places that provide semipermanent housing for otherwise homeless people, such as single-occupancy rooming houses, typically are located outside of residential areas in specialized facilities that also may provide counseling and other social services.

Housing for people with special needs can be controversial, especially when local residents oppose the location of such facilities in residential areas. Many communities have local regulations that place restrictions on the location, amount, and operations of special-needs housing in the community. For example, a community may restrict assisted-living homes for the elderly in residential areas to no more than six residents per home, require that there be staff at the home at all times, and place a limit on the total number of such facilities within the community.

Affordable housing

Since the crash of the U.S. housing market and the start of the economic recession in 2008, there has been a rising awareness of the costs of housing. But providing affordable housing has been a key challenge for many cities and towns for decades. A general rule is that housing costs of 30 percent of income or less are considered affordable, although various federal, state, and local housing affordability programs have different definitions.

Table 6-2 shows how much is spent for housing by different types of households in the United States. Overall, nearly four in ten households spend more than 30 percent of their income on housing, and about one in five households spend more than half of their income on housing. But some households are stretched even further. About half of African American and Hispanic households spend more than 30 percent of their income on housing, and six in ten households in poverty spend more than 50 percent of their income on housing.

Table 6-2	Percent of Household Income Spent on Housing		
	Number of Households	*Percent of Households Spending 30% or More of Their Income on Housing*	*Percent of Households Spending 50% or More of Their Income on Housing*
All U.S. households	111,800,000	39%	19%
Homeowners	76,400,000	32%	14%
Renters	35,400,000	53%	29%
African American	14,000,000	50%	27%
Hispanic	12,700,000	52%	27%
Elderly	23,000,000	39%	22%
Below poverty level	15,700,000	74%	60%

Source: U.S. Department of Housing and Urban Development, American Housing Survey (2009)

Many types of affordable housing may be present in a community, ranging from specific buildings and complexes for publicly supported affordable housing to houses in residential areas that are indistinguishable from surrounding houses in the neighborhood. Here's an overview of the kinds of affordable housing that typically are found in cities and towns:

- **Public housing buildings and complexes:** Many cities and towns have specific buildings and complexes for affordable housing that are supported by federal, state, and local funding. For example, many communities have local housing authorities that operate apartment buildings for low-income senior citizens.

- **Scattered site affordable housing:** Subsidized affordable housing is increasingly located alongside regular housing in urban and suburban neighborhoods. For example, the federal Section 8 housing program provides subsidies to low-income families that help them afford the costs of rental housing. Also, nonprofit organizations such as Habitat for Humanity help low-income families build and own homes in areas that may otherwise lack affordable housing.

✔ **Cheap housing:** For better or worse, every city and town has hous-ing in less-desirable areas and in less-than-perfect condition that are sometimes the only affordable housing available to low-income people and households. In her 1961 book *The Death and Life of Great American Cities* (Random House), famed urbanist Jane Jacobs railed against New York City's demolition of so-called blighted housing in the 1960s, lament-ing that such housing was a better-than-nothing option for many of the city's poorest families.

From the 1920s through the 1960s, the U.S. federal government helped build large-scale public housing projects throughout the country, including the well-known Pruitt–Igoe housing complex in St. Louis and Chicago's Cabrini–Green housing complex. In recent years, the federal government has shifted away from supporting large-scale affordable housing estates and has been working with cities and towns on programs that mix affordable housing into a wide range of urban and suburban neighborhoods.

Private homes + community facilities = Co-housing

Co-housing is a kind of housing development that combines private homes with community facili-ties that are used collectively by residents. Most co-housing communities are also "mini-democ-racies" where residents collaboratively make decisions about the design, development, and management of the community. Co-housing origi-nated in Denmark more than 50 years ago but has become increasingly popular in North America.

More than 100 co-housing communities exist in the United States and Canada. Most co-housing developments have 10 to 50 housing units that are arranged around the community's common house. The common house includes a kitchen and dining room for group meals, as well as space for group meetings, home offices, and childcare. In addition to creating a close-knit community, many co-housing communities have taken steps to reduce their environmental impact by planting community gardens to provide local food for residents and using alternative energy sources, such as wind and solar power.

Co-housing communities are located in lots of different kinds of places, from central Los Angeles to suburban Minneapolis and rural Virginia. If you're interested in learning more about co-housing communities, the websites of the Cohousing Association of the United States (www.cohousing.org) and the Canadian Cohousing Network (www.cohousing.ca) have lots of useful information and directories of existing and planned co-housing communities.

From Suburbs to Mixed Use: Types of Residential Areas

Housing can be located in many different parts of a city, ranging from stately homes in leafy suburban neighborhoods to converted loft apartments in industrial districts. Most housing is located in residential areas where housing is the primary land use, although other activities — such as schools and convenience shopping — often are located in these areas as well.

After World War II, the United States experienced a building boom in which millions of new houses were developed in subdivisions in suburban areas. One of the best known examples of suburban subdivision housing was built in Levittown, New Jersey, where builders constructed dozens of new residential neighborhoods that eventually held more than 15,000 single-family houses.

Since the 1940s, most new housing has been built as part of a subdivision, and more recent housing developments have included housing as part of mixed-use developments and used clustering layouts to preserve open space and natural resources.

Here are some examples of different types of residential areas:

✔ **Traditional neighborhoods (see Figure 6-7):** These areas typically feature a gridded street pattern with houses located on relatively small lots of land.

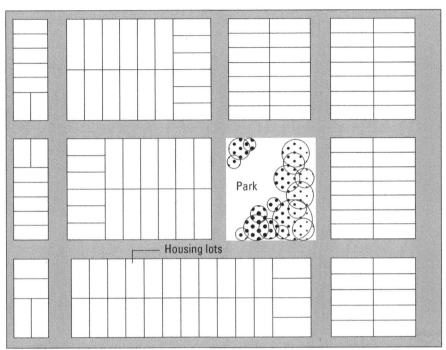

Park

Housing lots

Figure 6-7:
A traditional
neighbor-
hood.

✔ **Suburban-style subdivisions (see Figure 6-8):** These subdivisions feature cul-de-sac streets that branch off from a main street. Houses are
typically located on larger lots of land that provide a sense of privacy.

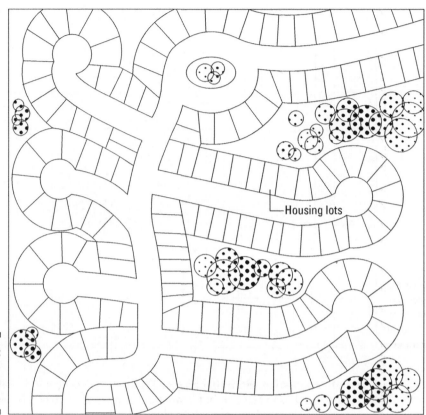

Housing lots

Figure 6-8:
A suburban-
style
subdivision.

✔ **Cluster development (see Figure 6-9):** Cluster developments place individual houses relatively close together on compact street patterns in order to preserve open spaces and undeveloped land. Using smaller lots of land for each house allows for more land to be conserved.

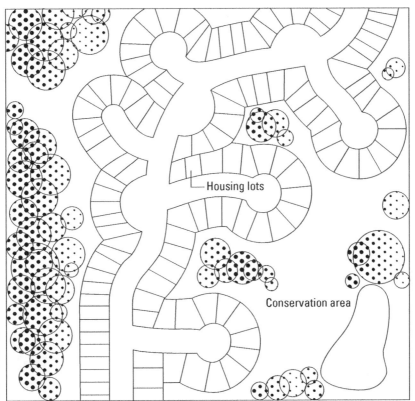

Figure 6-9:
A cluster
development.

✔ **Mixed-use development (see Figure 6-10):** Housing in mixed-use development can occur either as housing placed near other uses, such as offices and shopping, or as housing located in the same buildings as other uses.

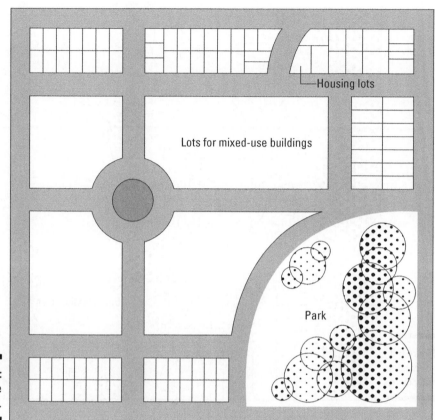

Housing lots

Lots for mixed-use buildings

Park

Figure 6-10:
A mixed-use
development.

Housing and the Urban Plan: Taking Stock of Housing in Your Community

An urban plan looks into many different aspects of the local housing situation so that the plan can recommend ways for the community to maintain and develop the right amount and right types of housing. Having a good sense of the community's current housing stock and future housing needs also helps urban planners make better decisions about related plan components, such as land use, transportation, and public services. The plan's housing component also can help homeowners and private real-estate developers better understand the local housing market and the future needs of the community.

Keeping up with demand: Is there enough housing?

One of the basic questions that plans ask about the community's housing situation is whether the community has enough housing to keep up with demand. Examining the current housing stock and comparing it to demographic projections of future population trends helps planners figure out if supply can keep up with demand.

✔ **Current housing supply** is the total amount of housing that is currently available in the community. This information is available from a variety of sources, including U.S. Census data and local records of property taxes or building permits. In addition to the total amount of housing, many specific housing characteristics — such as cost, condition, age, and location — are important factors related to housing supply (I talk more about these details in the next few sections).

✔ **Future housing demand** is the anticipated change in the total size of the community's population. The demographic details of future population change — such as income, age, household size, and lifestyle preferences — are also important in determining what types of housing may be called for in the future.

In places where there's a growing demand for housing or changes in the types of housing that are needed by the community, the community's plan can guide future development in ways that help meet these demands through supportive land use regulations and housing development programs. But in some cities, the demand for housing is actually shrinking. For example, the city of Cleveland lost more than 15 percent of its population between 2000 and 2010 and is trying to figure out good ways to reduce its housing stock and reuse vacant land.

What kinds of housing are available?

In addition to the overall *amount* of housing that makes up the housing stock of the community, the mix of different *kinds* of housing is also an important characteristic of the housing supply. Here are some of the important characteristics of housing that urban planners look for:

✔ **Different types of housing:** Looking into the different types of housing that are present in the community, such as single-family housing versus multifamily housing, is useful for urban planners. If population projections indicate that the number of smaller households is likely to grow in the future, planners need to know if the community has a sufficient number of smaller homes and apartments.

- ✔ **A mix of owner and renter-occupied housing:** As of 2009, about two-thirds of all U.S. housing was owner occupied and the remaining one-third was renter occupied. A mix of housing for homeowners and renters can accommodate a more diverse population, because many households may not be able to afford homeownership or may simply prefer the life-style offered by apartments and other rental housing options.

- ✔ **Housing costs:** A good understanding of the costs of housing in the community can be used to help plan for a mix of housing that reflects the income characteristics of the community. For example, a community with a significant number of low-income households may be concerned about the availability of affordable housing options.

Urban planners, real-estate agents, building developers, and other interested professionals use a wide range of information sources to research local housing markets, including data from the U.S. Census, property tax and building permit data, property sales data, and surveys of housing in specific neighbor-hoods or surveys of particular consumer segments (such as *empty nesters,* parents whose children have grown and left the house). A good sense of the mix of housing that is currently available in the community and that will be demanded in the future is used in urban plans to recommend land use regula-tions, zoning, and other policies and incentives that encourage the develop-ment of the right mix of housing.

This old house: Housing maintenance

Leaky roofs, peeling paint, broken windows — these are all part of the natural process that houses go through as they age. Without proper maintenance, even the most well-built housing can slip into disrepair. Understanding the condition of the community's housing stock helps planners identify strate-gies for maintaining and preserving its housing.

Here are some of the factors that urban plans examine when it comes to the condition of local housing:

- ✔ **Age of housing:** Roughly one-third of the entire U.S. housing stock is more than 50 years old. And many communities have substantial amounts of housing that date back a century or more. Age alone doesn't mean that a house is in poor condition, but communities with significant amounts of older housing tend to have greater needs for maintenance and upkeep. Information from U.S. Census reports and building department data often is used to determine the age characteristics of local housing.

✔ **Deficient housing conditions:** Planners can identify housing that is in poor condition in a variety of ways. Records of building code violations can help identify houses that are in poor condition and neighborhoods where there are significant numbers of poor-condition houses. Observational surveys of the exterior condition of the housing stock (also called *windshield surveys*) are used to assess housing conditions in specific neighborhoods or districts.

✔ **Ability of the population to maintain their housing:** Keeping a house in good shape requires time, money, and effort. Maintaining housing can be a stretch for many people, including low-income and elderly households. In addition to keeping an eye directly on housing conditions, understanding the underlying demographic and economic characteristics of the community can help identify households and neighborhoods that may require assistance in maintaining the housing stock.

Examining the maintenance and upkeep of local housing helps planners develop recommendations for improving the local housing stock, including programs and policies addressing housing conditions in specific areas, specific types of housing (such as older apartment buildings), and housing occupied by people who may require financial assistance.

Location, location, location: Is housing close to where people work and shop?

Understanding the location of housing relative to other places in the community — such as where people work, shop, or go to school — helps urban planners identify future locations for new housing or other land uses, as well as future improvements to the transportation system.

The housing component of a comprehensive plan often examines how people travel between places, especially whether people are able to walk, bike, or use public transportation to get to work. Another common measure of the relative location of housing is how long it takes people to get to work or other important places.

Another way of looking at the relative location of housing is to examine how many essential services are located in close proximity to households. In many urban and suburban areas, households are located several miles from the nearest grocery stores, banks, and hospitals.

Urban planners often use sophisticated maps to analyze location patterns, but you can get a quick sense of how well your neighborhood provides essential services and worthwhile amenities by checking out the Walk Score website (www.walkscore.com). This website lets you look up street addresses and rates their relative location on a scale ranging from "Car-Dependent" (worst) to "Walker's Paradise" (best), depending on what types of amenities are located nearby.

Housing that is located near other places that people use (such as grocery stores, restaurants, schools, and more) can provide both increased convenience for households and have a positive impact on the environment by reducing the amount of travel required to get between places. Understanding the relative location of housing in the community helps planners identify existing residential areas that could benefit from more diverse land uses, as well as commercial or mixed-use areas that may be appropriate locations for future housing development.

Looking at costs: Is housing affordable?

The cost of housing and the ability of people to pay for housing is a key concern of the housing component of a comprehensive plan. Most major cities and metropolitan areas in the United States receive federal and state funding that helps them provide affordable housing. Looking into the affordability of housing involves examining both the housing stock and the income characteristics of the population:

- ✔ **Looking at housing:** Planners can identify affordable housing in a variety of ways, including looking at housing costs for different types of housing based on information from U.S. Census data, databases of local real-estate transactions, and surveys of rental housing costs. Planners also try to identify specific areas of the community that have significant amounts of affordable (or unaffordable) housing.

- ✔ **Looking at the population:** The income characteristics of the population are an important indicator of the need for affordable housing. Even though U.S. housing prices declined during the economic recession that began in 2008, many people had a difficult time keeping up with housing costs due to unemployment and lost savings, which led, in turn, to a massive wave of housing foreclosures and evictions. In addition to information on income and employment trends, many communities are also keeping track of other measures of financial distress, including mortgage foreclosures and property tax delinquencies.

Examining local conditions helps planners determine the amount and types of affordable housing that are needed by the community. Goals for affordable housing can be coordinated with other plan components, such as using land use regulations and zoning to encourage the development of affordable housing. These goals also are addressed in other programs and policies that provide financial support for affordable housing and low-income households.

Going green: Environmentally friendly housing

Housing can have a significant impact on human health and the environment. Along with other efforts to improve local health and protect environmental resources, the housing component of a comprehensive plan can help identify and address environmental concerns:

- **Human and environmental health:** Many local plans identify housing conditions that may present hazardous conditions to both people and the environment. For example, some older homes contain construction materials treated with chemicals associated with asthma and other childhood illnesses. Housing conditions also can have environmental impacts, such as a house with a damaged sewer pipe or septic tank system that allows human waste to contaminate surrounding soils or groundwater sources.

- **Energy and resource conservation:** Housing uses a significant amount of energy and other resources on a day-to-day basis. For example, keeping the modern household running requires water, electricity, and heating fuels — all of which can have a significant impact on the environment. A plan's housing component can help identify opportunities for resource conservation by examining data on utility usage, getting information on resource use from consumer surveys, and conducting energy audits of older homes or in specific neighborhoods.

Efforts to reduce the presence of housing-based hazards and conserve resources often include building code enforcement, housing rehabilitation programs, and revisions to existing housing development standards. A growing number of communities are encouraging housing rehabilitation and development that meets the LEED standards of the U.S. Green Building Council by offering incentives such as financial support for environmentally friendly housing or expedited development approvals for proposed housing projects that meet green building standards.

For more information, go to www.usgbc.org/LEED or check out *Green Building & Remodeling For Dummies,* by Eric Corey Freed (Wiley).

Making homes healthier

Is your home a healthy place? According to the U.S. Department of Housing and Urban Development (HUD), many homes in the United States contain health and safety hazards that are particularly dangerous to children and the elderly. These hazards range from poorly maintained steps that can cause life-threatening falls for older people to the household presence of dangerous chemicals in paints, solvents, and other construction materials that can cause serious illnesses in infants and young children.

Since 1999, HUD's Healthy Homes initiative has been working with state agencies, local governments, and nonprofit organizations to reduce in-home hazards in five key areas:

✔ Reducing housing conditions that complicate childhood asthma and allergies

✔ Controlling mold and moisture problems

✔ Preventing unintentional injuries

✔ Reducing exposure to lead hazards

✔ Improving indoor air quality

In some cases, extensive housing rehabilitation measures are needed to reduce in-home hazards, such as the removal or treatment of asbestos-based construction materials. But many simple steps may improve in-home health and safety, including properly storing household chemicals and cleaners and installing carbon monoxide detectors.

For more information on healthy homes and a checklist to see if your home is healthy, go to www.hud.gov/healthyhomes.

Chapter 7

Moving the City: Transportation

In This Chapter

▶ Understanding why transportation matters

▶ Looking at different types of transportation

▶ Taking the measure of a community's transportation system

▶ Planning to meet a community's future transportation needs

*T*ransportation knits the community together by carrying people and things from one part of town to another. It also connects the local community to other places around the globe. Without good transportation, cities would come to a standstill and be unable to perform even their most basic functions.

Local transportation is what makes the city "go." It serves the needs of the community in many different ways:

✔ Transportation is used for many purposes, including personal travel and the movement of goods and supplies for businesses.

✔ Cities and towns use many different types of transportation, ranging from cars and trucks to planes and trains.

✔ People travel around the city for lots of different reasons, including commuting to work, going on shopping trips, and walking for leisure or personal health.

✔ Travel around the city involves trips of every possible distance, whether it's just a few blocks to the corner store or a round trip of dozens of miles back and forth to work.

The average American makes three or four trips away from home each day and logs more than 13,000 miles per year in some form of motorized transportation. Individuals spend a significant amount of time engaged in travel, and communities invest substantial resources in their transportation infrastructure and services.

In this chapter, I give you a tour of the transportation component of a local comprehensive plan. I offer an overview of the different types of transportation, how urban plans go about assessing local transportation conditions, and how urban plans can be used to improve local traffic conditions and reduce the environmental impacts of transportation.

Making Us Mobile: Why Transportation Matters

Transportation is a crucial component of a local comprehensive plan because it helps shape the form of the city and helps the community carry out its everyday functions. Here are some of the key considerations that go into planning for local transportation:

- **Transportation infrastructure is expensive and long lasting.** Providing infrastructure for transportation — such as roads, bridges, or airports — requires a substantial investment by the community. And most transportation investments are very difficult to alter after they're completed, so good planning is essential to getting it right the first time.

- **Transportation helps determine land use patterns.** Areas with different types of land uses require different kinds of transportation. For example, residential areas require access to roads and public transportation so that people can get to work. Coordination between land use plans and transportation improvements helps ensure that areas have access to needed transportation services and that transportation improvements are made in areas planned for future development.

- **Transportation has a significant impact on the environment.** At the moment, transportation in the United States is highly dependent on the use of fossil fuels. This means that transportation is responsible for a significant portion of pollution associated with fossil fuel use and contributes to emissions of greenhouse gases associated with global climate change. Transportation has other impacts on the environment, including covering natural soil surfaces with asphalt and other impermeable surfaces that can impact water quality.

Planning for local transportation requires a substantial degree of coordination between different government agencies, as well as private transportation businesses. The local transportation network often seems like a seamless web of streets and other features, but many different parties actually provide and maintain local transportation services. For example, a highway running through the community may be maintained by a state transportation department, while smaller roads are often maintained by county and local authorities, and some roads in residential areas are maintained by private homeowners associations.

The Transportation System: It's All Connected

Cities and towns have lots of ways for people to get around. These range from sidewalks that carry foot traffic to highways for cars and trucks to airports that move people and freight. A comprehensive plan helps determine what types of transportation need to be provided to the community and helps coordinate the development and operation of all the different modes of transportation in the community.

Roadways

Roadways are the most visible and important element of the local transportation system. They're essential for carrying passenger and commercial traffic by car, truck, and other forms of motorized transportation, as well as providing space for the movement of pedestrians, bicyclists, and other users of nonmotorized transportation.

Local roadway systems consist of many different types of roads. Most U.S. communities use the Federal Highway Administration's road classification system to plan for different types of roads:

- ✔ **Principal arterial roadways:** Principal arterial roadways are highways and freeways that are designed to have the highest capacity and fastest speeds within the overall roadway system. Highways and freeways have a limited number of road entrances and exits and typically don't have stop-and-go traffic signals. Traffic on highways and freeways is usually restricted to fast-moving cars, trucks, motorcycles, and buses.

- ✔ **Minor arterial roads:** Minor arterial roads usually have four or more lanes of motorized traffic and higher speed limits. They account for about 10 percent of all roadways but carry roughly half of all local traffic. Minor arterial roads usually have stop-and-go traffic signals to accommodate crossing roadways and adjacent land uses, such as shopping centers and office buildings. These roads typically have a limited number of pedestrian crossings and lack adjacent sidewalks.

- ✔ **Collector streets:** Collector streets are the connection between minor arterial roads and local streets. They typically have fewer lanes of motorized traffic and lower speed limits as compared to arterials. Driveways for homes and business may connect directly to the roadway, and pedestrian street crossings with traffic signals are located at regular intervals. Many collector streets also have dedicated space for non-motorized traffic, such as bike lanes.

✓ **Local streets:** Local streets make up the majority of street mileage in most communities. These are usually two-lane streets that provide immediate access to residential areas and small business districts. These streets have the lowest speed limits and typically have frequent street crossings that use stop signs (and other signage) instead of electronic traffic signals to control the flow of motorized traffic. (Check out Chapter 8 for more on urban design considerations for local streets, such as design features that improve road safety.)

In addition to different types of roadways, the community's overall road system may require specialized elements such as bridges and tunnels that have special planning and operational considerations. For example, many of the major bridges and tunnels in the New York City region are operated by a special public authority (for more information, check out the nearby sidebar on the Port Authority).

Port Authority: Planes, trains, and automobiles

The New York City metropolitan economy produces nearly a trillion dollars' worth of activity on an annual basis. Many of the region's most important social and economic functions are made possible by its extensive transportation infrastructure, much of which is operated by the Port Authority of New York & New Jersey, which serves the greater New York City area.

The agency was formed through an agreement between the two states in 1921. Although it doesn't oversee the region's roads or the NYC subway, a list of the Port Authority's facilities reads like a trophy case of transportation landmarks. In addition to five shipping ports, the Port Authority operates five airports (including John F. Kennedy International Airport, LaGuardia Airport, and Newark Liberty International Airport) and six bridges or tunnels (including the George Washington Bridge and the Lincoln Tunnel). The Port Authority's other transportation and commercial facilities include the Port Authority Bus Terminal, the PATH Rail Transit System, and the World Trade Center.

The Port Authority is a type of special-district public authority that doesn't receive tax revenues. Instead, it generates the income it needs for its operations from the users of its facilities. With an annual budget of more than $3.5 billion and facilities valued at $30 billion, the Port Authority is the largest regional transportation agency in the United States.

Public transportation systems

Public transportation is an essential element of the local transportation system. According to the American Public Transportation Association, public transportation systems in the United States carried passengers on more than 10 billion trips in 2009. Public transportation systems often are made up of several different types of transportation, and different elements may be operated by a range of state, regional, and local transportation authorities.

Bus services

Buses are the backbone of the public transportation system in the United States, and they account for about half of all public transportation rides. Bus service is a flexible and relatively low-cost public transportation option, as well as one that is becoming more environmentally friendly. Roughly a third of the U.S. bus fleet uses *alternative fuels* (fuels other than gasoline or diesel). Different types of bus service help people get around the city:

- **Local buses:** Local buses typically travel along set routes using the local street network and making stops at specific locations. Many places offer "express" bus services that make fewer stops between heavily used destinations. Local bus services are increasingly being connected to other types of transportation, such as transfers between buses and subway services.

- **Bus rapid transit (BRT):** This type of bus service allows buses to travel on dedicated roads where they're able to travel more quickly between stops. BRT requires special roadways but is a less costly option than rail-based rapid-transit systems.

  For example, the Port Authority of Allegheny County's East Busway in Pittsburgh uses a dedicated bus-only road to connect downtown Pittsburgh to the city's university district, neighborhoods, and nearby eastern suburbs.

- **Commuter buses:** Commuter bus services provide people with a way to travel long distances to work, usually 10 to 50 miles or more. These buses typically travel on existing highways and roadways, but they use specialized equipment that's more comfortable for long trips.

  For example, on weekday morning and evening rush hours, the Maryland Transportation Administration operates commuter bus services that link Baltimore and its suburbs to employment centers in the Washington, D.C., area.

Subways and rail services

Subways and rail services help millions of people travel around the city, whether they're commuting to work, going to school, or going on a shopping trip. Rail-based public transportation systems use a few different approaches and enable people to take trips that range from just a few blocks to dozens of miles:

- ✔ **Subways:** Subways carry about a third of all public transportation riders in the United States, although relatively few cities have extensive subway systems; these include Boston, Chicago, New York, and Washington, D.C. Most people use the term *subways*, but many routes travel above ground or on elevated tracks, as in Chicago. The more general term for these services, *heavy rail,* is used to describe local rail services that use dedicated infrastructure to carry large numbers of people.

- ✔ **Light rail:** Light rail services — including trolleys, trams, and streetcars — are rail-based systems that share roadways with car and truck traffic. For example, Toronto's extensive streetcar system includes rail paths that run down the middle of the street and requires streetcars to obey traffic signals at intersections with cars and trucks. Light rail systems are considerably less expensive to build than subway-type rail systems. Several U.S. cities have recently development light-rail routes, including Charlotte (North Carolina), Houston, and Minneapolis.

- ✔ **Commuter rail:** Commuter rail services are aimed at helping people commute to work over long distances, usually 20 to 50 miles or more. The most extensive commuter rail services are offered in large metropolitan areas, including Boston, Chicago, and New York. The New York City region is served by three commuter rail lines — including the Long Island Rail Road (LIRR) — which provide more than six billion miles' worth of trips each year.

Specialized public transit

Public transportation systems also include a variety of specialized public transit services that are essential to people who have limited transportation options.

Paratransit services are aimed at people with disabilities who are otherwise unable to access traditional public transportation services and facilities. Paratransit use makes up about 2 percent of all public transportation services. It often utilizes specially equipped buses, vans, and taxi-style vehicles.

Some specialized services cater to the unique geography of their communities. For example, both New York City and Seattle have extensive ferry-boat services that provide millions of rides each year. In a more unusual example, the Port Authority of Allegheny County in Pittsburgh, Pennsylvania, operates the 140-year-old Monongahela Incline, a funicular railcar service that climbs more than 400 vertical feet up a steep hillside. The incline originally connected hilltop housing with factories and steel mills in the river valley below, and the incline continues to serve both neighborhood residents and tourists looking for a great bird's-eye view of the city.

Pedestrians, pedals, and paths

Walking and bicycling, sometimes referred to as *non-motorized transportation*, are essential means of getting around for many people. Providing safe routes and services for walking and biking can help encourage people to make more of their trips on foot or by bike.

In many cases, pedestrians and cyclists share roadways with cars. Well-designed bicycle lanes and sidewalks can improve the safety of these roadways and help increase their usage by pedestrians and cyclists.

The city of Minneapolis boasts nearly 50 miles of on-street bike lanes and more than 80 miles of off-street bike paths, making it one of the most bike-friendly cities in the United States.

Biking and walking also can be used to connect people to other forms of transportation, such as walking to a nearby stop for public transportation. Some local public transportation systems are outfitted with equipment that encourages connections to walking and bicycling, such as buses with specially designed racks to hold bicycles.

Ultimately, a good local transportation system helps people get to where they want to go. Providing safe and direct roads or paths for pedestrians and cyclists that connect them to useful locations — such as schools or shopping areas — may require creating new routes or adding safety features to existing roads. For example, many communities are making an effort to provide children with safe ways to walk and cycle to school buildings (see Chapter 10 for more information).

Commercial transportation

Cities and towns rely on *commercial transportation* (transportation services and facilities offered mostly by private businesses or to meet the needs of businesses) to meet the demands of the local economy, whether it's cargo shipments headed for local factories or planeloads of tourists to visit beaches and museums. Some commercial transportation services and facilities, such as railroad tracks, are an everyday part of the urban landscape, while other types of commercial transportation, such as pipelines, often are hidden from plain sight.

Planes, trains, and buses for travelers and tourists

Air and rail connections are essential for making your community accessible to tourists and business travelers. While air, rail, and bus services usually are offered by private companies, many transportation facilities, such as airports and bus stations, are operated by public authorities:

- **Airports:** Airports provide an essential link between local communities and the rest of the world. In the United States, airports are organized into a *hub-and-spoke system* where smaller airports feed into larger airports in key locations such as Chicago, Detroit, Los Angeles, and New York City. The Hartsfield-Jackson Atlanta International Airport is the world's busiest passenger facility and moved nearly 90 million trips over its runways in 2009.

- **Rail service:** The dominant provider of intercity passenger rail services in the United States is Amtrak, which receives funding assistance from the federal government and operates 30 major routes that serve more than 500 locations. There is currently one high-speed rail route in the United States; Amtrak's Acela line reaches speeds as high as 150 miles per hour on its route between Boston and New York City.

- **Intercity buses:** Greyhound and other regionally based companies provide affordable long-distance transportation between cities. New York City's Port Authority Bus Terminal is the busiest bus station in the country and moves more than 50 million passenger trips a year through its Times Square location.

Intercity transportation facilities are increasingly being connected to local transportation systems, sometimes referred to as *intermodal* or *multi-modal transportation*. For example, the St. Paul–Minneapolis International Airport is connected to downtown Minneapolis by the MetroTransit Hiawatha Line light-rail service. This service allows visitors to the Twin Cities to step off their flight, walk directly to the airport's local rail station, and arrive at a downtown hotel in less than an hour.

Ports, planes, and pipes for commerce

Many people don't come into contact with transportation services and facilities for commercial freight on a regular basis, but they're essential to the success of the local economy. There are several specialized types of commercial transportation:

- **Trucking and warehousing:** Trucks carry roughly half of all commercial freight shipments in the United States. Most of this freight is carried over the interstate highway system. Local transportation plans often identify the best routes for use by heavy trucks and figure out where to locate warehouse facilities used by cargo trucks.

✓ **Commercial railroads:** Railroads are especially important to the long-distance movement of heavy commodities, such as coal and timber, as well as shipping containers that often are offloaded from shipping vessels for distribution to points across the United States.

✓ **Ports:** Shipping ports are essential to both the international and domestic movement of commercial cargo. Shipping ports often take cargo from shipping vessels and move it onto other types of transportation, such as trucks or railcars.

✓ **Air freight:** Air freight carries the least amount of cargo of any of the major types of commercial freight, and much of the value of air freight shipments is made up by high-priority, low-weight shipments, such as overnight mail and packages. The airports in Memphis and Louisville are among the busiest for air cargo in the United States; they are the centers of operation for FedEx and UPS, respectively.

✓ **Pipelines:** Commercial pipelines make up a mostly hidden distribution network for energy commodities, including oil and natural gas. These pipelines provide a cost-efficient means of transportation and help keep hazardous materials away from rail and roadway transportation routes.

Local planning for commercial freight services and facilities is closely coordinated with the overall land use component of a comprehensive plan, including locations for warehousing, manufacturing, and energy services. Commercial freight shipments also may involve hazardous materials — such as toxic chemicals or flammable substances — and the placement of facilities often necessitates extensive advance planning to manage local concerns about safety and potential hazards.

Assessing Transportation Conditions

Communities have to assess local transportation conditions to determine how well they're being served. In this section, I fill you in on some of the ways in which local plans examine traffic conditions and assess the transportation needs of the community. I also look into the relationship between transportation and environmental impacts.

Are we there yet? Assessing traffic problems

It doesn't take much for traffic congestion on car-clogged roadways to push even the most patient drivers to the edge of road rage. Most local plans examine traffic conditions in order to determine if local roadways are doing a good job of moving people to where they want to go. *Level of service* (LOS) ratings are used to evaluate different types of roads and intersections. Most transportation planning authorities use LOS ratings based on standards published by the Transportation Research Board.

LOS ratings use scores from A to F to describe how well a particular roadway or intersection handles traffic flow. Here are the ratings assigned:

- ✔ **LOS A:** At the highest level of service, traffic can move easily along the road at or near the speed limit of the road.

- ✔ **LOS B:** This rating describes traffic flow that is moving without major impediments but may be traveling at average speeds below the speed limit of the road.

- ✔ **LOS C:** Traffic is moving at a reasonable pace, but the roadway is crowded and there are minor delays due to slowing of traffic flow.

- ✔ **LOS D:** Traffic is moving at an average speed well below the posted speed limit, and there are significant delays due to traffic congestion. At this level of service (and lower), the roadway is considered inadequate for the purposes of handling the volume of traffic that it receives.

- ✔ **LOS E and F:** At the lowest levels of service, traffic is moving slowly and there are many delays due to stop-and-go traffic.

Urban planners and traffic engineers collect a wide range of data regarding the use of roadways and employ many methods other than LOS analysis to examine traffic problems. Complex computer models and simulations are increasingly being used to troubleshoot traffic problems, and many communities are using real-time traffic monitoring systems to help manage their traffic flow.

Serving the whole city: Can you get there from here?

Local plans for transportation strive to make sure that the needs of the community are met:

- ✔ **Are all areas of the community accessible?** Ideally, every geographic area within the community would be easily accessible by multiple modes of transportation. But some places that are easily reached by automobile can be very difficult to reach by public transportation, especially in suburban areas. A geographic assessment of the community's transportation system can help identify areas that are difficult to reach and identify ways to make them more accessible, especially when less accessible places provide essential services, including grocery shopping or medical care.

✔ **Can everyone get to where he or she needs to go?** People need to go lots of places for many different reasons. In the United States, automobiles provide many people with the ability to go anywhere at anytime. But many people lack access to automobiles and are dependent on friends, family, and public transportation to help them get where they're going. Understanding the transportation needs of the community helps planners make sure that adequate roadways and public transportation are available to help everyone get to work, school, or other vital locations.

Many sources of information can be used to examine local transportation accessibility. Governmental data sources, such as the U.S. Census, provide detailed information on transportation habits. Locally produced maps and information — based on service records from transportation agencies or passenger surveys, for example — also can be used to examine local transportation conditions.

Making an impact: Transportation and the environment

Local transportation systems are a feat of modern engineering that use many different energy sources to help people get where they're going. Whether it's elevated highways that carry millions of motorists or tunnels below the earth for subways cars, transportation infrastructure and services have a significant impact on the environment.

In many cases, there's a direct trade-off between environmental quality and transportation usage. More cars usually means more air pollution. Local plans are increasingly looking at the environmental impacts of transportation, including the following:

✔ **Pollution due to transit operations:** Worsening air pollution is one of the key impacts of local transportation systems. Due primarily to the use of fossil fuels in car and truck operation, air pollution contributes to a wide range of respiratory diseases in people and adds to global levels of greenhouse gases associated with climate change. Many communities are taking steps to support green transportation, which uses cleaner fuel sources (see Chapter 11).

✔ **Environmental impacts of transportation infrastructure:** The construction, placement, and operation of transportation infrastructure also can have a significant impact on the environment. The most obvious environmental impact occurs when construction converts undeveloped land into roads or other transportation features. But transportation infrastructure also can have broader impacts on the environment. For example, paved roadway surfaces require extensive drainage systems, which can alter water system patterns. In addition, excessive noise from roadways can disturb the habitats of vulnerable animal species.

In some circumstances, federal and state regulations require environmental impact studies of proposed transportation construction projects, such as freeway extensions or new subway lines.

There's a growing awareness of the global impacts of local transportation. According to the urban planning researcher Stephen Wheeler of the University of California at Davis, a growing number of communities are including the environmental impacts of transportation in local *climate-change inventories,* which track levels of greenhouse gas emissions by community.

Keeping Us Moving: Transportation Planning

Local transportation plans serve a variety of useful functions, including identifying locations for future investments in transportation infrastructure, planning for expanded public transportation services to serve the community, and coordinating improvements to the local transportation system with other components of the comprehensive plan. In addition to helping the local transportation system run safely and efficiently, local plans are increasingly looking for ways to improve local traffic conditions and reduce the environmental impacts of transportation.

Expanding and improving local transportation

A local comprehensive plan plays a key role in identifying the transportation needs of the community and proposing how these needs will be met by the various governmental agencies and private businesses that provide transportation services to the community.

In particular, local plans often look into the following questions:

✔ How will existing areas of the community be connected to newly developing parts of the community?

✔ What modes of transportation should be used to connect new development to existing parts of the community?

✔ Can existing transportation infrastructure and service be extended to serve developing areas?

✔ Does existing transportation infrastructure need to be upgraded or replaced?

✔ Do existing public transportation services adequately serve the community?

Local plans help identify what types of transportation are likely to be needed by the community in the future, as well as locations within the community that should be served by future transportation improvements and extensions.

Managing traffic: Old problems, new solutions

Americans spend a lot of time stuck in traffic. According to the Texas Transportation Institute, the average commuter in the United States spends 34 hours per year stuck in slow traffic. Improving traffic conditions is one of the key aims of transportation planning. Local planning uses a variety of approaches to help people get where they're going with as little frustration as possible.

Intelligent transportation systems

The U.S. Department of Transportation describes *intelligent transportation systems* (ITS) as cutting-edge technologies that can be used to "enhance the efficiency, safety, and convenience of surface transportation, resulting in improved access, saved lives and time, and increased productivity." This approach uses new technologies to make traffic run more smoothly, especially on congested highways and other arterial roads.

Here's a look at some of the key elements of ITS:

✔ **Computerized traffic signal systems:** High-tech traffic signals can be used to manage traffic flow and prevent traffic congestion.

✔ **Traffic detection and monitoring:** Surveillance cameras and sensors embedded in roadways are used to monitor traffic flow and provide real-time traffic information.

✔ **Traffic information systems:** A variety of communication methods — including electronic signs and web-based traffic updates — are used to provide transportation users with real-time information on traffic conditions and alternative routes.

✔ **Automated toll-road collection:** Some toll roads now use automated toll-collection services, such as the E-ZPass system, which help maintain traffic flow and reduce the need for traffic to stop at toll booths.

In addition to improvements to transportation infrastructure, federal and state funding for ITS programs has been used to establish local centers that operate real-time traffic management programs. For example, the Tennessee Department of Transportation's SmartWay Traffic Management Center in metropolitan Nashville provides real-time monitoring and management of traffic along the area's major thoroughfares.

Transportation management programs

A variety of approaches are being used to influence travel habits within the community in ways that help people use transportation infrastructure more efficiently and reduce traffic congestion, especially in heavily trafficked areas and during rush hour periods:

✔ **Time management programs:** One way to avoid the crush of rush hour traffic is to space out trips during different times of the day. Local transportation agencies often encourage major employers to stagger employee arrival and departure times in order to reduce traffic congestion.

For example, some federal agencies in the Washington, D.C., area give employees the option of arriving and leaving from work during different 15-minute periods, which helps reduce the rush hour traffic volumes.

✔ **Carpooling:** Carpooling programs help reduce the number of vehicles on the road and can help improve traffic flow. Many local programs support carpooling with ride-matching services, park-and-ride locations where carpool members can meet, access to high-occupancy vehicle lanes on roadways, and financial incentives for carpooling.

For example, the Los Angeles County Metropolitan Transportation Authority's Vanpool Program (www.metro.net/around/vanpool) provides low-cost leased vans to vanpool groups.

✔ **Parking management:** Parking management programs can have a significant impact on travel behavior, especially programs that change the cost or location of parking or the total number of available parking spaces. For example, changes to parking costs can increase or decrease the number of people who drive to work, and programs such as early-bird pricing discounts can encourage people to begin their commute before rush hour.

✔ **Road tolls:** Road tolls have been used in the United States for decades to help raise funds to maintain roadway systems, but road tolls also can be used to help manage traffic flow. Known as *peak-period pricing,* some toll roads are more costly to use during busy periods.

For example, tolls for truck traffic crossing Chicago's Skyway Bridge are higher during the peak daylight hours of 4 a.m. to 8 p.m.

✔ **Congestion pricing:** In some cities, an approach known as *congestion pricing* charges fees to cars and trucks for traveling to or through certain parts of the city.

The best known example is London, England's Congestion Charge Zone, which covers roughly a square mile of central London and charges most passenger cars between £9 and £12 just for driving in or through the zone. By some estimates, this has reduced traffic congestion within the zone by more than 30 percent. In 2007, New York City proposed a similar scheme for Manhattan, but the proposal failed to gain approval from New York's state legislature.

Making it green: Reducing environmental impacts

As a whole, the U.S. transportation system places a heavy burden on the environment. Some of the environmental impacts of transportation use are obvious at the local level, such as air pollution, while other impacts are being felt more broadly, such as the contribution of transportation to global emissions of greenhouse gases.

In the spirit of "thinking globally and acting locally," many communities are acting to reduce the environmental impacts of local transportation by

✔ **Encouraging the use of alternative fuels:** Local communities have been encouraging the use of alternative fuels in cars, trucks, and buses in a variety of ways, including

- Using alternative fuels in vehicles operated by government agencies

- Providing charging stations for electric vehicles

- Giving some energy-efficient vehicles access to priority lanes on highways

✔ **Reducing trips that use motorized transportation:** A variety of local efforts aim to reduce car and truck traffic by encouraging people to use other forms of transportation, including improving public transportation services and providing financial incentives for the use of alternative transportation. Check out the nearby sidebar on car sharing and bike sharing for some examples of new ways for people to reduce their use of cars and trucks.

✓ **Transit-oriented development:** Designing communities where essential locations are located close together is one way to reduce the need for transportation. Urban planners refer to this as *access by proximity.* A style of development known as *transit-oriented development* aims to locate mixed land uses close to each other and to transportation facilities.

For example, the state of California allows cities and towns to provide financial incentives for transit-oriented development. The state defines a *transit village* as "a neighborhood centered around a transit station that is planned and designed so that residents, workers, shoppers, and others find it convenient and attractive to patronize transit" and include "a mix of housing types, including apartments, within not more than a quarter mile." This approach to development helps create communities with compact land use patterns that minimize the need for automobile use.

Hitching a ride: Car sharing and bike sharing

Car sharing and bike sharing services are among the newest ways for people to get around cities. These services make cars and bikes available to people for short periods of time at affordable rates. Car-share and bike-share programs give people more transportation options and can help reduce the environmental impacts of automobile usage. Bike-share programs encourage people to bike instead of driving, and some communities are planning for car-share programs in order to reduce parking and land use demands.

A variety of car-share programs are offered throughout the United States by nonprofit organizations, governmental agencies, and green businesses. Zipcar (www.zipcar.com) is the largest private car-sharing company in the United States and offers shares for as little as 30 minutes. The company offers cars in more than 120 cities and caters to people who need to make occasional short-range car trips but can't afford car ownership or don't want to own a car.

Bike-share programs provide affordable access to bicycles for short-distance trips and are an alternative to driving and public transportation. During the 2000s, several European cities launched bicycle sharing programs, including Helsinki (Finland) and Lyon (France). In North America, the city of Montreal helped establish the BIXI (www.bixi.com) bike-share service in 2009. BIXI provides more than 5,000 bicycles for share that can be picked up or dropped off at any of 400 locations. New York City is set for a 2012 launch of the largest bike-share program in the United States, including a fleet of 10,000 bikes that will be available at more than 600 locations.

Chapter 8

The City Beautiful: Urban Design

In This Chapter

▶ Making places that people love

▶ Looking at the building blocks of the city

▶ Getting people involved in designing great places

*U*rban design helps make places that not only have strong visual appeal to a broad audience, but also work well as functional spaces. For example, a well-designed street block may contain several homes in complementary architectural styles, along with a small park and a few small shops with attractive storefronts, all linked together by safe sidewalks and pathways.

Thoughtful urban design can help make places that look good, work well, and are responsive to the needs and wishes of the people who live, work, and play in those spaces.

In this chapter, I look at what typically goes into the urban design component of an urban plan. I explain how urban design is used to make attractive places that also contribute to other objectives of the plan, such as environmental sustainability. I cover approaches to designing different elements of the community, including buildings, blocks, and neighborhoods. And I share ways to get people involved in designing their communities and planning tools that you can use to help implement urban design programs.

The Role of Urban Design: Making Meaningful Places

The urban design component of an urban plan addresses the physical form of the city and typically includes detailed designs for various elements of the city (such as buildings, blocks, and streets) as well as general guidelines for the physical appearance of different parts of the city (from street signs to storefronts). A plan's urban design component also can help support the plan's overall goals and connect to other planning components, such as transportation and natural resources.

In addition to visual appearance, the urban design component of an urban plan can help strengthen other features of the community, including

- ✔ **Functionality:** Good urban design helps make places that function well. For example, a well-designed housing subdivision would have both attractive homes and a street layout that can be patrolled easily by police and used easily by fire services in case of emergency.

- ✔ **A sense of community:** Urban design can help create a sense of community by using local historic and cultural features — such as designing new buildings that complement the architectural heritage of older buildings — and creating spaces that encourage people to interact, such as parks and public plazas.

- ✔ **Sustainability:** Good design also can help preserve and conserve natural resources. For example, a group of homes could be designed to sit closer together and make room to conserve some existing natural features, such as creeks or old-growth trees.

Interest in urban design has grown significantly in recent years, and good urban design has become a priority for many communities. One of the most important developments in this area has been the increasing popularity of the urban design style known as *New Urbanism* (also known as *neo-traditional design*). This approach to design has been promoted widely by an organization called the Congress for the New Urbanism (www.cnu.org), which defines the goals of New Urbanism as creating "diverse, walkable, compact, vibrant, mixed-use communities" that "contain housing, work places, shops, entertainment, schools, parks, and civic facilities essential to the daily lives of the residents, all within easy walking distance of each other." Many communities have adopted urban plans that incorporate the New Urbanism approach, and some aspects of the New Urbanism have been adopted by the U.S. Department of Housing and Urban Development (HUD) and the Environmental Protection Agency (EPA).

Design Elements: The Building Blocks of Cities

I'd bet that many urban designers, if not most, grew up playing with a big set of toy blocks that they used to create everything from small houses to entire cities. Real urban design isn't that much different. A city is made up of lots of different pieces and can be designed at different scales, from buildings to neighborhoods to entire cities.

Buildings, lots, and blocks

Individual buildings and their lots are the most basic urban design elements of a community. The key elements of buildings and lots that are addressed by urban design are the following:

- **Building form:** The shape of a building — including its overall height, width, and length — is a key design element. Variations in building design can be used to shape structures that have different designs but the same amount of interior space. For example, a building with 12,000 square feet of floor space could be designed as a skinny three-story building that's 40 feet wide and 100 feet deep, or as a squat one-story building that's 150 feet wide and 80 feet deep.

- **Appearance:** The appearance of a building is its architectural style and other outside features, such as attached signage or roof antennas.

- **Lot coverage and placement:** Good urban design considers how much of the lot will be covered by the building and where the building will be placed on the lot. Minimizing lot coverage can allow for the preservation of open space, and careful placement of buildings on lots can help preserve natural features.

- **Accessory elements:** Building and lot design also includes placement and appearance of accessory elements, such as landscaping, lighting, parking, and driveways.

In some cases, the design characteristics of buildings and lots are established in urban design plans for streets and neighborhoods that help give entire areas a distinctive look and feel. The next step up from building and lot design is the design of *street blocks,* which are groups of lots and buildings that are surrounded by a common boundary, usually streets. The design of street blocks typically considers the following:

- **Block size:** The size of street blocks in some places has been set for decades or centuries. Most of Manhattan's street grid pattern has been in place for more than 200 years. But urban designers often get the chance to design street block patterns in newly developing areas, as well as to retrofit street block patterns in existing areas.

    Small street blocks help create a more walkable setting, especially in residential areas, and lend places a more intimate feeling. Large street blocks allow for larger buildings to be developed but can feel less walkable and less user-friendly to some people.

✔ **Coverage and placement:** The design of a block considers how much of the surface area will be used for buildings and other improvements (such as parking or sidewalks), as well as where different uses will be placed on the block. Good block design can help create places that provide more open space and preserve natural features.

✔ **Appearance:** Urban design also considers the overall architectural appearance of a block. Some block designs emphasize a generally uniform appearance among buildings that helps to establish a specific identity for the block, whereas other designs may mix complementary architectural styles in order to create greater visual appeal.

Streets

Designing city streets is a challenging task because streets serve two functions that are sometimes at odds with each other. On the one hand, streets are conduits for transportation that help you get from point A to point B; on the other hand, streets are destinations that people go to. Because of this dual role, street design considers some diverse elements, including the following:

✔ **Traffic flow and layout:** The layout of a street considers what features are needed to manage traffic flow through the street and what features are needed by the other activities happening on the street. For example, Figure 8-1 shows a cross-section of a street where there are good sidewalks for people to walk on, traffic lanes for cars and trucks, and trees and a median strip to help separate pedestrians from the roadway traffic.

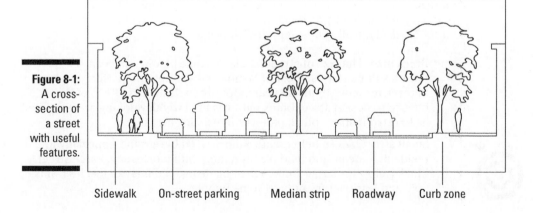

Figure 8-1:
A cross-section of a street with useful features.

Sidewalk   On-street parking   Median strip   Roadway   Curb zone

✔ **Appearance:** A variety of design features can be used to increase the visual appeal of streets. For example, a consistent and distinctive style for light poles or tree plantings can lend aesthetic appeal to a street and also help give the length of street an easily recognizable appearance.

✔ **Streetscape elements:** Additional street features such as decorative lighting, bike racks, seating benches, planter boxes, and even lowly rubbish bins are referred to by urban planners as *streetscape elements.* Good streetscaping helps encourage greater use of sidewalks by pedestrians and creates streets that are more attractive to shoppers and other visitors.

An increasing number of communities are working to improve the design of their streets. For example, New York City recently published a *Street Design Manual* that you can find at http://on.nyc.gov/29ftw. The nearby sidebar, "Complete streets," talks about nationwide efforts to improve street design.

Neighborhoods and districts

Urban design also is used to help shape attractive and well-functioning sub-areas within the city, such as neighborhoods or business districts. The following sections cover some of the key elements that designs for neighborhoods and districts address.

Complete streets

For the past several decades, most streets have been designed to meet the needs of automobiles rather than people. But over the last several years, a coalition of organizations advocating everything from bicycle safety to preventing heart disease to representing the needs of older Americans has been working with communities to plan for complete streets.

The National Complete Streets Coalition (www.completestreets.org) defines a *complete street* as one that serves everyone in the community and is designed to be used not just by cars and trucks, but also by pedestrians, bicycles, and public transportation. Unfortunately, many streets aren't accessible to everyone who needs to use them. For example,

someone who uses a wheelchair or motorized scooter to get around may not be able to use a street's sidewalks if its curb ramps are too steep or aren't in good repair. And many streets aren't safe places for everyone, such as children walking to school who have to cross busy roads that lack safe crosswalks.

Several states have started programs encouraging local communities to improve their streets, and some states are providing funding for these improvements. Completing streets is a way to improve their design and serves other important purposes as well, including providing more transportation options and keeping people safe.

Street pattern

The street pattern within a neighborhood determines the shape and size of street blocks and establishes the pattern of transportation routes that allow people and cars to move around the area.

A neighborhood's street pattern also contributes to the overall aesthetic feel of the community. For example, a rectangular street grid pattern may lend a feeling of openness and encourage people to walk short distances within the neighborhood, while a street pattern that uses dead ends and cul-de-sacs may help create a sense of privacy and security for the area but also tends to discourage walking due to longer distances.

Coverage and placement

The design of neighborhoods and districts also considers how much of the area should be developed and how much should be used as open space and natural preserves. The placement of development within the area also helps determine how different land uses will relate to each other (for example, will houses be near shopping or far away?), the overall building density of the neighborhood, and what natural areas will be left undisturbed.

Appearance

Like other urban design building blocks, a neighborhood may benefit from a relatively uniform architectural appearance or may appear attractive by blending complementary architectural styles. You can read more about how communities use design districts and design guidelines in the "Place-making approaches: Using urban design techniques" section, later in this chapter.

Cities and regions

Most urban planners and designers don't get the chance to design entirely new cities from scratch. But some approaches to urban design suggest ways that cities and metropolitan areas can benefit from a coordinated pattern of development. The *transect planning* approach popularized by the New Urbanist architect Andres Duany and urban planning professor Emily Talen illustrates how different urban design patterns can be used in different parts of a metropolitan area.

Figure 8-2 shows an urban design transect where the most intense urban development takes place at the center of the area. The amount of development gradually tapers off with increasing distance from the center. Each area along the transect has its own distinctive design characteristics, including different building types, different road types and street patterns, and varying amounts of open space and preservation of natural areas.

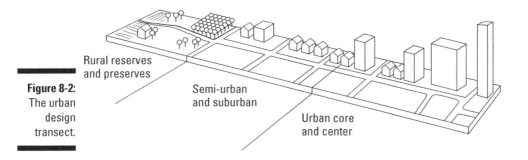

Figure 8-2:
The urban design transect.

Rural reserves and preserves

Semi-urban and suburban

Urban core and center

The transect planning approach uses an idealized version of how entire cities and regions could be designed, and most places don't actually look like this. But this approach is being used by communities to help understand how their places fit into the broader area and what design features will most benefit both their community and the region as a whole.

Urban Design: Blending Form and Function

The urban design component of an urban plan is where form meets function. In this section, I look at some urban design approaches that not only help create places that are enjoyable to look at, but also address broader planning goals, such as environmental conservation.

Making places attractive and user-friendly

Urban design techniques can be used to make places that are both visually appealing and user-friendly at the same time. In this section, I cover a few general approaches that are often used in the urban design component of a plan.

Using diverse and complementary architectural styles

Good design is often a balancing act. A place that uses a single architectural style — such as a residential street full of identical ranch-style houses — can seem boring and homogenous. And a place with a jumble of design styles can seem incoherent and unsightly.

Good urban design often can find an attractive middle ground, such as design variations within the same style or different styles that complement each other. For example, architectural design standards for the Mission District in the city of San Gabriel, California, require that new houses use one of three design styles that blend in with the district's existing architecture: Spanish Colonial, Mission Revival, or Spanish Colonial Revival.

Mixing land uses

Designs with mixed-land use patterns can help create areas that have diverse uses and are lively spaces. For example, a mixed-use district that includes buildings with residential apartments, offices, and shops is likely to have people coming and going at different times throughout the day. Perhaps it's just about safety in numbers, but people tend to be attracted to places that are well used by lots of other people.

Making places easy to get to

Good urban design makes sure that places are well connected to each other, especially by more than one type of transportation. For example, a neighborhood park may have parking for cars and be connected to the neighborhood by a separate path for walking and bicycling.

Creating a sense of place

Good urban design creates places that people feel good about. Some urban planners call it *place attachment* when people develop a meaningful and emotional connection to a specific place. Planning for urban design uses a variety of approaches to help bring out a place's unique character.

Making space for people to mix

People like places where they can interact with other people, even if it's just doing some people-watching. Places ranging from small parks to busy boulevards give people a chance to see old friends and meet new people.

Using historic features

Using historic features helps create places that are unique and different from other places. For example, building designs for a business district may repeat a common historic motif, such as a signature color or architectural style.

Accentuating natural features

Another way to bring out a place's distinctive charm is to accentuate its natural features.

For example, the city of San Antonio's River Walk district blends walking paths, residences, and businesses with a naturally winding waterway that gives it a distinctive identity that is attractive to both local residents and visiting tourists.

Encouraging sustainability

There's a strong connection between the physical form of the city and its impact on the environment. Good urban design can help lessen the impact that cities have on the environment and create places that are more sustainable. In this section, I cover some ways that urban design can encourage long-term sustainability.

Balancing development with natural features

Urban design techniques can be used to shape land use patterns in ways that allow for new development while also preserving existing natural resources. For example, a good design plan could help a housing development preserve more land as open space by creatively arranging houses relatively close to each other but still allowing adequate privacy for each house.

Encouraging access by proximity

Places where things are relatively close together and can be reached easily by walking and bicycling are referred to by urban planners as *access by proximity.* This means that you can get from one place to another easily because they're not very far apart to start with. For example, when important services — such as grocery stores and restaurants — are located close to residential areas, more people have the option of walking to them, which helps reduce pollution that may otherwise be generated by a car trip; plus, the walk helps people stay healthy.

Taking advantage of natural features

Good urban design uses the natural landscape to its advantage, such as locating buildings in areas that are naturally cooler and, therefore, require less energy to heat. Urban planners often refer to this approach as *ecological design,* which ecologists Sim Van der Ryn and Stuart Cowan define as "any form of design that minimizes environmentally destructive impacts by integrating itself with living processes."

Designing the Community

In this section, I fill you in on some planning tools that can be used to encourage public participation in planning for urban design and to help communities implement their plans for urban design. Getting people directly involved in the design of their community is a great way to ensure that an urban plan will create a place that people will use and enjoy, and makes it more likely that the implementation of the plan will be supported by the community.

Participatory design methods: Engaging the community

Planners can get people involved in urban design in a variety of ways. In my experience as a professional urban planner, I've found that people are especially enthusiastic about participating in urban design planning. I believe this is because the appearance of a community is very important to most people and also because a community's design features are a tangible part of people's everyday lives.

Community design charrettes

A *community design charrette* uses community input to help create an urban design plan, especially for small areas or specific projects such as a new park or redevelopment of a neighborhood business district. In a charrette, a design team of urban planners, designers, and architects works directly with community members, property owners, local officials, and other stakeholders in a series of workshops, usually held over a few days or weeks.

Here's the typical process for a design charrette:

1. **The design team gets input from the public.**

   For example, in a charrette to design a neighborhood park, some people may want something specific, like playground equipment, while other people may have more general suggestions, like giving the park a "welcoming feeling."

2. **Using the participants' ideas and suggestions, the professional design team goes to work making several alternative designs.**

3. **The design team presents its designs to the participants for their feedback.**

4. **The design team uses participant feedback to create a draft version of a final plan.**

   The final plan may be based on the most favored alternative design but also use specific elements from other alternatives that people liked.

5. **The team presents a final draft of the plan to the participants.**

   Additional minor adjustments to the plan can be made if necessary.

The result of a community design charrette is an urban design plan that not only is technically feasible, but also has the support of the community.

Visual preference surveys

In the 1960s, the U.S. Supreme Court heard an important case on free speech and obscenity. In his opinion, Justice Potter Stewart famously said that he couldn't provide an exact definition of what was or wasn't obscene, but that "I know it when I see it." Urban design is sort of the same way. Many people know what they like and don't like about the design of their surroundings, but they can't always express exactly what they like or dislike.

Visual preference surveys are a way to find out how people feel about the design of their community and what design approaches they would like to see used in plans for their community. In a visual preference survey, people in the community are shown a series of different images — such as architectural drawings or photographs — and asked to respond to each image. Popularized by urban designer Anton Tony Nelessen, these surveys are typically conducted by urban planners and urban designers at public meetings, in focus groups, and sometimes through websites.

Finding out about people's visual preferences for urban design helps make better plans in two ways:

- ✔ **It identifies what people like and don't like.** A visual preference survey can help determine how people feel about specific design elements. For example, in response to a photograph of a group of storefronts, some people may identify the stores' signs as being particularly attractive. Knowing what people like and dislike can help urban planners and designers come up with designs that accentuate positive features and minimize those that are seen as negative.

- ✔ **It helps planners choose among alternatives.** Visual preferences can be used to help choose among different design alternatives for the same site. For example, people may be shown architectural drawings or pictures of different designs for the same place and asked to choose their favorite or rank the images from best to worst.

Visual preference surveys have typically used architectural drawings and photographs. But new design technologies are making it easier to use other types of images, including 3-D computer models and video-game-style virtual tours, to help understand what people like and don't like about urban design.

Place-making approaches: Using design techniques

Communities can implement the urban design component of a plan in a variety of ways. In some cases, communities enact new laws, codes, and ordinances requiring that properties be developed using certain standards. Other communities may have voluntary guidelines for urban design. Many real-estate developers also incorporate urban design approaches into their building projects in order to make their properties more attractive to potential consumers.

Design guidelines

Many communities have adopted mandatory or voluntary *design guidelines* to guide the character of physical development. Design guidelines sometimes apply to the entire community. But because different parts of a community often have different design features, it's common for design guidelines to apply to specific neighborhoods or districts, commonly referred to as *design districts*.

Design guidelines usually address how buildings are to be placed on lots, the appearance and form of buildings (such as architectural styles or building materials that may be used), what types of landscaping are expected, and allowable styles for signage and other decorative features. Many communities use a process known as *design review* before approving the development of projects that are subject to mandatory urban design guidelines.

Pattern books

A *pattern book* is a document — usually produced by architects and/or urban designers — that visually defines urban design features for a community using drawings, sketches, photographs, blueprints, maps, and other graphic elements in addition to written descriptions of design features. An urban design pattern book that includes a variety of compatible design styles allows for development to be consistent with the community's overall goals for urban design, while also providing flexibility and a range of choices for builders and developers.

You can check out the following real-world examples of urban design pattern books:

- *A Pattern Book for Norfolk Neighborhoods:* `http://1.usa.gov/ vIltZ5`
- *Miramar Town Center Pattern Book:* `http://bit.ly/svm1JL`

Form-based codes

A *form-based code* is a type of local law or ordinance that serves a function similar to a traditional zoning code and requires that properties be developed in a manner consistent with certain design standards. The use of form-based codes to guide design and development is a relatively new approach that has become increasingly popular since the early 2000s.

Two important differences between form-based codes and traditional zoning are that form-based codes prescribe very exact urban design standards and place fewer restrictions on the specific use of land than traditional zoning does. For example, a traditional zoning code may designate that a property is to be used specifically for commercial purposes and leave open many details about exact architectural characteristics. In contrast, a form-based code would provide detailed regulations on the design of the building and allow for a wider range of uses. A form-based code allows buildings to more easily change their use over time; a building that starts out as a retail store may later be converted to residential town houses, for example.

In Chapter 21, you can find an example of an urban plan from Fayetteville, Arkansas, that uses a form-based code to implement its urban design recommendations.

Chapter 9

The Great Outdoors: Natural Resources, Open Space, and More

In This Chapter

▶ Understanding why conservation matters

▶ Planning for different types of parks and open spaces

▶ Creating an inventory of natural resources and monitoring environmental change

*O*ne of New York City's most popular residents goes by the nickname of "Pale Male." He lives on Fifth Avenue on Manhattan's Upper East Side, and, like many New Yorkers, he spends a lot of his time in Central Park. He also eats mice. Pale Male is a Red-Tailed Hawk who lives among the hustle and bustle of the city. For more than a decade, Pale Male and his family have nested above an arch outside the 12th floor of an apartment building. Even in the biggest of big cities, nature has found a way to coexist with the urban landscape.

In this chapter, I look at the components of an urban plan that deal with the preservation and conservation of the environment:

✔ **Natural resources:** The basic air, water, and land resources that serve the community, as well as local plant and animal species

✔ **Conservation areas:** Habitats, wetlands, forests, dunes, floodplains, and coastal areas that are environmentally sensitive, contribute to biological diversity, and help protect the quality of air, water, and land resources

✔ **Open space:** Different kinds of planned areas that contribute to both conservation and human enjoyment, including nature preserves, greenbelts, and other open spaces used as agricultural and *recreational areas* (areas that are used for recreation purposes and contribute to the conservation of open space and natural resources)

Cities and towns occupy a wide range of natural settings, and a growing number of communities are heeding the advice of renowned landscape architect Ian McHarg to "design with nature" in ways that improve human quality of life while also conserving natural resources.

Planning for conservation areas, open space, and recreational areas is closely coordinated with the land use planning component of an urban plan. These types of areas are directly related to land use and are immediately impacted by land use decisions, such as the conversion of undeveloped woodlands or productive farmland into suburban housing developments.

Saving the Future: Conserving and Protecting the Environment

In the United States, planning for the protection and conservation of the local environment involves a combination of local initiatives and federal or state regulations. The federal government plays a broad role in local environmental protection, although perhaps not as active a role as some environmental advocates would like. Many federal regulations apply to local environmental issues, including the Clean Air Act, the Clean Water Act, the Endangered Species Act, and the Comprehensive Environmental Response, Compensation, and Liability Act (commonly know as the "Superfund" program). These regulations typically apply to individuals, businesses, state and local governments, and the federal government itself.

In addition to federal regulations, several states have adopted environmental regulations that exceed federal standards. For example, the state of California is well known for requiring automobiles to meet pollution and emissions standards that are stricter than those of the federal government. Many states also are adopting formal and informal goals for the protection of the environment at the statewide level. For example, the state of Washington has adopted regulations mandating a statewide reduction in "overall emissions of greenhouse gases in the state to 1990 levels" by the year 2020.

Some states also require that local urban plans address specific environmental goals and issues. For example, the state of California requires that local urban plans address conservation and open-space issues, Wisconsin mandates that local plans address "Agricultural, Natural, and Cultural Resources," and the state of Washington recommends that a section on "Open Space, Habitat, and Recreation" be included in local plans.

Although a wide range of federal and state goals and regulations may apply at the local level, local plans play an important role in the protection and conservation of environmental resources.

Planning for the protection and conservation of local environmental resources provides a wide range of benefits to cities and towns:

✔ **It helps provide essential services and protect the community.** Protecting and conserving local resources can help local areas provide basic services, such as municipal water services, and help manage potential natural hazards, such as landslides and wildfires.

✔ **It contributes to the community's overall quality of life.** Many efforts to preserve and protect the local environment help people enjoy and appreciate the community, such as recreational areas that also serve as protected open space.

✔ **It can improve human health.** Reducing pollution and protecting natural resources can have significant impacts on human health, especially among younger and older populations that are at risk for environmentally sensitive diseases, such as asthma.

The benefits of local environmental planning don't stop at the city limits. Acting locally can help globally. Many places are planning for the local environment in ways that may reduce local contributions to global environmental problems.

For example, New York City has adopted aggressive goals to reduce climate changing greenhouse gas emissions to protect the local environment and because New York City is vulnerable to rising sea levels caused by climate change. But the benefits of New York City reducing its greenhouse gas emissions don't stop at the Hudson River — those benefits contribute to the overall reduction in greenhouse gas emissions of the planet, which helps everybody.

Planning for the protection and conservation of local environmental resources can be coordinated with many other components of an urban plan, from urban design to housing and transportation. For example, planning for public transportation, bicycling, and walking can help preserve and protect the environment by reducing automobile traffic that can lead to air, land, and water pollution. In addition, housing developments that use land conservation techniques can provide the community with additional open space and natural areas (see Chapter 6).

Identifying Elements of the Urban Environment

Cities and towns have many important and valuable environmental features. Elements such as air, water, and land provide the basic building blocks of the natural environment. Some specific environmental features — such as wetlands or woodlands — require protection and conservation because they are highly sensitive to pollution or provide homes for endangered animals. Other areas provide people with spaces for recreation and enjoyment, while still preserving their environmental integrity.

In this section, I talk about the ecological resources, conservation areas, and open spaces that are part of the urban environment.

Ecological resources

Cities, towns, and suburbs are home to all the Earth's basic ecological resources, including air, water, and land resources that provide habitats for people, plants, and animals. The natural resources component of an urban plan identifies both the quantities and qualities of the community's ecological resources. For example, a community may have what seems to be an ample water supply, but potential contamination of the water supply by toxic chemicals could sharply reduce the amount of usable water available to the community and have significant impacts on the health of both people and wildlife.

Air

Poor atmospheric conditions can have significant impacts on cities and towns, including worsening the health of people with respiratory diseases and spreading pollution into the water supply. A rising global awareness of the role of greenhouse gases in accelerating climate change is leading many communities to work toward lowering local greenhouse gas emissions.

Air quality

In the United States, the federal government plays an active role in promoting local air quality. Under the provisions of the Clean Air Act, the Environmental Protection Agency (EPA) sets standards for local and regional air quality. The EPA's National Ambient Air Quality Standards measure the presence of six key air pollutants: carbon monoxide, lead, nitrogen oxides, ozone, sulfur dioxide, and particulate matter.

The EPA has established local air quality standards for more than 240 Air Quality Control Regions, such as the Metropolitan Los Angeles Air Quality Control Region. Regions that fail to meet air quality standards are termed *non-attainment areas,* and governmental agencies representing these areas may be required to prepare supplemental plans to improve air quality and can be subject to reduced federal funding for local transportation programs.

Greenhouse gas emissions

An increasing number of communities are tracking local emissions of greenhouse gases (GHGs) that contribute to global climate change, including carbon dioxide, methane, nitrous oxide, sulphur hexafluoride, hydrofluorocarbons, and perfluorocarbons.

The reduction of worldwide GHG levels is addressed by the Kyoto Protocol, an international agreement that has been ratified by more than 190 countries, including Japan, Russia, and the countries of the European Union. As of 2011, the United States was one of the few countries that had *not* committed to the agreement.

Despite the U.S. holdout from the Kyoto Protocol, an increasing number of North American cities — such as Chicago, New York, and Vancouver — are making plans to address GHGs, including measuring local GHG emissions and identifying major sources of GHGs (such as factories, power plants, and automobiles). New York City's plan aims to reduce local GHG emissions by 30 percent between 2005 and 2030. Vancouver expects that by 2012, its local GHG emissions will reach their lowest levels in more than 20 years. You can check out these cities' plans online:

✔ *City of New York PlaNYC 2030: Climate Change:* http://on.nyc. gov/evfRGs

✔ *Chicago Climate Action Plan:* www.chicagoclimateaction.org

✔ *City of Vancouver Climate Protection:* http://bit.ly/6TgvRG

Portland's LUTRAQ solution

LUTRAQ. No, it's not the name of a prescription drug or a newly discovered planet. LUTRAQ is an acronym that stands for "Land Use, Transportation, Air Quality."

In the late 1980s, state and local authorities in Oregon proposed a bypass freeway that would cut across the western side of the Portland metropolitan area. 1000 Friends of Oregon (www.friends.org), a statewide nonprofit advocacy organization, argued that the new freeway would promote urban sprawl and have a negative impact on the region's environment. The organization presented an alternative proposal, called *The LUTRAQ Connection,* which argued that a combination of land use planning and improved public transportation would be an effective and more environmentally friendly alternative to a new highway.

The LUTRAQ alternative in Portland recommended using light rail and express bus mass transit services to connect the communities of Hillsboro, Beaverton, Tigard, and Tualatin, as well as concentrating new development in these areas in mixed-use centers and in areas easily accessible by public transportation, called transit-oriented developments (TODs).

Studies of the LUTRAQ alternative found that it would meet the standards of the federal Clean Air Act and produce significantly less air pollution and greenhouse gas emissions than a new freeway would. The proposal for a new freeway was eventually shelved, and Portland's regional planning agency adopted a coordinated land use and transportation plan that reflected the LUTRAQ approach. Many other communities have since adopted some elements of the LUTRAQ approach and are using new land use and transportation planning techniques to protect and improve local air quality.

Water

Water resources play a broad role in sustaining cities and towns. Not only is water an essential resource for human health, but many cities are situated along bodies of water that are used for economic and recreational purposes. Assessing the local water supply and the quality of local water resources is a key concern of urban plans, as well as related federal and state regulations.

In addition to identifying water sources and monitoring water quality conditions, urban plans also may examine a wide range of underlying factors related to water supply and quality. For example, changes in transportation and land use conditions — such as increased pollution from cars and factories — may lead to the contamination of local water supplies.

Assessing the water supply

A community's water supply for general uses, including clean drinking water, may consist of a wide range of areas and types of resources, including surface sources of water (such as lakes and rivers) and groundwater sources (such as underground aquifers). Some communities use local water resources for their water supply, while other communities may use water resources drawn from lakes, rivers, and reservoirs located many miles away. (See Chapter 10 for more on water supply issues.)

Maintaining water quality

Water quality is a key concern of local environmental planning. Monitoring water quality measures helps ensure the safety of the water supply and prevents the contamination of natural habitats. In the United States, a variety of federal regulations mandate that state and local authorities monitor local water quality:

- The Clean Water Act aims to reduce water pollution among the nation's bodies of water and requires states to establish water quality standards that must be regularly monitored by states and their local areas.

- The Safe Drinking Water Act establishes water quality standards for most local water supply systems and also requires monitoring of water supply sources.

- The Environmental Protection Agency sets standards for wastewater quality known as Total Maximum Daily Load, which limits the amount of pollutants in discharged wastewater.

Land

Cities and towns are home to many different types of land resources. Land resources may have different levels of suitability for urban development and may be regulated by particular federal, state, or local provisions.

In Chapter 5, I explain how local communities plan and manage local land use. One of the techniques that local areas use to identify land areas for development or conservation is *suitability analysis*. Suitability analysis examines land characteristics, including soil types, topography, geologic and hydrological conditions, the presence of plant and animal species, and other ecological features. Some information on local land conditions can be found in maps and information from federal and state data sources. Many communities maintain additional land records or may conduct their own surveys and field research to document local conditions.

Some local land areas may have attributes causing them to be regulated by state and federal provisions. For example, a variety of federal and state regulations define specific areas as wetlands or habitats for endangered species, and urban development on these lands requires special permitting by federal or state agencies. (I discuss these types of areas a bit more in the "Conservation areas" section, later in this chapter.)

Many urban plans also identify land areas that are contaminated by toxic or hazardous substances. These areas are known as *brownfields*. Common sites for brownfields include areas formerly used as dry cleaners, gas stations, industrial factories, and power plants. Contaminants common to brownfields include industrial solvents, pesticides, lead, asbestos, volatile and semi-volatile organic compounds (called VOCs and SVOCs), polychlorinated biphenyls (PCBs), fuels, and toxic metals (such as mercury). A variety of federal and state programs help local communities identify, clean up, and redevelop contaminated areas. (I talk more about brownfield redevelopment programs in Chapter 12.)

Conservation areas

Conservation areas are places that have valuable ecological features that help protect the community's natural resources and biodiversity. These areas can range from small plots of land to large preserves. There are many different types of conservation areas and some of these — such as wetlands and floodplains — are defined and marked for protection by various federal, state, and local provisions. In some cases, conservation areas also serve as areas for complementary uses, such as recreation and agricultural activities.

Habitats and biodiversity

Habitats are areas that are home to important plant and animal species or that provide essential resources to valuable plants and animals. By identifying and protecting conservation areas, communities can protect valuable habitats and promote the biodiversity of plant and animal species. Several states have developed statewide biodiversity plans and are encouraging communities to address biodiversity in their local plans.

Local areas often contain many different kinds of areas that may serve as important habitats. For example, Kalamazoo County in Michigan is home to more than 240,000 people, but only about 60 percent of the county is occupied by human-oriented land uses, including developed and agricultural areas. Table 9-1 shows a breakdown of habitat types in the county.

Table 9-1	Types of Land Cover Habitats in Kalamazoo County, Michigan	
Land Cover Habitat Classification	Square Miles	Percent of Total
Human land use	**325.14**	**57.3%**
Developed	87.60	15.4%
Agriculture	237.54	41.9%
Aquatic	**18.83**	**3.3%**
Open water	18.83	3.3%
Forest and woodland systems	**141.95**	**25.0%**
Deciduous dominated forest and woodland	141.49	24.9%
Mixed deciduous/coniferous forest and woodland	0.46	0.1%
Shrubland, steppe, and savanna systems	**0.63**	**0.1%**
Deciduous dominated savanna and glade	0.63	0.1%
Recently disturbed or modified	**16.75**	**3.0%**
Harvested forest	7.58	1.3%
Managed forest (plantations)	6.93	1.2%
Other disturbed or modified	2.24	0.4%
Riparian and wetland systems	**64.09**	**11.3%**
Freshwater herbaceous marsh, swamp, or baygall	20.72	3.7%
Floodplain and riparian	43.37	7.6%
TOTAL LAND AREA	567.39	100.0%

Source: U.S. Geological Service, Gap Analysis Program, National Land Cover Viewer

In addition to documenting the presence of different types of habitats, many communities are carrying out plant and wildlife inventories that document what types of species are present in local habitats. Identifying local habitats and species allows local urban plans to designate conservation areas and coordinate future development with the protection of valuable ecological resources.

Wetlands, floodplains, and beaches

Wetlands, floodplains, and beaches are areas with specific natural and hydrological characteristics that may be critical to the protection of ecological resources and may also be areas that are not well suited for urban development. Many cities have been founded near bodies of water — especially oceans, lakes, and rivers — and these communities often are home to wetlands, floodplains, and beaches.

Wetlands

Wetlands is a broad term for a wide range of areas, including certain types of marshes, swamps, and bogs. In general, wetlands are covered by water for at least some period of time during a typical year and are characterized by the presence of specific soil types and aquatic plants called *hydrophytes.* Some wetlands are regulated under the provisions of the Clean Water Act, and alterations to these areas may require permitting by the U.S. Army Corps of Engineers.

Floodplains

Floodplains are areas that are adjacent to rivers that may experience flooding. The U.S. Federal Emergency Management Agency (FEMA) works with state authorities to identify floodplain areas and rates the risk of flooding in terms of its likelihood to occur. For example, a 100-year floodplain is an area where there is a 1 percent chance of a flood each year. Development in floodplains is typically restricted by state and local regulations due to the risk to lives and property, and also because development in floodplains often has negative impacts on river flow and can worsen the impacts of a flood event.

Beaches

Beaches are made up of banks of sand and gravel at the edges of certain bodies of water, including oceans, lakes, and some rivers. Not only do beaches provide people with access to shorelines and recreational spaces, but they're also valuable environmental resources that are home to a wide range of unique habitats for plants and animals. Beaches also are among the most fragile of natural resources and can be damaged easily by everything from overuse by people to water pollution to changing weather patterns.

The U.S. Coastal Zone Management Act encourages states to limit coastal beachfront development, and many states have enacted statewide regulations to protect beaches. Some states also require that local urban plans specifically address beach resources. For example, the state of Oregon requires that local plans "provide for diverse and appropriate use of beach and dune areas consistent with their ecological, recreational, aesthetic, water resource, and economic values, and consistent with the natural limitations of beaches, dunes, and dune vegetation for development."

Forests

The outer edges of many urban areas are home to forested areas that serve a variety of purposes, including recreational areas, tree farms, timber-harvesting areas, and natural forests that provide habitats for plants and animals. Due to their wide range of uses, forested areas provide cities and towns with many recreational, economic, and environmental benefits.

Measures to protect and manage forested areas are increasingly being included in local plans due to the risk of wildfires. As cities and their suburbs have sprawled ever farther into the countryside, a substantial number of homes and businesses are located in areas that are prone to wildfires.

Urban planners, environmentalists, and fire safety specialists have begun referring to these areas as the *wildland urban interface* (WUI). In 2011, after a summer of record-setting hot and dry conditions, the Austin metropolitan area in Texas was besieged by a series of wildfires. Austin's wildfires spread into some heavily populated suburban areas, forcing major evacuations and destroying more than 1,500 homes.

Many communities are taking steps to identify WUI areas and make plans that will guide future development in ways that minimize risks to people and property. For example, the state of California publishes Fire Hazard Severity Zone maps that help local communities identify fire-prone areas. Missoula County in Montana has adopted a *Community Wildfire Protection Plan,* which shows areas that are most vulnerable to wildfires and recommends ways to minimize the risks of development near WUI areas.

Open space and parks and recreation

Planning for open space and recreational areas can provide communities with resources that help conserve and protect the local environment, while also providing places that people can use and enjoy.

Open space

Open space includes areas that are left undisturbed (sometimes called *passive open space*), as well as environmentally valuable *active open space* (which balances conservation with complementary activities, such as recreation). Local urban plans typically identify and plan for a variety of different types of open spaces:

- ✔ **Open space conservation areas:** These are passive open space areas whose primary purpose is the protection of environmentally sensitive areas, including wetlands, floodplains, woodlands, and habitats. In addition to dedicated preserves and parks, some housing and mixed-use development sites use conservation development techniques that preserve open space areas (see Chapter 6).

- ✔ **Urban open space:** Urban and suburban areas are increasingly looking for new ways to integrate green elements with their built environments. In the concrete jungle, even the smallest patch of green is a useful asset, and many small features can contribute to the community, including small parks, playgrounds, tree-lined streets, landscaped plazas and boulevards, walking and cycling trails, urban gardens, and even *green rooftops* (gardens and planted areas on top of buildings).

- ✔ **Agricultural areas and "working landscapes":** These areas feature complementary active open space uses, such as low-intensity farms and agricultural areas, hunting ranges, and commercial forestry areas that use sustainable management practices. These types of areas can help preserve open space while still serving valuable economic purposes.

Frederick Law Olmstead's "Emerald Necklace"

Frederick Law Olmstead (1822–1903) is best known as the co-designer of Central Park in New York City. In 1858, Olmstead and his partner, Calvert Vaux, won the design competition for Central Park and helped create a green jewel in the very center of Manhattan. For more than 150 years, Central Park has served as refuge from the city's concrete jungle and has been copied in cities around the world.

In later years, Olmstead turned his attention to designing parks that ringed the edges of a city, rather than being placed in a central location. Urban planners now refer to these types of parks as *greenbelts* or *greenways*. In Boston, Olmstead designed the city's "Emerald Necklace" system of parks and parkways that formed a crescent around the central city. The

1,100-acre system spans more than 7 miles and consists of eight parks (including the historic Boston Commons) linked by parkways and waterways.

Many communities now use parks as greenbelts and greenways to provide recreational areas, protect environmental resources, and help control land use development patterns. For example, Boulder, Colorado, is mostly surrounded by a 45,000-acre open space greenbelt that consists of both publicly and privately owned properties. The Canadian national capital of Ottawa is encircled by a protected greenbelt that encompasses nearly 80 square miles of nature preserves, recreational areas, and sustainable farming.

Open space areas provide communities with a wide range of benefits, including encouraging biodiversity, preserving the aesthetic appeal of undeveloped and rural areas, and helping to protect air, water, and land resources. Many communities are making plans that coordinate open space preservation with traditional land use planning in order to accommodate growth and new development in ways that also preserve their natural landscape.

Parks and recreation

Recreational areas can serve as both open space and areas where people can interact with each other and the environment. Here are some of the different types of recreational areas that also provide valuable environmental benefits:

- ✔ **Neighborhood and community parks:** These types of parks typically serve a specific neighborhood or community, such as a small suburban area, and can range in size from 1 to 30 acres (although neighborhood parks of 6 to 10 acres are a good size for most communities). Neighborhood parks often feature a combination of natural areas and park improvements, such as playgrounds, community centers, or athletic fields.

- ✔ **Regional parks and preserves:** These types of facilities are designed to serve large communities and may range in size from dozens to thousands of acres featuring a combination of natural areas and park amenities.

For example, the Cuyahoga Valley National Park encompasses more than 30,000 acres within the greater Cleveland area, including bicycle and skiing trails, historic sites, swimming, horse trails, and nature preserves that are home to nearly 200 kinds of birds.

✔ **Small parks:** Sometimes called *pocket parks,* these parks may take up just a few hundred square feet in cities, towns, and suburbs. Small parks often are located at street intersections or in between buildings on busy streets to provide a green respite from their urban surroundings.

✔ **Greenways and trail systems:** Also called *linear parks,* greenways and trail systems are recreational areas that are organized as trails for walking or bicycling, and as narrow stretches of open space that often form a green boundary around a community or neighborhood. Greenways and trail systems also are used to connect local park systems and give people more options for non-motorized transportation between different facilities. Some trails and greenways also are intended to serve as safe migration paths for animals.

There are a variety of ways to look into the recreational needs of the community to help plan for future improvements. These include surveys to determine what kinds of recreational areas are wanted by the community and reviews of usage statistics for recreational areas and facilities. A variety of professional organizations and government agencies also publish recommended standards and guidelines for local recreation areas and facilities.

For example, *Florida's Statewide Comprehensive Outdoor Recreation Plan* (http://bit.ly/ul5ts8) establishes priorities for the statewide park system and helps local communities identify the demand for specific types of recreational activities.

Monitoring and Managing the Environment

Making plans to take good care of the local environment can be a very complicated task, especially when the community doesn't have a good understanding of its local situation or local efforts aren't well coordinated with federal or state policies. Local plans and efforts to conserve and protect the environment can be improved by creating an inventory of natural resources, monitoring local environmental conditions, and coordinating local efforts with federal, state, and regional programs and regulations.

Keeping an inventory and monitoring conditions

An increasing number of communities are developing inventories of their natural resources and implementing programs to monitor the condition of the local environment. These efforts can help improve local planning by showing what types of natural resources may benefit from environmental conservation and improvement programs.

Taking an inventory of natural resources

The main purpose of a local natural resource inventory is to identify all of an area's important and unique environmental characteristics, including those that may be protected by state and federal regulations. A local inventory of natural resources would typically include unique or protected plant and animal species and habitats; environmentally sensitive areas; and other air, land, and water resources. The locations of these resources can be shown on a map, along with other documentation about their features, such as specific types of habitats or the total amount of the resource.

A local natural resources inventory can be drawn from a variety of information sources, including state and federal maps and data sources, local land use records, and local research studies. A good inventory of local natural resources can be used to guide future decisions about urban development, make plans for the conservation of natural resources, and help raise awareness of the community's environmental assets.

Monitoring environmental conditions

Monitoring local environmental conditions includes looking at the following:

- ✔ **Local environmental conditions:** Existing state and federal programs measure and monitor a wide range of environmental and weather-related conditions, including local air and water quality. Many local areas also have begun monitoring a range of locally specific conditions, such as emissions of greenhouse gases reported by local factories and tracking of animal species carried out by volunteers.

- ✔ **Local health impacts:** Communities are becoming increasingly aware of the relationship between environmental conditions and human health. Keeping track of particular health conditions related to environmental conditions — such as a rise in the number of people suffering from asthma — can help communities identify priorities for local environmental improvement and make plans to assist populations whose health may be at risk due to environmental conditions.

Monitoring these conditions can help communities plan for improved conditions in the future and find ways to minimize or mitigate negative impacts on human health.

Coordinating the management of natural resources

Many aspects of environmental quality and a wide range of local natural resources are regulated by federal, state, and local provisions. These provisions often apply not just to publicly owned areas, but also to privately owned areas and related activities, such as pollution controls for manufacturing facilities. Because local areas are covered by a patchwork of federal, state, and local laws and regulations, it's a good idea for local plans to document what local resources are regulated by different policies and government agencies.

In some cases, the protection or development of local land may be regulated by state or federal policies. For example, the development of lands in federally designated wetlands or floodplains may be prohibited or require extensive review by the U.S. Army Corps of Engineers. Other types of areas or resources also may be protected or regulated by state or federal provisions in addition to local regulations, such as a "critical habitat" designated by the U.S. Fish & Wildlife Service under the Endangered Species Act.

Changes in federal and state policies also can impact local environmental conditions. For example, proposed changes to federal regulations for automobile fuel economy standards — known as Corporate Average Fuel Economy regulations — are intended to increase fuel efficiency and may help to reduce pollution and improve local air quality. Keeping track of changing state and federal policies can help communities plan for coordinated local efforts to conserve and protect natural resources and human health.

Chapter 10

Infrastructure and Public Services: Something for Everyone

In This Chapter

▷ Coordinating infrastructure and public services with land use, housing, and natural resources

▷ Planning for energy, water, schools, telecommunications, and public safety

▷ Assessing community needs, improvement costs, and environmental impacts

*I*nfrastructure and public services are essential to any city or town, but their importance is overlooked by most people. Most of us just expect that our homes will have clean water coming out of the faucets or reliable electricity to power our gadgets. Keeping a city's lifelines in good working order may not be the most glamorous aspect of urban planning, but it's one of the more important because it's the foundation on which most other activities are built.

In this chapter, I dig into the different systems and services supporting cities and towns. I cover ways that infrastructure and public services support the community. I delve into planning approaches for different types of infrastructure and services. And I explain how urban plans not only assess community needs for infrastructure and public services, but also find locations for needed operations and improvements.

A good comprehensive plan helps identify the community's needs and options for infrastructure and services that will be provided by public utilities, other government agencies, and private businesses and utility companies. Plans for infrastructure and services help shape the overall development of the community because most residential, commercial, and industrial activities require locations with different types of infrastructure and services.

Transportation and recreation are often closely coordinated with the infrastructure and services component of the plan. I take an in-depth look at how transportation and recreation fit into urban plans in Chapters 7 and 9.

Keeping the City Running

The comprehensive plan component dealing with infrastructure and public facilities is concerned with a wide range of elements that make up the essentials of any city, such as water, power, waste disposal, schools, communication services, and police stations. Some elements of a community's infrastructure and public facilities may be provided by local government agencies — such as municipal water and sewer services — while other items are provided by other governmental agencies, private businesses, or non-profit organizations.

Providing infrastructure and services: Why they're important

Providing infrastructure and public services is often a dirty, daunting, and complex task involving significant expenses and financial risks. But adequate infrastructure and public services are a necessity of any community. Here's why:

✔ **They're essential to the health of the community.** Services like clean water, reliable power, and safe streets contribute to what planners call the "health, safety, and welfare" of the community and its residents. Essential services and infrastructure also support the economic stability of the community because they're depended on by factories and other businesses.

✔ **They need to be coordinated with other plan components.** There's a close relationship among infrastructure, public service, and the other components of a plan — especially land use, because most land uses rely on some type of infrastructure or service. For example, plans for new residential areas may need to be closely coordinated with plans for water system expansion and the installation of sewer lines.

✔ **They're expensive and long-lasting.** Improving and maintaining infrastructure and public services can be very costly. Making plans that get it right the first time can save money. And good planning is also essential because most infrastructure and public service improvements are long-lasting — with lifetimes of 30, 50, or 100 years or more — and can't be easily changed after they're put in place.

✔ **They have a significant environmental impact.** Communities are increasingly aware of the environmental impact of these infrastructure and public services, such as the pollution generated by power plants and the ecological issues associated with water usage. Good planning helps minimize the impacts of essential services by introducing new technologies and promoting resource-efficient practices that help avoid negative impacts.

Coordinating infrastructure and services with changing cities

One of the key challenges of planning for infrastructure and public facilities is keeping up with how the community is changing. Urban plans typically consider a combination of demographic, economic, and geographic trends that are related to infrastructure and public services.

Demographic trends

A change in the size or makeup of the population can influence the demand for infrastructure and services. For example, a community experiencing rapid population growth is probably also facing increasing demand for basic utilities, such as electricity and drinking water, as well as new schools.

Changes in the makeup of the population also have an impact on what types of services are needed. For instance, a community with an aging population may need to plan for expansions in hospitals and other healthcare services.

Economic trends

The needs of local businesses also drive the demand for services, and different types of businesses have different needs. An area with a growing number of office buildings may need to expand its access to electricity and sewer services. But an area experiencing industrial growth may need to provide a different set of services, such as access to natural gas lines for industrial use.

Geographic trends

The areas where services are needed can change over time, especially when expanding services to newly growing areas within the community is necessary. Most communities have specific standards for services that must be located in developing areas, such as for new office parks or housing developments. These standards ensure that new development has adequate access to needed services. Adding some services too late in the game can be expensive and disruptive (such as digging up a street to expand a too-small sewer pipe).

Some states and communities require that certain types of infrastructure and public facilities be put in place before the construction of new development. Many communities use what are known as *development impact fees* to help pay for the costs of expanding their infrastructure and services to keep up with new development. A development impact fee is a special charge by a local or county government on new development — such as a new office building or new apartment complex — that is used to pay for the cost of additional services that are indirectly demanded by new development, such as expansions to sewers or public parks.

The Backbone of the City: Utilities and Services

The provision of energy, water, and other specialized utilities and services are essential needs of every community. Every community should consider the role of utilities and related services, but the extent of planning varies widely from place to place, because different communities have different needs. In some cases, planning for utilities and related services is a mandatory component of local plans, as in the state of Washington, where communities are required to prepare plans that include a utilities component addressing electrical, natural gas, and telecommunications services.

Energy

Cities use energy — lots of it. Energy is a basic element of the modern lifestyle, and people use it for everything from running factories to heating homes to charging cellphones. But providing energy is an expensive proposition and one that has significant environmental consequences. Local planning for energy considers not only the needs of the community but also ways to reduce costs and environmental impacts.

Providing a community with energy resources and services is a complex undertaking that involves many different working pieces. Here are the main elements of the local energy system that need to be coordinated with other plan components and are typically addressed in plans:

- **Electrical generation facilities:** These facilities transform raw sources of energy into electricity; they include plants that are powered by coal, oil, or natural gas, as well as hydroelectric and nuclear power plants. These plants often are difficult to place in urban areas either because of concerns about pollution and environmental impacts or because of their need to be located near specific resources (such as dams or water currents for hydroelectricity). In many cases, cities are served by power plants that are located dozens or hundreds of miles away.

For example, metropolitan Detroit uses electricity generated at the Fermi nuclear power plant, which is located roughly 30 miles away.

✔ **Substations and storage:** Locations are needed for the storage of energy resources, such as oil and coal stocks, as well as facilities for electrical substations that connect important points in the local electrical grid system. These facilities often are located in industrial areas, but they may need to be located close to residential and commercial areas in order to provide adequate access to the energy system.

✔ **Supply lines:** The most widespread element of the local energy system is the wires and conduits making up the distribution system that carries power to all the buildings in a city or town. In some areas, electrical wires are strung aboveground, but electrical wires are buried underground in many newly developed or retrofitted communities.

✔ **Large on-site facilities:** A variety of major institutions, such as factories and large hospitals, operate their own power generation facilities.

✔ **Small on-site facilities:** The growing popularity of alternative energy sources — such as wind, solar, and geothermal — is helping to turn an increasing number of homes and buildings into mini-power plants. In some cases, small sources of energy located in homes and buildings generate enough power to "sell" electricity back to the grid, instead of "buying" from it. Many communities are changing their local land use regulations in order to accommodate alternative energy use in residential and commercial areas.

Urban plans have traditionally been concerned with making sure that communities have adequate access to energy supplies. However, today many communities are looking at ways to reduce energy use and minimize the environmental impacts of energy infrastructure, including using alternative and renewable sources of energy, and promoting the use of green buildings, which are energy efficient and environmentally friendly.

Water and sewer

The provision of water is essential to working cities. The most obvious use of water is for drinking and household uses, but water is also used for a wide range of other activities. The United States uses more than 400 billion gallons of water every day, although the public use water supply makes up only about 10 percent of this total. Nearly half of all water is used for the production of thermoelectric power, while agricultural irrigation uses another third.

Planning for local water and sewer services involves managing the natural aspects of the community's water system, providing water supplies to different users within the community, and providing sewer and wastewater treatment.

National trends in energy usage

Communities use a wide range of energy resources, and the specific kinds of energy resources that are used vary from place to place. According to the U.S. Department of Energy, 2009 estimates show that energy demanded for residential, commercial, and industrial uses — typically supplied through local utilities — makes up about 60 percent of overall demand; the remaining 40 percent of the total is used for transportation and draws mostly from petroleum supplies.

The main sources of energy in the United States are nonrenewable fossil fuels. Oil and petroleum provide about 37 percent of all energy, although the vast majority of this is supplied for transportation. Energy sources typically used by utilities include natural gas (which makes up 25 percent of all energy sources); coal (21 percent); nuclear power (9 percent); and other sources including wind, solar, and geothermal energy (8 percent).

So-called "raw" sources of energy must be converted into electricity for use by homes and businesses. About half of all electricity in the United States is generated using coal, while an additional 21 percent is generated by nuclear power plants, 17 percent is generated using natural gas, and 6 percent of all electricity is produced using hydroelectric resources. But there's a lot of regional variation in electricity production based on locally available resources. For example, West Virginia uses coal to produce 98 percent of its electricity, while Idaho produces more than 80 percent of its electricity using hydroelectric plants, and two-thirds of Vermont's electricity is produced by nuclear power plants.

Water supply and distribution

The focus of local water system planning is typically the production and distribution of sanitary potable water for bathing, drinking, cooking, and other general uses by households, business, and other users. But water systems also may provide nonpotable water for commercial, industrial, and agricultural uses.

Here's an overview of the main elements of local water supply systems:

✔ **Water source:** A typical water supply system includes access to one or more supply sources, including surface and groundwater sources. Roughly half of the public use water supply originates from surface sources, such as rivers and lakes. The other half comes from groundwater sources that are underground pockets of water that are accessed by wells and other means of extraction. Some places are able to access local water resources, while others must tap into resources in more distant locations.

For example, a significant portion of New York City's potable water supply comes from protected watershed areas located up to 100 miles away and is pumped into the city through an extensive system of pipelines.

✓ **Treatment and storage facilities:** These facilities purify the public use water supply prior to use and store potable water until it's needed. Water towers are common to most communities and are a good reminder of our need for water. Many water storage facilities are located relatively close to developed areas, often in elevated areas where the downward pull of gravity helps to maintain water pressure within the usage area.

✓ **Pipes:** Pipes connect the local water system from sources to storage to users. Pipes extending from treatment facilities or storage areas eventually reach all the homes, buildings, and other users in a community. Pipes are a crucial part of the infrastructure system and often are best appreciated when they don't work as planned — broken water mains and other damaged pipes not only stop the flow of water but also lead to other problems, such as traffic disruption or land erosion due to flooding as well as contamination of the water supply.

In most cities, much of the community is connected to the water system. However, *on-site water supplies* are common in suburban and semirural areas. In these areas, individual homes and small buildings sometimes are serviced by small wells that draw groundwater directly into homes and buildings. Additionally, some large facilities — like industrial factories and energy utilities — may collect their own water directly from surface and groundwater sources.

Trading for toilets in Santa Fe

Running a city in the middle of a desert isn't easy. In Santa Fe, New Mexico, the water supply is extremely limited, and the city has struggled to keep up with demand for many years. With few ways to increase the amount of water available to the city, it has relied on increasingly aggressive conservation programs to keep the city *water use neutral* (which means using the same amount of water, just more efficiently).

In 2002, the city introduced an innovative water-saving measure known as the Toilet Retrofit Program. Due to the limited water supply, builders of new homes and other buildings were required to find older toilets in existing homes and buildings and replace them with water-saving, low-flow toilets in order to offset the amount of water to be used in newly built structures. Between 2002 and 2009, more than 4,000 vintage toilets were replaced with water-saving versions.

In fact, the local water authority discontinued the program in 2010 because nearly 100 percent of the city's vintage toilets had been replaced. The toilet retrofit program was replaced by a broader approach using a Water Bank system that gives builders a variety of new ways to earn water conservation credits. But if you know anyone with an old toilet in Santa Fe, tell him it might just be a "collector's item."

The availability of water is a key constraint on development. Water system plans help determine which areas of the community will be developed and serviced by the water system, as well as the need for other improvements to centralized sourcing, treatment, and storage facilities. Places with limited water supplies or water system capacity may face significant limits on how much future development can be supported. For an example, check out the nearby sidebar on Santa Fe's efforts to conserve water and support local development.

Wastewater and sewer services

Used water is typically treated before being discharged back into the environment. Local wastewater and sewer systems collect water that has been used by households, businesses, and other users. However, used water containing certain contaminants may require special treatment:

- **Domestic wastewater** is water that has been used by households and businesses; it doesn't contain any special contaminants. After use, domestic wastewater moves into the sewer system through pipes and pumping stations to treatment plans where it can be treated to meet federal, state, and local water quality standards. Treated water is typically released into local water bodies. Some communities are looking for ways to recirculate large amounts of domestic wastewater (sometimes called *graywater*) for agricultural and industrial uses.

- **Industrial wastewater** is water discharged by factories and other establishments that contains hazardous or toxic contaminants. Industrial wastewater is usually subject to special regulations and may have to be pretreated on-site to remove contaminants before entering the domestic wastewater system or specially processed in separate facilities.

Wastewater systems typically consist of sewer pipes that carry wastewater away to treatment facilities. Treatment facilities themselves allow for the accumulation of waste and sludge, which are problems because people don't want these wastes in their own backyards or neighborhoods. Wastewater and sewer services are closely coordinated with land use plans in order to determine what areas will be sewered and the overall capacity of the sewer system. Like facilities for water supply, a lack of adequate wastewater facilities can limit the locations or amount of development that can occur in a community.

Some wastewater is managed on-site, including homes that use septic tank systems. On-site treatment and storage of wastewater is limited by how the waste is treated and where it's stored, because only a finite amount of waste can be stored in one place over a certain time period. When septic tank systems and other forms of on-site treatment reach their capacity, excess wastewater can begin to contaminate surrounding lands and groundwater.

Storm water and drainage facilities

Cities also need infrastructure to handle rainfall and the flow of natural bodies of water, such as rivers and lakes. Infrastructure for these purposes may be integrated with the sewer system (called a *combined sewer system*) or may use a separate system where runoff water is not treated. For example, many sewer grates that line the sides of streets are marked with the words sewer drains directly to river or lake, to make people aware that water runoff is not treated before discharge and to discourage people from using these sewers to dispose of contaminated water or hazardous substances.

Storm water and drainage facilities are important elements in the overall water system because they help prevent soil erosion and flooding and can be used to help recharge groundwater sources. Some communities in flood-prone areas have specialized infrastructure to handle potential disasters, including storm basins, levees, dams, and other controls. These facilities often are funded through a combination of local, state, and federal programs. (I talk more about how communities make plans to avoid environmental problems and recover from disasters in Chapter 14.)

Other utilities and related services

In addition to needing infrastructure that helps communities manage their energy and water resources, communities also require a variety of other facilities and related services. Depending on the needs of the community, the nature of these facilities and related services varies significantly from place to place.

Telecommunications

In the digital age, telecommunications are an important element of the local infrastructure system that serves households and local businesses. These facilities and services typically are subject to a variety of federal, state, and local regulations. Local plans help identify locations for major facilities and routes for cable and telephone transmission lines. Even wireless communications facilities have land use considerations — the locations of cellphone towers can have a significant impact on the community and are seen as eyesores by some residents.

Solid waste disposal and recycling

Facilities for solid waste disposal and recycling deal with the processing and storing of garbage and recyclables, including landfills, transfer stations, short-term storage facilities, incinerators, and processing plants. People don't really want to have very much to do with these facilities or have them located near their homes. These facilities also can have significant environmental impacts and tend to be located away from environmentally sensitive areas.

Many communities are working to reduce burdens on their solid waste disposals systems through recycling programs and other innovative methods such as *cogeneration power plants,* which turn burned trash into electricity.

Special-purpose districts

Special-purpose districts are governmental agencies that collect special fees to maintain specialized infrastructure or provide specific services. For example, some communities in California use street-lighting districts to provide public street lighting and traffic signals. In Illinois, some communities are served by flood prevention districts that operate levees and other flood control infrastructure along the Mississippi River.

Community Facilities and Services

Community facilities provide the public with a broad range of essential services, such as public safety and schooling. These services are offered by a variety of public agencies, private businesses, and nonprofit organizations. For example, many schools are operated by public school districts, but most communities have additional private schools operated by churches and other nonprofit organizations. The primary concern of planning for community facilities is determining the types and amounts of community facilities needed by the community, as well as adequate locations for community facilities.

Public safety

Community facilities for public safety include locations for police, fire, and other emergency response services. These facilities need to be coordinated with the community's land use patterns and offer services that are appropriate for different parts of the city. For example, a fire station in a residential neighborhood may house different staff and equipment than a fire station serving an industrial area.

Police departments and other local law enforcement facilities typically include a variety of different buildings, including administrative headquarters, jails, and precinct or neighborhood stations and substations. Precinct and neighborhood stations typically provide patrol services and respond to emergency calls from small areas. Fire and rescue stations provide the community with first response services to fires and emergencies. These services benefit from locations that allow for quick response times to emergency calls.

Standards for the provision of public safety facilities vary from place to place, but the need for pubic safety facilities and personnel is generally driven by the size of the population, the types of services needed by the community, and what locations need to be served. For example, some service standards suggest a certain ratio between police officers and the size of the population, such as 2.5 police officers for every 1,000 people. For services where distance is the most important factor in determining response time, such as emergency response by fire services, a service goal standard may be for every residential structure to be within five minutes of a fire station.

Like other infrastructure and services, public safety services may need to be expanded or cut back, depending on changes in the community. Public safety services also need to be coordinated with other components of an urban plan and can be a major consideration in the development patterns of some communities. For example, it may be necessary to limit development in areas that can't be reached easily by public safety services, and even minor differences in street layouts and traffic patterns can cause delays in emergency response times.

Schools

The emphasis of planning for school facilities is to provide adequate locations for schools given the size and composition of the population. This typically considers the types of public and private school sites and buildings that will be needed to serve the population, including elementary schools, middle schools, and high schools, as well as administrative buildings and specialized school facilities.

Planning for school facilities is driven by demographics and the locations of populations that need to be served. Many public school districts are required to conduct long-range enrollment projections looking ahead 10 or 20 years in order to help them budget for their services. Many school districts also aim to locate school facilities within a limited distance from the population.

Planning for school facilities can be coordinated with other plan components in a variety of ways, including the following:

- ✔ Coordinating land use planning with school facilities expansions in growing areas.
- ✔ Making transportation plans that provide students with safe routes to schools that encourage walking when possible and reduce traffic accidents. For more information, check out the National Center for Safe Routes to School at www.saferoutesinfo.org.

Other services and facilities

Other types of community facilities and public services required by communities range significantly from place to place and can include everything from animal shelters to post offices. Here are some of the other services and facilities that often are addressed in local plans and incorporated into the community's future land use map:

- **Hospitals:** A plan may consider the different types of hospitals and healthcare facilities needed given the size, composition, and geographic distribution of the community's population. For example, a community may plan to have a certain number of general care hospital beds in proportion to its population or may make plans to have every residential area within a certain distance of a trauma center.

- **Libraries:** Many communities operate public library systems and incorporate planning for the locations of their facilities into the comprehensive plan. Especially important are the locations of new facilities to serve growing areas of the community or other ways of serving less accessible areas of the community (such as traveling bookmobiles).

- **Social services:** Some urban plans include land use and service requirements for various social services benefiting the population, including childcare facilities, community centers, and centers serving the elderly.

Making tough choices: Closing schools in Detroit

The population of the city of Detroit decreased by nearly one-third between 1990 and 2010, falling to just over 700,000 people. And the number of students attending its public schools has declined even more dramatically, with public school enrollments falling by more than half between 2002 and 2010, from about 165,000 to just over 80,000.

Along with difficult questions about educational quality and mismanaged finances, Detroit's public schools are dealing with the painful reality that having fewer school buildings may be the best way to serve a smaller population. In 2010, the school district unveiled a plan to close more than 50 school buildings in an effort to "eliminate empty spaces and reduce costs."

In addition to closing schools, the district plans to "build and modernize" a limited number of school buildings in areas of the city with stable populations.

The school district's proposal to close so many schools has been extremely controversial, not just because of the importance of education to the city's children, but also because schools often play important roles in the neighborhoods where they're located. In this shrinking city, the loss of a neighborhood school is one more unwelcome reminder of the city's decades-long decline — but it may be an essential part of planning for a "smart decline" that provides a realistic approach to offering fewer services for fewer residents.

For an example of a comprehensive plan with a community facilities component that deals with things ranging from post offices to cemeteries, check out the city of Dublin, Ohio's plan in Chapter 21.

Are You Being Served? Evaluating Infrastructure and Services

Like all aspects of planning for the future, it's impossible to know exactly what may happen as time progresses. But making plans that are too far off the mark can have serious consequences for communities. Due to their high costs and long lifetimes, infrastructure and service improvements that turn out to be unnecessary may be a financial burden on the community, while underestimating the need for improvements may have a negative impact on the community's quality of life and limit future development.

The infrastructure and public services component of an urban plan assesses the community's current situation and helps determine future courses of action. In this section, I cover some of the main considerations that go into planning for infrastructure and services.

Are community needs being met?

A plan should assess the need of the community for infrastructure and services to determine the following:

- **How much will the community need?** One basic consideration is the total amount of services needed by the community, such as an estimate of how many gallons of clean drinking water will be used per day or how many schools will be needed, given the number of children in the community.

- **What kinds of services will the community need?** In addition to total amounts of services, each element may need to consist of a certain mix of services, depending on how they're used by the community. For example, a public school system typically has different kinds of buildings for different types of students, including elementary, middle, and high schools.

A needs assessment of the community is used to help determine what improvements will need to be made in the future. A well-researched estimate of future needs based on existing conditions and reasonable projections can help communities make realistic plans for the future, instead of leaving the community underserved or saddled with the costs of unnecessary infrastructure and services.

There are a variety of ways to measure and examine what a community needs:

- **Reviewing usage information:** Information on the usage of existing facilities can provide a baseline measure of community services.

- **Looking at demographic and economic trends:** The demand for services is driven by population and economic changes, both positive and negative. Estimates of population and business trends can help determine future needs.

- **Surveying the community:** Surveys of the community can help measure how satisfied people are with existing services and what kinds of services people would like to have in the future.

Are there adequate locations for future improvements?

One of the key considerations of the infrastructure and services component of an urban plan is to determine locations for needed facilities and services. These include determining the service areas and finding appropriate site locations:

- **Service areas** are the geographic areas of the community that are served by a particular service or facility. For example, a water storage tank may provide water to households within a half-mile radius, while a public high school may serve the needs of an entire school district. Each of these service areas must be defined in the plan.

- **Site locations** are the places where infrastructure and public facilities are located. Some elements have specific site location requirements. For example, sewage treatment plants often are located in industrial areas because of their potential to produce odors and generate pollution.

One way to coordinate the locations for future improvements with the overall comprehensive plan is through a *community facilities map,* which identifies the locations of current infrastructure and service sites, as well as desirable locations for future improvements that can be coordinated with the community's plans for land use, housing, transportation, and natural resources.

Some cities and regions have established *urban service boundaries* (also known as *urban service areas*), which are geographic areas of a community within which a full range of infrastructure and services will be offered. But the availability of infrastructure and services may be limited outside the urban service boundary; this is intended to discourage future development beyond the service boundary area. This approach can help lower the costs of infrastructure and services by encouraging future development in areas to which existing infrastructure and services can be more easily expanded.

How much? The costs of capital improvements

Clean water isn't cheap. Operating, maintaining, and improving local infrastructure can be very costly and requires major long-term investments in a wide range of facilities. These facilities, such as power plants or water treatment facilities, often are referred to as *capital improvements* and may be in service for decades.

Local urban plans often are coordinated with local capital improvement programs, especially for services that are offered by local governments (such as water and sewer services). Local urban plans often include rough estimates of the costs of providing infrastructure and services, as well as identifying potential sources of funding for maintaining and expanding needed infrastructure and services.

A variety of methods are used to estimate the costs of infrastructure improvements, including estimates based on per capita industry averages for providing services, estimates based on costs of services in similar communities, and estimates based on the past costs of providing local services. For the purposes of a comprehensive plan, a rough estimate of the costs of capital improvements can be used to coordinate infrastructure projects with local government budgets and with funds that may be available from state government, federal agencies, and private utilities.

What are the environmental impacts?

Infrastructure can have a significant impact on the environment. For example, coal-fired electrical power plants can emit large quantities of pollution into the air and water. Urban plans are increasingly examining the potential environmental impacts of infrastructure improvements and operations in order to find ways to minimize impacts on the environment.

Some types of infrastructure have both direct and indirect impacts on the environment. For example, a wastewater treatment facility could have a direct impact on the environment by changing the water quality of the body of water, such as a river or lake, into which it discharges treated water. And a change in water quality could pose additional indirect impacts on the environment, such as having a negative impact on the plants or animals that make up the aquatic food chain, leading to a loss of species diversity.

Infrastructure also can have local and global impacts on the environment. For example, a coal-fired electrical power plant may emit pollutants into the air that have a small impact on local air quality but would probably contribute to worldwide greenhouse gas emissions. Balancing local impacts with global impacts on the environment is a key challenge for local urban plans and is an example of one way that plans can "think globally and act locally." Many communities are looking for ways to incorporate new technologies and efficient resource use into their plans in order to minimize their local and global environmental impacts.

Part III

Hot Topics and Urban Planning Challenges

The 5th Wave   By Rich Tennant

"His only suggestion is to add more hotels."

In this part . . .

Today's cities are home to more people than ever before in human history. And the challenges faced by people and their cities also are greater than ever before. This part talks about urban planning techniques and approaches that are being used to help cities and their residents rise to meet these challenges.

Chapter 11 explores how cities are using sustainable development approaches to make cities cleaner and greener. Chapter 12 digs into cities that are on the rebound and looks at urban revitalization efforts. Chapter 13 dives into the topic of urban sprawl and looks at how urban planning is being used to create a balance between cities and their suburbs. Chapter 14 looks at how cities are planning to be less vulnerable to disasters, from floods to terrorist attacks, and what cities can do to heal and rebuild after a disaster. Chapter 15 shows how cities are growing their local economies in ways that support residents and local businesses. The part finishes up with Chapter 16, which takes you on a trip around the world to look at global urban planning and how cities across the globe are coping with the world's ever-growing population.

Chapter 11

Greening the City: Making Sustainable Places

In This Chapter

▶ Thinking globally and planning locally

▶ Designing greener cities

▶ Planning using green tools

*T*he number of people living in cities across the planet is growing rapidly. Sustainable urban development will be one of the key challenges facing both local communities and the world at large in coming decades. Well-planned cities and good local decisions are essential ingredients in the world's efforts to improve the state of the global environment, as well as a means of improving the livability of cities and towns at the local level.

Sustainability is a popular term, but its exact meaning can vary from person to person and it can be a difficult concept to apply — especially in a broad field such as urban planning. One of the most influential definitions of *sustainability* comes from the World Commission on Environment and Development convened by the United Nations:

> Sustainable development is development that meets the needs of the present without compromising the ability of future generations to meet their own needs.

In this chapter, I look at how cities and towns are using sustainable planning and development approaches to create a greener planet and communities that will provide a higher quality of life for generations to come. Some cities and towns have developed specialized plans addressing sustainability — such as action plans for anti-climate-change initiatives. However, sustainable planning concepts can be applied throughout a comprehensive urban plan, especially in the areas of land use, transportation, environment, housing, and economic development.

Examining the Pillars of Sustainability

Making cities more sustainable involves balancing long-term efforts to conserve and protect the environment with economic and social concerns. The pillars of sustainability, or the three Es, are

- **Environment:** Planning for urban sustainability considers both the quality of local ecological resources and human health, as well as the regional and global impacts of local activities.

- **Economy:** Sustainable approaches to urban development recognize that the world's growing population requires the economical use of resources to meet growing demands.

- **Equity:** Often referred to as *social equity,* this element of sustainability considers fairness in the distribution of resources and aims to reduce social inequality for improving conditions for all.

The three Es are fundamentally interrelated: Changes in one element typically resonate with the others. For example, overuse of the world's economic resources due to growing rates of consumption could lead to unchecked destruction of the world's ecological resources. Many communities are developing plans and development programs that aim to meet the *triple bottom line* of sustainability that coordinates environmental quality with social and economic considerations.

The challenge ahead for cities and towns is to nurture great places that offer an outstanding quality of life and preserve possibilities for future generations. To meet these aims, cities will have to find new ways to think globally and plan locally.

Planning for Sustainable Communities

Sustainability has quickly become a key element of urban planning. An increasing number of communities are setting goals for local sustainability and carrying out efforts intended to reduce environmental impacts and improve the community's overall quality of life. Although many places have initiated sustainable planning efforts in order to improve local conditions and respond to local concerns, some states have begun requiring their cities and towns to address sustainability issues in local plans. Additionally, a variety of state and federal programs are providing funding to support local efforts to create sustainable communities.

Tackling climate change

Global climate change is a multifaceted issue for cities and towns. On the one hand, cities and towns contribute to global climate change by virtue of the activities that are located in their areas, including everything from auto-mobile pollution to energy plant operations. Cities and towns also are on the receiving end of the potential consequences of climate change — rising sea levels, increased temperatures, and changes in weather patterns may have significant impacts on local communities in the coming decades.

Cool cities: Reducing greenhouse gas emissions

The United States has not adopted the United Nations–sponsored Kyoto Protocol on climate change, an international agreement between more than 190 countries that calls for the reduction of greenhouse gas emissions (see Chapter 9 for more on greenhouse gases). However, many U.S. cities are engaged in local efforts toward anti-climate-change planning and the reduc-tion of greenhouse gas emissions. These efforts focus on changing local con-ditions that promote the use of fossil fuels.

Some cities and towns have established clear goals for the reduction of green-house gas emission and have instituted monitoring programs that inventory and track local conditions. For example, the city of Seattle conducts a commu-nity greenhouse gas inventory every three years and has set a goal of reducing greenhouse gas emissions by 90 percent by the year 2050. You can check out Seattle's ambitious plans online at `http://1.usa.gov/j5ioPA`.

Improving energy use

Fossil fuels used in the generation of electricity account for nearly one-third of all greenhouse gas emissions in the United States. States and cities are working to use energy more efficiently and change their energy portfolios to include more sources of renewable energy. In some places, public utilities are under mandates to shift to alternative sources of energy or use cleaner fossil fuels. Many public authorities are leading the way by purchasing *green energy* (energy that comes from a renewable source, such as wind, solar, geother-mal, or hydroelectric power) for municipal use.

Reducing vehicle emissions

Transportation accounts for more than a quarter of all U.S. greenhouse gas emissions. Cities are taking steps to reduce vehicle emissions by encouraging the use of alternative fuels, promoting the use of public transportation, and promoting what urban planners refer to as *location-efficient land use patterns,* which shorten the distance of trips away from home.

Building better buildings

Making buildings more energy efficient is a key goal of local planning efforts. Many places are promoting or requiring the use of green building standards in government facilities and privately built structures. For more information on this subject, check out "LEED-ing the way: Eco-friendly buildings," later in this chapter.

Making industry cleaner and greener

Factory operations and other activities of heavy industries account for about 20 percent of all greenhouse gas emissions. Although some emissions by private businesses are regulated by state and federal agencies, local areas also are trying to help by promoting green business practices, such as purchasing recycled materials when possible or using green buildings (see "LEED-ing the way: Eco-friendly buildings," later in this chapter). In some communities, companies that use greener practices are eligible for financial incentives offered by local government agencies or expedited approvals of development permits.

The hot club: Adapting to climate change

In addition to reducing their impacts on climate change, a growing number of cities also are making advance preparations to adapt to changing environmental conditions as a result of climate change. In 2010 and 2011, the White House's Interagency Climate Change Adaptation Task Force issued reports urging local communities to begin planning for "resilience to climate change," noting that "federal agencies are working with diverse stakeholders in communities to prepare for a range of extreme weather and climate impacts (for example, flooding, drought, and wildfire) that put people, property, local economies, and ecosystems at risk."

Although there is some popular disagreement about the nature of long-term climate change, some places are acting on the best available science to incorporate climate change adaptation into their local plans. For example, the coastal community of Chula Vista, California, recently adopted an action plan for climate change adaptation that addresses a wide range of issues — including water supply levels, wildfire risk, biodiversity, coastal protection, and economic losses — that may arise due to changing environmental conditions, such as rising temperatures and sea levels.

Using local resources

Using local resources strengthens the local economy, reduces the need for some products to be transported domestically or internationally, and can help lower the costs of some goods and services. In this section, I cover some of the approaches that cities and towns are using to "go local."

Supporting local food systems

Most urban areas depend on the global food system to stock the shelves of their local grocery stores. According to some estimates, the average food purchased at a grocery store travels 1,500 miles. And many residents of urban areas are not located near good quality grocery stores and lack regular transportation to travel for groceries.

For example, it's estimated that roughly half of the residents of the city of Detroit lack access to a good quality grocery store and some of the city neighborhoods are described as *food deserts,* where a majority of the population is unable to shop at a good quality grocery store, either because no such stores are within walking distance or because people don't have regular access to a car or reliable public transportation to get to such a store. In some urban neighborhoods, food supplies are scavenged from lower-quality and higher-priced establishments, such as convenience stores and gas stations.

In order to improve local food systems, many cities and towns have adopted programs promoting locally grown food. Urban agriculture programs promote the growing of food within urban neighborhoods and range in approach from community gardens that help provide fresh food for local families to small commercial farms in urban areas. Farm-to-city programs help link rural growers with farmers markets in urban neighborhoods and can provide fresh foods to urban dwellers at reasonable costs.

Developing alternative energy resources

Many communities are encouraging the development of large-scale alternative sources of energy, such as wind farms that can supply relatively large amounts of electricity.

Some places also are encouraging the use of small-scale alternative energy sources that can directly supply homes and businesses, such as wind, solar, and geothermal. The use of these sources typically requires communities to revise their local building and zoning regulations to accommodate elements such as solar panels or small wind turbines.

Promoting local buying

Sometimes known as *import substitution,* this approach connects local suppliers with local purchasers for different goods and services. Some local government agencies have established programs to "buy local" and to "buy green" from local suppliers. These efforts can help jumpstart the market for new products and give community-based businesses a chance to expand.

LEED-ing the way: Eco-friendly buildings

The Leadership in Energy and Environmental Design (LEED) Green Building Rating System is a voluntary standard for green buildings developed by the U.S. Green Building Council (USGBC; www.usgbc.org/leed). In this program, building owners pay a fee and apply to have their buildings evaluated by the USGBC.

LEED standards are in place for several types of buildings and development projects, the best known of which is the LEED certification and awards program for new and existing buildings. These LEED programs use a set of technical standards to evaluate buildings based on six criteria:

- ✔ Site selection
- ✔ Water efficiency
- ✔ Energy and atmosphere
- ✔ Materials and resources
- ✔ Indoor environmental quality
- ✔ Innovation in design

Buildings that meet certain standards are LEED certified and may be awarded silver, gold, or platinum status for meeting additional green building goals. Since the inception of LEED in 2000, more than 8,000 buildings have been certified and awarded status as LEED green buildings; more than 20,000 new green building projects in some stage of planning or construction are registered with the USGBC.

In 2010, the USGBC introduced a LEED standard for large-scale development known as LEED–Neighborhood Development (ND), which rates the quality of neighborhood-scale and mixed-use development projects. One of the first developments to receive LEED-ND status was the Gulch, a 60-acre mixed-use transit-oriented development in central Nashville, Tennessee, that features reused buildings, energy-efficient infrastructure, and excellent access to local jobs and public transportation.

LEED standards for green buildings are used by many government agencies to promote the construction and renovation of government-owned facilities that are environmentally friendly. Many communities also are incorporating green building standards into their local zoning and building codes, as well as providing incentives and financial assistance for green building projects.

For example, the city of Gainesville, Florida, aims to update many public buildings to qualify for LEED certification and offers a discount on building permit fees to private contractors who are building LEED-qualified projects.

Planning greener cities

Sustainable planning techniques can be woven throughout the various topics addressed in an urban plan, and sustainable development initiatives can be carried out across a wide range of areas, from housing to infrastructure. In this section, I look at some of the specific ways in which cities and towns can "green up" the community and how different approaches can be used throughout a comprehensive urban plan.

Land use

Compact land use patterns promote sustainability by using less land, making it easier for people to reach nearby locations, and encouraging the active use of public spaces. Here are two approaches to creating more compact and efficient places:

- **Urban design and zoning:** Urban design elements — including narrower streets, small common parks instead of large yards for each house, and pedestrian paths that replace small streets — can help conserve space and promote a sense of community. These approaches can be reinforced by zoning and building codes that give property owners and developers greater leeway to use greener design approaches.

- **Redevelopment:** The reuse of existing land in urban areas helps conserve land, directs development to areas that often are served by existing infrastructure, and promotes the revitalization of the community. *Infill redevelopment* is the development of vacant lots in urban areas. *Brownfield development* cleans up polluted properties and prepares them for redevelopment. Both of these approaches can be supported by changes in zoning regulations and financial incentives to encourage redevelopment.

Housing

Housing uses lots of ecological resources — from building materials to energy for heating and cooling — and many communities, individuals, and builders are coming up with ways to make housing greener:

- ✔ **Green housing:** Many communities are working to support the construction of energy-efficient housing and green retro-fitting for existing homes. Some places have updated their zoning and building codes to accommodate elements such as solar panels. Communities also are using financial incentives to promote green upgrades and providing building density incentives for green housing.

    For example, the city of Seattle allows developers to build a larger number of units per acre in some areas when they construct green housing.

- ✔ **Smaller houses:** The average size of a newly built single-family home in the United States peaked in 2007 at 2,500 square feet, an increase of nearly 50 percent compared to homes built in the 1970s. However, many people and families are rediscovering the joys of smaller living, a concept popularized by books such as Sarah Susanka's *The Not So Big House: A Blueprint for the Way We Really Live*. Smaller houses require less resources to build and maintain, use less land, and can be more affordable than larger homes. Some cities and towns have revised their zoning and building codes to allow the development of smaller homes in areas that previously were restricted to larger dwellings.

- ✔ **Multifamily housing and mixed-use development:** Many communities are using zoning regulations and financial incentives to encourage the development of multifamily housing, including apartments and town houses in mixed-use development areas. These types of housing tend to be more energy efficient, require less infrastructure, and sometimes provide the community with additional affordable housing.

Transportation

Most urban areas in the United States are dependent on conventional automobiles as a primary form of transportation, but many communities are promoting green alternatives to a car-driven lifestyle.

Promoting transportation alternatives

Walking, bicycling, and using public transportation are alternatives to car use. Many communities are using public service campaigns to urge people to consider alternative forms of transportation. They're also making improvements to sidewalks, bicycles paths, and public transportation facilities to encourage greater public use of alternative forms of transportation.

Supporting green vehicles

A growing number of cars, trucks, and buses are running on alternative fuels such as natural gas, electricity, and biofuels. Some communities are working to provide networks of charging stations for electric vehicles. In some places, green vehicles receive preferential treatment on roads and highways, such as access to high-occupancy and express lanes.

Using transit-oriented development

Transit-oriented development (TOD) is an approach to urban design that places mixed land uses — including residential areas — closer to public transportation centers, especially subway, light-rail, and bus services. This approach promotes the use of public transportation and conserves the amount of land used for residential development. (You can find more information on TOD in Chapter 7.)

Becoming car-free

In Venice, Italy, locals travel by gondola, but few other truly car-free cities exist in Europe or North America. Some cities — such as Salzburg, Austria, and Montreal, Canada — have significant *car-free zones* where the use of cars is severely restricted. Many cities have enough walking, bicycling, and public transportation options that many people are able to live car-free lifestyles, where getting to work, shopping, and engaging in other activities don't depend on owning a car.

Infrastructure

Green infrastructure is a concept that has recently been adopted in urban planning to describe how features of the natural environment can be used to complement the use of traditional infrastructure, such as storm-water drainage systems. The use of green infrastructure can help preserve and restore ecological systems and may be a cost-effective alternative to some types of traditional infrastructure.

For example, the Green Topeka program (www.greentopeka.org) in Topeka, Kansas, uses areas planted with native grasses that absorb storm water that contributes to flooding. The program has converted vacant lots into bio-retention ponds that reduce the amount of rainwater going into the sewer system.

Curitiba, Brazil: A model sustainable city

The Brazilian city of Curitiba is home to more than 1.5 million residents and is located about 250 miles south of São Paulo. Since the 1960s, Curitiba has been experimenting with new ways to manage rapid growth while encouraging environmental sustainability and a high quality of life for its residents. The city has been awarded the prestigious UN Environmental Award by the United Nations Environmental Program, and many urban planners and environmentalists view the city as a model sustainable city.

Here's a look at some of Curitiba's signature green planning projects:

✔ **Rapid transit:** The city has made extensive investments in a bus rapid transit system that carries roughly 70 percent of all commuters. The express bus system uses specially designed buses and a vast network of futuristic-looking high-speed bus stops. Broad use of public transportation has helped the city maintain low levels of air pollution and greenhouse gas emissions. The bus system also is relatively inexpensive to operate and provides an affordable means of travel for poor workers.

✔ **Recycling and waste management:** Curitiba also is well known for its unique approach to recycling and waste management. The city maintains a garbage diversion program that encourages people to donate or resell items that might otherwise end up in the city's only landfill. The city Cambio Verde (Green Change) recycling program encourages poor residents to bring litter and recycling to waste centers in exchange for fresh food and vouchers for other household supplies. This program and others help to improve the city's sanitation and public health conditions, as well as provide some benefits for the city's poorest residents.

✔ **Public parks:** The city also has developed an extensive park system of more than two dozen major parks that cover more than 5,000 acres. Some park locations were formerly sites of abandoned industrial buildings or deteriorated housing. Today these sites are used for recreational purposes and have been planned as green infrastructure that helps the city clear its air and manage storm water.

Curitiba's population has increased by more than a million people since the 1970s, and the city continues to be challenged by rapid growth. Although some of the city's green experiments have not gone as well as others, the words of the city's former mayor Jamie Lermer sum up Curitiba's approach to sustainable urban planning: "Cities are not the problem; they are the solution."

Growing the city's greenprint

Throughout this chapter, I talk about the city's ecological footprint and many of the ways in which cities consume all types of ecological resources. But the news isn't all bad. Many cities are working to grow their *greenprints* (green footprints) by protecting, restoring, and enhancing their natural features, including the following:

✔ **Habitats and corridors:** These spaces are dedicated to habitats for plants and animals. They also can be used by animals to safely move about and migrate. Habitats and corridors protect and enrich the area's biodiversity and may serve as low-impact recreational areas for human uses (such as walking, hiking, or birding). These areas also can be used as greenbelts or greenways to help define the rural edge of the community and discourage the spread of urban sprawl.

✔ **Urban forestry:** Trees provide cities with everything from cool shade to clean air to the absorption of pollutants. Urban forestry programs aim to improve the health of trees in the community and increase the number of trees.

Several major U.S. cities — including Denver, Houston, Los Angeles, and New York — have initiated "million-tree city" programs with the aim of planting one million or more new trees. You can check out the progress of Los Angeles and New York City at www.milliontreesla.org and www.milliontreesnyc.org, respectively.

✔ **Natural systems restoration:** Also known as *ecological restoration,* these projects aim to restore the natural functions of environmental resources that have been changed or impacted by urban development or natural disasters.

For example, in the greater Chicago area, the North Branch Restoration Project (www.northbranchrestoration.org) is a volunteer organization that works to restore the native prairies, woodlands, and wetlands that border the Chicago River. These efforts protect the environment from the impacts of urban development, help remove invasive plant and animal species, and improve local biodiversity.

✔ **Open space:** Open spaces for conservation and recreation not only provide places where people can enjoy nature, but also serve ecological purposes, such as cleaning the air and water or providing habitats for plants and animals. (See Chapter 9 for more information.)

✔ **Urban agriculture:** The transformation of vacant urban land into areas for urban agriculture has both social and environmental benefits. In recent years, urban agricultural projects have grown to include a wide range of community gardening and urban farming projects.

In Detroit, hundreds of community gardens have sprouted from the city's many vacant lots. The city also is becoming home to a growing number of urban farms, such as Brother Nature Produce (http://on.fb.me/t8NMqH), a 2-acre farm in central Detroit's Corktown neighborhood.

Denver's greenprint

Since 2006, the city of Denver's Greenprint Denver initiative (www.greenprint denver.org) has been working to put sustainability at the center of the city's growth and development. Greenprint Denver aspires to "incorporate triple bottom-line analysis, seeking to balance economic, social, and environmental considerations into all city policy and program decisions" and "partner with community organizations, cultural institutions, and businesses to achieve broad impact."

The city's action plan for sustainable development aims to

✔ Reduce greenhouse gas emissions

✔ Increase the number of trees in the city

✔ Reduce waste

✔ Increase recycling

✔ Increase the use of renewable energy sources

✔ Promote mass transit use

The city also is active in supporting business development efforts that will "position Denver as a regional center for renewable energy and green industries."

Not only is Denver planning for a greener future, but it's also leading by example. The city has adopted municipal policies that require the use of green building standards for municipal buildings and the use of energy-efficient vehicles.

Using New Tools to Plan for a Greener Future

Urban planners are using some new tools to plan for a greener future. Here are some green planning techniques that are being used to identify opportunities for sustainable planning, set goals for sustainable development, and monitor the implementation of plans and changing conditions in the community:

✔ **Ecological footprint analysis:** An *environmental footprint* measures the total amount of biological and earthen resources — including resources taken from air, water, and land supplies — that people consume. By some estimates, the world's current environmental footprint consumes natural resources at a rate that is 50 percent higher than can be naturally renewed each year and many wealthy countries — including the United States, Canada, the United Kingdom, and Australia — have environmental footprints that are roughly two to three times the world average. Due to an increasing awareness of the limitations of the world's natural resources, some communities are using the environmental footprint approach to measure their local use of resources.

For example, the city of Calgary, Canada's *Ecological Footprint Baseline Report 2008* (http://bit.ly/uN6aMc) found that its ecological footprint was 30 percent larger than the Canadian national average. The report calls for the city to consider planning for "mixed land uses, compact form, higher densities, more transportation choices, high-quality transit service, and with green building infrastructure and technologies" if it hopes to achieve "long-term reductions" in its ecological footprint.

✔ **Community indicators and report cards:** Community indicators and report cards help cities and towns better understand local conditions and how well local programs are working to meet sustainability goals.

In Minnesota, the city of Minneapolis's Sustainability Indicators program (http://bit.ly/nHLcIB) measures a wide range of conditions related to sustainability, including air quality, employment in green jobs, asthma rates, and availability of affordable housing. These indicators help the community determine how well it's working toward ten-year targets that have been established for local sustainability.

In California, the city of Santa Monica's *Sustainable City Report Card* (http://bit.ly/bJXKe7) measures the community's progress toward meeting goals in resource conservation, environmental and public health, and human dignity. The city's grades are based on yearly indicators of how much progress the community is making in reaching the goals that it has set, including a survey of the community and data taken from public service operations. From 2008 to 2010, the city improved its grade in the area of Resource Conservation from a C+ to a B–, noting rather dryly that "resource use is down and sustainable practices are increasing."

✔ **Green maps:** A *green map* illustrates the locations of the community's environmental resources. Green maps raise community awareness of environmental issues, allow people to find and use green resources, and help identify green spots that may need to be preserved and protected.

Artist Wendy Brawer is credited with creating one the first green maps in the United States in the early 1990s for New York City. The current version of NYC's "Green Apple Map" (www.greenapplemap.org) includes everything from farmers markets and places for birding to wetlands and toxic hot spots.

Many other cities in the United States and around the world have developed green maps. As a part of its 2003 comprehensive plan, the city of New Haven, Connecticut, developed a green map to help the community gain a greater appreciation of its natural resources and develop a better understanding of how its environmental assets contribute to the community's overall quality of life.

You can find more information and examples of green maps from around the world at the Green Map System website (www.greenmap.org).

✔ **Bio-regional plans:** A bio-regional approach to planning emphasizes the natural geography of environmental systems, such as animal habitats or watersheds. In many cases, these natural resources occur over broad geographic areas and involve the territories of many different cities and towns. Bio-regional plans promote cooperation among places to plan for the sustainable treatment of shared environmental resources.

For example, a nonprofit organization called EcoCity Cleveland developed a *Citizens' Bioregional Plan for Northeast Ohio* (http://bit.ly/sSZ4xv), which uses a community-based approach to understanding the best ways to balance the needs of greater Cleveland's cities and suburbs with the conservation of the region's environmental resources.

Green planning is really just the tip of the iceberg. Movement toward more sustainable cities requires action by communities and their stakeholders.

Many cities have begun programs to stimulate interest in sustainable planning and development through "green leadership" programs that identify outstanding local efforts and help train leaders and social entrepreneurs. For example, local governments in Indianapolis and Boston have established sustainability awards programs to recognize and encourage local businesses and community leaders to go green.

Chapter 12

Urban Revitalization: Cities on the Rebound

. . . .

In This Chapter

▶ Turning around declining downtowns

▶ Jumpstarting waterfront redevelopment

▶ Promoting the arts and attracting tourists

▶ Preserving historic architecture

▶ Making urban neighborhoods great places to live

. . . .

*I*n recent years, many U.S. cities have experienced prolonged periods of decline that have resulted in the loss of people and jobs, a decline in the city's physical conditions, and worsening social conditions among the current population. Since the 1950s, the cities of Boston, Cleveland, Detroit, Philadelphia, Pittsburgh, and St. Louis all have lost a substantial portion of their peak populations. Some cities, such as Chicago, have begun to lose population more recently. And even cities that are gaining population, like Houston and Los Angeles, have a variety of urban problems within their borders.

Planning for urban revitalization addresses a broad range of concerns, including population loss, aging downtown areas, poor conditions in urban neighborhoods, and declining quality of life for residents. In many central cities, urban revitalization is the primary goal of the local plan and development efforts and local redevelopment and revitalization programs often are supported by federal and state efforts, as well as those of the business community and nonprofit organizations.

Although some cities have experienced long-term decline, the overall outlook for central cities has great possibilities. The U.S. population is expected to grow significantly in coming decades and will provide new opportunities for cities to grow and improve their quality of life. As the Baby Boomers get older, many empty nesters may relocate from suburbs to central cities, and recent surveys of the *millennial generation* (those born in the 1980s and 1990s) show that many younger adults are interested in living and working in diverse and active urban areas.

Every place is unique, and a wide range of communities are making plans that not only identify opportunities for improvement and revitalization, but also maintain their current strengths.

In this chapter, I explain the challenges of revitalizing urban areas and the diverse ways in which communities are working to improve and maintain themselves, including redeveloping waterfronts; jumpstarting downtowns; promoting tourism; improving the quality of life in urban neighborhoods; preserving historic areas; and enhancing the city with arts, culture, and entertainment.

Making Dynamic Downtowns

Downtown areas play a special role in the overall success of communities. Downtowns are often both the commercial and civic centers of communities, and a declining downtown can have a negative impact on the local economy and become a demoralizing symbol for the community. Improving and maintaining downtown areas is a priority in many places, and a wide range of communities have adopted specialized plans for downtown areas and established special governmental authorities to carry out downtown planning and development.

How cities are bringing people and businesses back to Main Street

Downtown areas are the heart of the community and can serve a wide range of social and economic functions. Many communities have devised plans and development strategies to improve and maintain their downtown areas in ways that support existing businesses, attract new businesses, and promote increased local use as well as tourism:

- **Promoting a range of uses:** Downtown areas with a mix of lively uses can attract a broader range of users and tourists. This mix isn't just about supporting different types of businesses, although that's important. It's also about widening the range of land uses to include residential and civic uses, ranging from combined live-work spaces for artists to specialized entertainment venues.

- **Designing attractive and distinctive downtowns:** A wide range of approaches can be used to improve downtown spaces in ways that improve the physical look of the area and give it a unique flair.

For example, the city of Greenville, South Carolina, adopted a *Downtown Streetscape Master Plan* (http://1.usa.gov/u58ymB) that aims to enhance the character of downtown streets by providing spaces for outdoor restaurant dining, preserving trees and increasing planted areas, and renovating the facades of historic buildings.

✔ **Encouraging activity around the clock:** Many downtown areas have bustling daytime populations but turn into virtual ghost towns outside the 9-to-5 workweek. Cities have many options for promoting the full-time use of downtown areas, including improving nighttime safety so that visitors will feel comfortable visiting bars and restaurants, and holding special events on weekends to draw in shoppers and other visitors.

In addition to local planning and support, a variety of statewide and nonprofit programs help support downtown areas in big cities, suburbs, and small towns. For example, the state of Colorado provides for the establishment of local downtown development authorities that can tap into a variety of funding sources and provide financial incentives for downtown redevelopment. The state of Wisconsin uses its Main Street Program (http://bit.ly/s4zkGn) to support local downtown development initiatives. The nonprofit National Trust Main Street Center (www.mainstreet.org) works with communities across the United States on the planning and development of downtown and neighborhood commercial districts.

Pittsburgh's Golden Triangle: Reinventing an industrial city

The city of Pittsburgh's downtown area sits at the confluence of three rivers — the Allegheny, Ohio, and Monongahela. Originally described as the Golden Triangle in the early 1900s, this section of downtown Pittsburgh was long occupied by some of the city's most important industrial facilities. But by the 1940s, the Golden Triangle had lost its shine and the area was described by the city's mayor, David Lawrence, as "an ugly jumble of warehouses and railroad trackage."

Starting in 1946, the city's redevelopment authority acquired and cleared nearly 60 acres of the Golden Triangle, transforming it from a smoking industrial eyesore to a green and modern downtown centerpiece. More than 30 acres at the tip of the triangle were turned into what's now known as Point State Park, an open space featuring an elegant fountain, a historical center, and green fields that often are used for concerts and festivals. The remaining area of nearly two dozen acres that flows into the rest of downtown Pittsburgh was redeveloped during the 1950s and 1960s as a complex of office and apartment buildings known as the Gateway Center.

The redevelopment of the Golden Triangle brought national acclaim to Pittsburgh as a city that was capable of progressing beyond its industrial past and was heralded by other industrial cities as a successful example of what would later be known as "urban renewal."

The new wave of downtown housing: Lofts, high-rises, and urban villages

Some cities have maintained vibrant downtown residential populations for decades, while many others have very small residential populations because their downtowns are dominated by commercial and office activities. But today some areas are seeing an increase in the demand for downtown living spaces, and, unlike many urban and suburban areas that are dominated by single-family homes, downtowns tend to offer different types of housing:

- **Lofts and industrial conversions:** Many new residential developments in downtown areas are of buildings that used to serve as factories and warehouses. These buildings often have high ceilings and open floor plans that make them ideal for conversion to loft apartments and condominiums. Some new downtown housing developments emulate the look of former industrial buildings and offer loft-style apartments (sometimes called *loft-a-likes* by urban planners).

New York City's TriBeCa neighborhood is well known for the conversion of its former industrial buildings into luxury lofts and condos during the 1970s and 1980s.

- **High-rises:** Not every city has a critical mass of consumer demand to support the development of downtown high-rise apartment buildings, but many cities are seeing an increase in high-rise development.

Downtown Chicago is home to more than 30 high-rise condominium and apartment buildings. The most recent and tallest of these is the Trump International Tower and Hotel, which offers residential condominiums ranging from a 500-square-foot studio to a 7,000-square-foot penthouse valued at more than $10 million. Another recent addition to Chicago's high-rise skyline is the 215 West Apartments, a 50-story apartment building that's LEED-certified as environmentally friendly by the U.S. Green Building Council.

- **Urban villages:** Another option for downtown housing is the development of *urban villages,* which use medium-density housing to create areas that have a sense of community and may be smaller in scale than surrounding downtown areas.

One example is downtown Toronto's Portland Park Village, a redevelopment of a former parking lot that features a nine-story mixed-use apartment building and 74 town houses. A common courtyard, attractive landscaping, and an adjacent public park give the development a less-dense feel, even though it's just six blocks away from downtown Toronto's iconic CN Tower, which rises more than 1,800 feet above the ground.

Just Add Water (fronts): Capitalizing on Proximity to Water

Waterfront areas can offer unique opportunities for recreation and tourism that incorporate both scenic beauty and unique activities. In recent decades, many cities have transformed their underused and formerly industrial waterfronts into mixed-use areas that draw in both locals and tourists.

Here are some examples:

- ✔ **Baltimore's Inner Harbor:** During the 1970s and 1980s, the city's historic harbor was transformed into a vibrant urban district that now includes hotels, restaurants, museums, an aquarium, and shopping areas. The harbor's signature project is the Harborplace "festival marketplace," which opened in 1980 and attracted more than 18 million visitors during its first year. The redevelopment of the Inner Harbor helped put Baltimore back on the map as a tourist destination and has helped to provide jobs to city residents who live in nearby neighborhoods.

- ✔ **Toronto's Harbourfront:** The transformation of Toronto's waterfront began in the 1970s. The opening of the Queen's Quay Terminal as a mixed-use complex in 1982 signaled a major change for the area. The Harbourfront is now a major entertainment destination for both locals and tourists. It's connected by light-rail mass transit to the city's downtown area, and it features a year-round schedule of artistic and cultural events.

- ✔ **The Indianapolis Canal Walk:** The Canal Walk cuts a mile-long ribbon of blue water through the heart of downtown Indianapolis. The canal dates from the early 1800s and has been redesigned to offer a range of activities on and off the water, including bicycling, walking, kayaking, and paddle-boating. The Canal Walk connects to parks, hotels, restaurants, apartment buildings, museums, universities, and office buildings in the downtown area and draws tourists into the core of the city.

Keeping It Cool: Arts, Culture, and Entertainment

Supporting arts, culture, and entertainment contributes broadly to the revitalization of urban areas. New and improved amenities can bolster the local quality of life, help create a distinct image for downtown and neighborhood areas, promote new destinations for tourists and other visitors, stimulate the redevelopment of arts and cultural districts, and contribute to the economic health of the community.

Creative cities: Cultural amenities that strengthen urban development

In his 2002 book, *The Rise of the Creative Class,* Carnegie-Mellon University professor Richard Florida observed that cities that are able to attract or hang on to creative workers and entrepreneurs are more likely to prosper than those that don't. For example, the economies of places such as Austin, San Francisco, and Washington, D.C., have thrived in part because they offer social and cultural amenities that are attractive to what Florida calls the "creative class" of workers who are essential to the development of innovative and profitable businesses.

Since the early 2000s, many communities have made plans and developed programs to provide enhanced amenities that appeal to creative workers and help revitalize urban areas. Here are two examples:

- **Michigan's "cool cities":** In 2003, the state of Michigan began its Cool Cities initiative (www.coolcities.com) to help transform the state's economy and improve local communities by improving the cultural amenities that may help retain and attract "knowledge workers" in innovative industries, such as new media and advanced manufacturing. Some of the efforts that have taken place through the program include support for the renovation of a downtown entertainment district in Lansing and improvements to Ypsilanti's Riverside Arts Center, a multipurpose cultural arts venue.

- **Getting creative in Dayton:** Dayton is a midsize city in southwestern Ohio that has a long history of economic innovation, including a pair of brothers named Wilbur and Orville Wright who invented a little something they called the "flying machine." In recent years, the city has taken a number of steps to recapture its innovative past. One of these efforts is a "creative incubator" building in downtown Dayton, known as C{space (www.cspacedayton.org), which hosts a wide range of artistic events and provides opportunities for collaboration between local artists and entrepreneurs.

Performance spaces: Promoting arts districts and cultural facilities

Arts and culture always have played an important role in urban life, and centers of arts and culture are often integral to the life of the city, ranging from the theaters of ancient Rome to the music halls of Vienna and the museums of New York City.

Branding a city: How cities use events and advertising to promote tourism

Some cities don't mind being a "best kept secret," but many communities are using signature events and cutting-edge marketing techniques to make sure that the word gets out about what they have to offer. Many communities have developed specific events that both draw in tourists and contribute to the city's overall reputation as a vibrant place that's worth a visit. Here are some examples:

✔ **The Indy 500** (www.indianapolis
   motorspeedway.com/indy500):
   Since its inception in 1911, the Indy 500
   has become one of the best-known sporting events in the world, and the race draws international attention to the Indianapolis Motor Speedway and its home city. In addition, the race's long history and great success have helped Indianapolis develop as a global center for automotive technology and sports-related businesses.

✔ **Austin's music scene:** Austin, Texas, has claimed the title of "live music capital of the world" and boasts more than 200 live-music venues. Its South by Southwest (SXSW) music festival (www.sxsw.com) is one of the most important annual events for the U.S. music industry and has recently branched into additional SXSW events for the film, gaming, and social media industries. SXSW and other local efforts, including the long-running *Austin City Limits* music series (www.austincity
   limits.org), have helped Austin establish itself as a center for both entertainment-related tourism and innovation in music, film, and new media.

A good slogan is another element of a city's brand image that can be used to promote tourism and create a theme along which additional tourism-related activities can be planned. We all know that "Virginia Is for Lovers" and that

"What Happens in Vegas Stays in Vegas," but here are some city slogans that you may not have heard of:

✔ **"The Little Apple"**: Everyone knows that New York City is the Big Apple, but 1,300 miles away, the city of Manhattan, Kansas, has staked its claim as the Little Apple. This Manhattan is a small city of about 52,000 people located 120 miles west of Kansas City. But it's a thriving city that's home to a large public university, Kansas State. The Little Apple wants everyone to know that even though its Manhattan is smaller and a little out of the way, it's still a place worth visiting.

✔ **"Keep Austin Weird"**: The unofficial slogan of Austin, Texas, celebrates everything that's a little off-center about this quirky city, ranging from vegetarian cowboy restaurants to tattooed roller-derby queens and the crowds that gather to watch the colony of bats that roost under one of the city's downtown bridges. The slogan has been informally adopted by many of the city's locally owned businesses to emphasize their importance to the local economy and their contributions to the city's eclectic social scene that draws in tourists who want to visit someplace that isn't like anywhere else.

✔ **"NYC I DO"**: Shortly after the legalization of same-sex marriage in the state of New York in 2011, New York City's mayor, Michael Bloomberg, announced the city's "NYC I DO" campaign to encourage couples to consider wedding in the city, a move that could generate millions of dollars in additional tourism business. You can find the city's same-sex wedding planner online at www.nycgo.com/nycido.

Many communities are now making plans that use artistic and cultural facilities not only to enrich the community, but also to serve as a catalyst for the redevelopment and improvement of surrounding areas. Here are two shining examples:

- ✔ **Collecting the arts in Dallas:** They say that everything's bigger in Texas, and the Dallas Arts District (www.thedallasartsdistrict.org) claims to be the largest arts district in the United States. In the 1970s and 1980s, plans were made to concentrate the city's major artistic and cultural institutions in downtown Dallas. This area now covers 19 city blocks and features a range of artistic activities, including the Dallas Museum of Art, a symphony hall, and an opera house. Some consider the district itself a work of art, because it features buildings and public art pieces by many notable artists and architects, including Edward Larrabee Barnes, Rem Koolhaas, Renzo Piano, I. M. Pei, and Andy Warhol.

- ✔ **Making music in downtown Los Angeles:** The Walt Disney Concert Hall (http://bit.ly/eYk8t) in downtown Los Angeles is a wonder of twisted metal that has become one of the city's modern landmarks since its opening in 2003. Designed by noted architect Frank Gehry, the hall is home to the Los Angeles Philharmonic Orchestra and has helped generate new interest in the downtown area, which has recently added new shops, restaurants, and apartment buildings. Although many construction projects have been delayed due to the economic recession that hit in 2008, the concert hall remains a centerpiece of an arts-and-entertainment-based approach to revitalizing downtown Los Angeles.

Preserving History

As the saying goes, "Rome wasn't built in a day." Cities are built up in layers over hundreds or even thousands of years. They reflect the city's social, economic, cultural, and architectural past. Efforts to preserve the community's historic character — known as *historic preservation* — can contribute to the revitalization of the community by accentuating its aesthetic and cultural appeal, as well as by using existing resources in an efficient manner.

In addition to state and federal efforts to preserve historic buildings and areas, many communities have adopted local plans and programs to promote historic preservation. A wide range of nonprofit organizations — including the National Trust for Historic Preservation (www.preservationnation.org) — are actively involved in assisting communities in their preservation efforts.

Using historic districts to preserve the city

In the United States, the National Historic Preservation Act created the National Register of Historic Places, which provides federal recognition of both individual buildings and *historic districts*. Many communities also have established local programs to recognize and protect local historic districts, including regulations limiting development and redevelopment that alter the historic quality of the area. A variety of federal, state, and local programs also provide financial support and incentives for the preservation and improvement of historic districts.

The size of urban historic districts ranges from a single block containing just a few buildings to large areas that make up entire neighborhoods, such as Charleston, South Carolina's central historic district, which covers more than 4,000 buildings in 3 square miles. Here's the scoop on a couple other notable historic districts:

✔ **Philadelphia's Society Hill:** The Society Hill district lies just southeast of the city center and was drawn into city founder William Penn's 1682 plan for Philadelphia. Its earliest residents were a mixed bag of laborers and wealthy business owners, as well as some of the city's early African-American residents. The area includes a range of 18th- and 19th-century buildings that are classic examples of Georgian, Federal, Greek Revival, and Italianate architecture. Society Hill was placed on the National Register of Historic Places in 1987. The district also is protected by local historic preservation regulations that limit changes to existing buildings and provide design guidelines for the construction of new buildings.

✔ **Denver's Lower Downtown:** The Lower Downtown district in Denver — also known as LoDo — is a centrally located area of more than 20 city blocks whose settlement dates back to the 1850s. By the 1970s, the area had fallen into decline, and a significant number of buildings were demolished. The city designated LoDo as a local historic district in the 1980s, and it has become a vibrant urban neighborhood with bars, restaurants, retail boutiques, and converted living spaces. LoDo's historic district designation protects more than 120 buildings and contains design guidelines for the continued development of the area in ways that preserve and enhance its historic character.

Restoring the past: New uses for old buildings

One approach to maintaining a city's history and the character of its historically important architecture is to find modern uses for historic buildings, especially those that may be unused or have fallen into disrepair. Urban planners call this *adaptive reuse*. The adaptive reuse of historic buildings ranges from making mild renovations to carrying out major reconstruction.

Here are two examples of adaptive reuse:

- **Pittsburgh's Church Brew Works** (www.churchbrew.com): From the outside, this building looks a lot like any of the other ornate churches built in Pittsburgh during the early 1900s. But on the inside, it's hard not to notice the gleaming copper beer brewing tanks that sit on what was once the church altar. Decommissioned by the local Catholic diocese in 1993, the building was later transformed into a restaurant and micro-brewery while preserving the building's stately Northern Italian–style architecture.

- **Kansas City's Union Station** (www.unionstation.org): In Kansas City, Missouri, the adaptive reuse of the city's Union Station transformed a derelict train station into a multiuse complex. Built in 1914 and listed on the National Register of Historic Places, Union Station was a major freight and passenger railway station that served as many as a million people a year at its peak. But by the 1980s, the demand for train service had declined precipitously, forcing the station out of use. During the 1990s, the station was renovated and now features a science center museum, restaurants, retail shops, and an IMAX movie theater.

In many cases, the cost of reusing an existing building may be less than the cost of demolishing an existing building and constructing a new one. And reusing existing buildings contributes to environmental sustainability by making good use of existing resources. But successful adaptive reuse projects often require local building codes and land use regulations that easily permit changes in how buildings are used. Adaptive reuse also can be promoted by land use and historic preservation plans that designate certain areas or build-ing classes as priorities for adaptive reuse initiatives.

Strengthening Urban Neighborhoods

Many urban neighborhoods have experienced decades of decline and neglect, especially in older industrial cities, such as Baltimore, Cleveland, Detroit, and St. Louis. However, many cities have been working hard to improve their urban neighborhoods in ways that attract new people and investment into the heart of the city, as well as improve the lives of existing residents.

Revitalizing urban neighborhoods with improved housing and services

Since the late 1960s, many cities have been working to improve conditions in their urban neighborhoods using a wide range of approaches to what is often called *community development*. In particular, planning for community devel-opment aims to improve both the physical conditions within neighborhoods and the social conditions for people who live there.

Reimagining Cleveland for a smaller population

In 1950, the city of Cleveland tallied a peak population of more than 900,000 people and was the seventh largest city in the United States. But the city's population has been declining steadily since its peak, and the 2010 U.S. Census reported that Cleveland's population had fallen to just under 400,000 people. As Cleveland's population has fallen, the amount of vacant land in the city has increased due to the destruction of houses and other buildings. As of 2008, it was estimated that there were more than 3,300 acres of vacated land within the city and another 15,000 vacant buildings awaiting either demolition or rehabilitation.

A local initiative known as Reimagining Cleveland has begun looking into how Cleveland's vacant land and abandoned buildings can be used in ways that will allow Cleveland to become a better city with a smaller population. In addition to redeveloping some vacant areas as replacement housing and new businesses, Reimagining Cleveland's suggestions for the reuse of vacant land include building up the city's "green infrastructure" (including managed open space and the restoration of natural ecosystems) and transforming vacant land into "productive landscapes," including spaces for urban agriculture and wind or solar power generation.

You can check out this effort and take a look at the *Reimagining Cleveland: Ideas to Action Resource Book* online at www.reimagining cleveland.org.

Stimulating new development

Many urban neighborhoods have experienced a decades-long loss of people and jobs. A wide range of planning approaches have been used to encourage people and businesses to locate in urban neighborhoods, from programs to support small local businesses to initiatives to develop new homes in older neighborhoods.

Making it clean and safe

One of the priorities of community development is to address poor physical conditions, such as deteriorating buildings and crumbling streets. In some cases, it may be possible to renovate and rehabilitate buildings that are in poor condition, but sometimes demolition of failing structures can be the best available option.

Promoting affordable housing

Access to safe and decent affordable housing is a struggle for many residents of urban neighborhoods. In addition to governmental efforts to provide public housing, community-based nonprofit organizations known as *community development corporations* (CDCs) have played a key role in improving housing conditions in urban neighborhoods. Since the early 1990s, CDCs have preserved or produced nearly a million units of affordable housing in cities across the United States.

Increasing social and economic opportunities

In many ways, a neighborhood is only as strong as the people who live there. A variety of community development approaches have been used to improve social and economic opportunities for residents of urban neighborhoods, from community organizing programs that help residents look for solutions to common problems and job training programs that connect local residents with local redevelopment efforts, such as the construction of new homes.

Improving services and amenities

Providing better services and enhanced amenities can improve the quality of life for existing residents and help attract new residents to urban neighborhoods. For example, many cities are working to improve parks and recreational areas in urban neighborhoods, as well as provide urban neighborhoods with needed services, such as grocery stores and affordable childcare facilities.

Expanding social services to reach distressed urban neighborhoods

Helping people gain access to social services has become an important element of local plans to improve urban neighborhoods. Many communities are involved in initiatives that help connect residents with a wide range of governmental agencies and nonprofit organizations that can provide needed services.

Community outreach programs

Community outreach programs help bring social services to people in neighborhoods who may be unaware of available services or are unable to travel to centralized locations. For example, local governments and public health agencies often work with local hospitals and other healthcare providers on programs to provide services to urban neighborhoods, ranging from visiting "health-mobiles" to the establishment of community health centers that can provide basic medical services.

Comprehensive community development initiatives

A comprehensive community development initiative combines bricks-and-mortar neighborhood redevelopment with efforts to provide improved social services.

For example, a comprehensive community development initiative in the Nystrom neighborhood of Richmond, California, augmented the development of new mixed-income affordable housing with a wide range of services for the community, including a community garden and a youth nutrition program.

Chapter 13

Rushing to the Suburbs: Managing Sprawl

In This Chapter

▶ Defining urban sprawl

▶ Recognizing the consequences of urban sprawl

▶ Recognizing sprawling land use patterns

▶ Solving sprawl with regional planning solutions

▶ Balancing new development with investment in existing communities

---

*M*ost metropolitan areas of the United States have sprawling land use patterns where dense urban neighborhoods give way to suburban shopping malls, office parks, and housing cul-de-sacs that run for miles before eventually tapering off into the countryside. But, in Portland, Oregon, there's a line where the city stops and the countryside starts. It's called an *urban growth boundary* (UGB), and it's Portland's unique way of managing regional land uses in a way that limits the spread of urban sprawl.

Established in 1979, the Portland metropolitan UGB surrounds nearly 400 square miles, including most of the city of Portland, plus all or part of 23 other cities and towns. Nearly 90 percent of the population of the Portland metropolitan area lives inside the UGB. Since the inception of the UGB, employment and population in the region have both increased by more than 50 percent. But the amount of land allocated for urban growth has increased by just 12 percent, far less than in most other U.S. metropolitan areas. Many experts believe that the UGB has helped the area use its land resources more effectively, protect the environment, and help the region maintain a high quality of life.

But not everyone in Portland agrees that the UGB is a fair or effective way to regulate regional land use. Over the years, the UGB has faced numerous legal challenges and ballot referenda attempting to weaken or overturn the growth boundary restrictions. Nonetheless, many communities look to Portland as a leading example of how to manage urban sprawl, and many urban planners wish that managing regional land use patterns were as easy as simply drawing a line between city and country. In most places, efforts to prevent urban sprawl and encourage regional land use planning involve a complex mix of cooperation and coordination among dozens of different communities.

In this chapter, I talk about sprawling land use patterns. In particular, I look at a variety of regional and local approaches that can be used to discourage the spread of urban sprawl and strengthen existing communities. I also fill you in on ways to help guide development in new areas that conserve land, use resources efficiently, and provide a high quality of life.

What's Urban Sprawl?

The term *urban sprawl* often is used to describe the way in which most metropolitan areas in the United States have expanded over the last several decades to include vast outlying suburban areas that used to be undeveloped or agricultural. More and more people are living at the outer edges of metropolitan regions. A 2006 study of U.S. metropolitan areas by the Brookings Institution's Metropolitan Policy Program found that about 24 percent of the population lived in central cities, 38 percent lived in older suburbs, 29 percent lived in newer suburbs, and about 9 percent of the population lived in newly developing "exurbs" at the outermost edges of metropolitan areas.

Sprawl also comes with a negative connotation and is often used to describe suburban and exurban areas that display a haphazard or poorly planned pattern of land development, although many people disagree about what exactly constitutes urban sprawl.

Here are five characteristics typically associated with urban sprawl:

- ✔ **Low-density development:** One indicator of sprawl is low-density land development, especially in locations where increases in land development have occurred more rapidly than increases in the population. For example, a 2001 study led by urban planners William Fulton and Rolf Pendall found that urban and suburban areas in the United States used 47 percent more land in 1997 than they did in 1982, even though population in the same areas grew by only 17 percent.

- ✔ **Leapfrog development:** *Leapfrog development* (also known as *scattered development*) is land development that skips over previously developed areas in favor of more distant locations. Housing developments, office parks, and shopping centers sometimes leapfrog across undeveloped areas in search of low-cost land that can be developed most profitably.

✔ **Single-use areas:** Large areas that feature a single land use — especially residential, retail, and office areas — often are associated with urban sprawl. So-called "bedroom suburbs" and "commercial strips" tend to encourage low-density development and often put things out of walking distance, making it necessary for people to use cars to get from one place to another.

✔ **Poor-quality design:** A common critique of sprawling areas is that they are either "ugly" (imagine a busy commercial road lined with fast food signs and billboards) or too "homogenous" (such as a housing subdivision full of identical houses). Poor quality design also may fail to provide the community with well-planned public spaces, such as parks and town centers.

✔ **Dependence on automobiles:** Traveling by car is often a necessity in suburban and exurban communities. In some suburban and exurban areas, the nearest "corner store" may be at a shopping center several miles away. Some places have great roads for cars but lack sidewalks, crosswalks, and other safety features that encourage walking and bicycling. And, somewhat ironically, some suburban and exurban areas are not well served by public transportation because it's typically more expensive to offer public transportation in areas with low population density.

Of course, not every newly developed neighborhood at the outer edge of a metropolitan area is sprawling. Many new communities have well-designed features and contribute to an overall pattern of regional development that conserves land and uses resources efficiently. By the year 2050, the number of people living in U.S. metropolitan areas may increase by more than 100 million people, and every region will have to figure out efficient and effective ways to accommodate growing populations.

Costs and Consequences: Why Urban Sprawl Matters

Sprawling land use patterns can have significant impact on multiple aspects of the community. For example, when farmland is converted into a housing subdivision, the most obvious consequence is that the land is no longer productive as an agricultural resource. But the impacts of development often are felt more broadly because new development requires more services — such as water and electricity — to be delivered to more distant areas or may cause increased traffic congestion.

In this section, I discuss the costs and consequences associated with urban sprawl, including how urban sprawl is related to concerns about environmental, economic, and social issues.

Spreading too far? Environmental impacts of urban sprawl

Sprawling land use patterns can have both direct and indirect impacts on the environment. For example, a housing subdivision built on a former cornfield transforms an agricultural land use into a residential land use. And changes in land use can indirectly impact the environment by increasing the overall use of resources.

The use of previously undeveloped and agricultural areas for suburban and exurban development may disturb environmentally sensitive areas, such as natural habitats or watersheds. The provision of infrastructure — such as water and sewer services — for new development may have additional impacts on the environment, especially when land or water resources have to be altered in order to provide additional services.

Sprawling land use patterns tend to increase automobile usage and traffic congestion. More miles on more cars means more pollution, especially air pollution due to automobile emissions.

Paying more, getting less: Sprawl and government spending

Poorly planned land use patterns can have a significant impact on governmental budgets, especially in areas where new development in sprawling areas requires increasing spending on the construction and maintenance of infrastructure and public services.

Here are two ways that urban sprawl can strain public resources:

- ✓ **Construction and maintenance of roads and highways:** Building and maintaining new roadways to service sprawling development at the outskirts of the metropolitan area is expensive. Providing roads and highways to areas with low-density development patterns also is less cost-efficient. For example, 1 mile of roadway that provides access to 200 homes is only half as cost-efficient as 1 mile of roadway that provides access to 400 homes.

✔ **Duplication of public services:** Sprawling areas typically demand the construction and operation of a wide range of public services, including schools or police stations. However, many governmental agencies wind up paying not just for new services in sprawling areas, but also to maintain public services in older areas that may be losing population to suburban and exurban areas.

Metropolitan areas with growing populations require additional spending on needed public services. However, the costs of sprawl are sometimes "hidden" when people and businesses follow sprawling land use patterns from one part of the metropolitan region to another. When this happens, one community's gain is often another community's loss. But, at the regional level, the costs of sprawl are often a zero-sum game, where the same number of people bear the costs of providing for increased spending on public services.

Growing apart: Sprawl and social issues

Sprawling land use patterns also are associated with a variety of social issues, including how urban sprawl is related to employment opportunities and health conditions. Many urban planners have expressed a growing concern over the potential social impacts of sprawl related to both the movement of people and businesses to the outer edges of metropolitan areas, as well as issues related to poorly planned, low-density land use patterns that are sometimes found in newly developed suburban and exurban areas. In the following sections, I cover some of these concerns.

Loss of a "sense of community"

A key concern of some architects and urban planners is that poorly designed low-density areas may not provide communities with public spaces that encourage social interaction, such as town squares or public plazas.

Health issues

There's growing concern that sprawling low-density areas may have a negative impact on long-term health conditions. Recent studies have suggested that the design of low-density areas can make people more dependent on automobiles in ways that discourage physical activity and may be linked to increased rates of obesity and high blood pressure.

Access to employment

Although many suburban and exurban areas are centers of employment for retailing, services, and office work, many of these employment opportunities aren't accessible to a significant portion of the population. As businesses move farther away from existing urban areas, they often become inaccessible by public transportation and difficult to reach for workers who lack regular access to an automobile.

Strengthening inner-ring suburbs

Inner-ring suburbs are older communities that are sandwiched between central cities and newer suburbs. This includes places such as Shaker Heights, just outside of Cleveland, Ohio, or Evanston, Illinois, just north of the city of Chicago. Many inner-ring suburbs were founded in the early 1900s and gained substantial populations after World War II. But today, some inner-ring suburbs are losing population and facing many of the same planning challenges as central cities, including housing abandonment and growing poverty.

In the Kansas City metropolitan area, a coalition of inner-ring suburbs has been working since 2002 to come up with solutions to their problems and advocate for state and regional policies to help direct reinvestment into existing communities. The First Suburbs Coalition (www.marc.org/firstsuburbs) includes 19 member communities in the states of Kansas and Missouri that are on a mission to "promote

sustainable communities with healthy environments, vital economies, and a high quality of life for all current residents and future generations by promoting the preservation, reinvestment, and revitalization of first suburb neighborhoods, commercial areas, and infrastructure."

The First Suburbs Coalition is working to promote increased investment in the transportation infrastructure, promote reinvestment in the housing stock, and promote the redevelopment of inner-ring commercial areas. Similar organizations exist in other parts of the United States, including the Michigan Suburbs Alliance (www.michigansuburbsalliance.org), which focuses on issues facing older suburbs in the Detroit region, and Ohio's First Suburbs Consortium (www.firstsuburbs.org), which represents communities in the Cincinnati, Cleveland, Columbus, and Dayton metropolitan areas.

Growing Smart and Sprawling Less

A wide range of approaches to local and regional planning can be used to curb sprawling land use patterns. Some approaches to growth management focus directly on land use issues and attempt to limit the amount or types of land that can be developed in a community or region, while other approaches deal with other planning components that are indirectly related to sprawling land use patterns, such as transportation, housing, and urban design.

The *smart growth* approach to local and regional planning uses techniques that allow communities to both keep up with the demand for new development and develop in ways that use resources efficiently and provide a high quality of life. The Smart Growth Network (www.smartgrowth.org), a collaborative partnership between the U.S. Environmental Protection Agency (EPA) and more than 40 other organizations and government agencies, works with communities and regions to promote planning and development using the Ten Principles of Smart Growth:

✔ Mix land uses.

✔ Take advantage of compact building design.

✔ Create a range of housing opportunities and choices.

✔ Create walkable neighborhoods.

✔ Foster distinctive, attractive communities with a strong sense of place.

✔ Preserve open space, farmland, natural beauty, and critical environmental areas.

✔ Strengthen and direct development toward existing communities.

✔ Provide a variety of transportation choices.

✔ Make development decisions predictable, fair, and cost effective.

✔ Encourage community and stakeholder collaboration in development decisions.

Many communities and regions have adapted the smart growth approach to local and regional planning in ways that are sensitive to local and regional conditions and meet the planning goals of their local and regional communities. The smart growth approach also has been used in different types of places, ranging from major metropolitan areas to rural regions:

✔ **Metropolitan San Diego:** The San Diego Association of Governments' 2004 *Regional Comprehensive Plan for the San Diego Region* (http://bit.ly/r3NnK0) uses smart growth principles to develop a long-range approach to the growth and development of the metropolitan area that "provides people with additional travel, housing, and employment choices by focusing future growth away from rural areas and closer to existing and planned job centers and public facilities, while preserving open space and natural resources and making more efficient use of existing urban infrastructure."

✔ **Hudson Valley, New York:** In upstate New York's Hudson Valley region, the Hudson Valley Smart Growth Alliance (www.sustainhv.org) has adopted a set of seven locally oriented principles to guide the future development of the region, including the following:

   • **Building close-knit, interconnected communities:** "Encourage compact, mixed-use development patterns, in and around existing centers and in locally identified priority growth areas, linked to more cost-efficient infrastructure and public services."

   • **Protecting our landscape legacy:** "Adopt protection measures for farmlands, important open space, parks, and critical natural and wildlife areas that create connected greenspace systems across municipal boundaries and through the region."

The Big Picture: Regional Strategies

Regional strategies to manage urban sprawl and encourage smart growth (see the preceding section) emphasize limiting the extent of new development, guiding the character of new development in ways that create enjoyable and efficient places, and directing growth to existing areas whenever possible. In some cases, regional plans are driven by statewide mandates requiring local and regional planning, while other regional planning initiatives are driven by "bottom-up" cooperation between local and regional agencies and organizations.

Promoting regional planning

Promoting smart solutions to avoid urban sprawl often requires the use of regional approaches that encourage cooperation between different communities. Regional planning allows for goals and objectives to be defined in broader terms and gives individual communities an overall framework for coming up with local approaches that help meet regional planning goals.

Here's an overview of some of the ways in which state, regional, and local communities can work together to promote regional planning:

- **Statewide plans and goals:** A growing number of states are taking a proactive approach to regional issues by developing statewide land use planning goals, creating statewide land use plans, and mandating regional planning.

  For example, the state of Oregon has adopted a set of 19 statewide planning goals that address issues including urban land use, transportation, and housing. And a few states — including Hawaii, New Jersey, and Rhode Island — have recently prepared statewide land use plans outlining desirable future development patterns.

- **Regional comprehensive plans:** A growing number of states are adopting regulations that mandate or promote comprehensive regional planning, and communities in many other metropolitan areas are working together voluntarily to create regional plans.

  For example, the state of Washington's Growth Management Act requires local and countywide comprehensive plans that consider regional development issues. In the greater Los Angeles area, the Southern California Association of Governments' 2008 *Regional Comprehensive Plan* (www.scag.ca.gov/rcp) "serves as an advisory document to local agencies in the Southern California region for their information and voluntary use for preparing local plans and handling local issues of regional significance."

✔ **Specialized regional plans:** Most metropolitan areas have agencies that produce specialized regional plans that address specific planning issues at the regional level. For example, federal regulations for transportation funding require most major metropolitan areas to have regional agencies known as *metropolitan planning organizations* and produce regional transportation plans that address local and regional transportation needs.

Visioning regional development patterns

One of the most valuable tools for promoting smart growth and avoiding sprawling land use patterns is a regional plan for future land use. A regional land use plan allows each community within the region to understand its role in the development of the region, develop local strategies to guide local development, and come up with local ways to meet regional land use objectives.

The most important function of a regional land use plan is to identify where future development will and won't take place:

✔ **Evaluating the development capacity in existing areas:** A regional plan looks at the existing pattern of development to locate areas within existing communities that have the capacity for additional development. This allows for future development to be guided toward existing areas that already have adequate access to public services and infrastructure.

✔ **Identifying the best areas for new development:** If additional land area is needed to accommodate future growth, a regional land use plan can help identify areas for possible expansion that will minimize negative impacts on the environment and can be connected easily to existing roadways and infrastructure.

✔ **Identifying conservation areas:** Regional land use plans also identify the areas within the region that are least suitable for development. This includes environmentally sensitive areas, as well as potential development sites that are distant from existing developed areas and may promote sprawling land use patterns.

In the same way that many local communities develop an overall conceptual vision for their future land use plans, a growing number of metropolitan and regional areas are developing regional visioning plans to envision the future shape and character of their region as a whole. These exercises not only help give direction to the entire region, but also provide each community with a specific role in directing the future of their region. For some examples of this approach, check out the nearby sidebar on regional visioning in Texas.

Taming the Texas Triangle?

The state of Texas gained more people than any another state in the United States between 2000 and 2010. During the 2000s, the population of the Lone Star State increased by nearly 4.3 million people, and much of that growth was concentrated in the Texas Triangle, a mega-region that connects four major metropolitan areas — Austin, Dallas–Fort Worth, Houston, and San Antonio — and stretches across 57,000 square miles in 66 counties. The four major metropolitan areas in the Texas Triangle areas grew by a combined 25 percent from 2000 to 2010 to a population of more than 16 million people. And, by some estimates, the entire Texas Triangle could be home to as many as 35 million people by 2050. However, much of this growth is taking place in sprawling suburban and semirural areas in ways that are straining the region's environmental resources, creating increasingly congested traffic patterns, and generating significant new costs for state and local governments.

In recent years, many of the communities in the Texas Triangle have started looking for regional planning solutions that can help the area keep up with rapid population growth. Regions including Austin, Dallas–Fort Worth, and Houston have recently developed regional vision plans that aim to tame sprawl and plan for sustainable futures:

✔ Around the Austin metropolitan area, the Envision Central Texas regional planning project asked the question: "What if a million more people lived in central Texas?" Envision Central Texas (www.envision centraltexas.org) worked with a broad range of community stakeholders to come up with a recommended strategy for the region's future land use that has a "greater developed area than today, but more compact and denser, considering how many more people live in the region." The plan also suggests that future development be concentrated near "an efficient transportation network of transit and roadways linking more densely populated areas" and that a dense development pattern will help preserve areas that are "green, with clean creeks and rivers, wildflower vistas, and open space."

✔ Vision North Texas launched its regional visioning effort in 2005 to develop a plan for a 16-county region including the Dallas–Fort Worth metropolitan area. One of the driving ideas behind Vision North Texas (www.visionnorthtexas.org) was that "business as usual" was likely to produce a future land use pattern characterized by low-density development in outlying areas, leading to the loss of more than 900,000 acres of agricultural land, strained infrastructure, and worse traffic. In addition to a regional vision that suggests guiding new development toward existing community and neighborhood centers, the Vision North Texas plan also includes an "action package" of steps that can be taken by the region's stakeholders to work toward making the vision a reality.

✔ In 2005, the Houston-Galveston Area Council (www.h-gac.com) began its initiative "to create a regional 'vision' or strategy to help successfully manage future growth." Known as Envision Houston Region, this effort sought ways to accommodate up to three million new residents over the next 30 years. Local leaders and community stakeholders came up with two new approaches to regional development that would focus new mixed-use development into town centers near existing transportation and mass transit routes, as well as additional mixed-use development areas in the region's satellite cities. These approaches can help communities through the Houston metropolitan region use less land, avoid traffic congestion, reduce pollution, and spend less on new infrastructure for water and sewer services.

Coordinating land use regionally

A growing number of states and local communities are adopting planning programs and policies that regulate and promote regional land use patterns. Some approaches directly regulate land use at the state and regional level, while others encourage cooperation in local planning and the provision of public services.

Urban growth boundaries

A limited number of metropolitan areas use urban growth boundaries to control land use patterns at the regional level. The states of Oregon and Washington provide metropolitan areas with special powers and regulations that allow them to designate urban growth boundaries and regulate the use of land inside and outside those boundaries. Many other areas indirectly influence the pattern of land development through controls on the provision of public services and infrastructure.

Urban service areas

An urban service area is a regional area where local and regional agencies are able to influence the character of future land use patterns by agreeing on what areas will be served by essential public services, such as roadways, utility services, and water systems. The designation of service areas typically is coordinated with local zoning and land use regulations to help guide new activities to areas designated for future development.

Coordinated planning

Several states have statewide provisions requiring local areas to plan in a coordinated fashion. For example, the state of Michigan's Coordinated Planning Act requires that communities allow adjacent communities to comment on their comprehensive plan prior to approval. The state of New Jersey has used a process known as *cross-acceptance,* in which local plans are reviewed by state, regional, and other local authorities in order to promote cooperation and consistency between communities.

Regional plans for coordinating local plans and the provision of public services can play an important role in promoting smarter regional development, but they're effective only when individual communities carry out the implementation of new strategies and approaches.

Conserving open space

Efforts to conserve open space not only help protect valuable natural and agricultural areas, but also promote a more compact pattern of regional development by establishing a "green" edge to the metropolitan area. A wide variety of approaches are used to conserve open space. These include land regulations and financial support for open space conservation, as well as efforts to preserve undeveloped areas and existing agricultural lands.

Preserving natural areas

The creation of greenways and beltways at the edges of metropolitan areas can provide the region with natural and recreational resources and help demarcate an informal growth boundary. In some cases, governmental agencies and non-profit organizations purchase land to be used as greenways and beltways.

Conservation easements also are used to promote the preservation of natural areas. A conservation easement allows a property owner to retain ownership and some use of the land, while transferring most of the development rights to a public agency or nonprofit organization.

Farmland preservation

Farmland preservation efforts typically involve a combination of regulatory and financial initiatives. Specialized zoning can be used to encourage the continued use of agricultural areas. Some communities have established programs that provide financial, marketing, and technical support to help farmers maintain the economic productivity of their land.

More than 20 states have established programs to encourage the *transfer* or *purchase of development rights* that allows owners of farmland to retain the active agricultural use of their land while granting a permanent conservation easement against further development to a government agency. Private non-profit organizations, known as *land trusts,* also work with agricultural land-owners to establishment conservation easements to protect farmland.

Making smart public investments

Sprawling land use patterns can create burdensome expenses for state, regional, and local government agencies that provide infrastructure and public service.

In the mid-1990s, the state of Maryland launched a statewide smart growth initiative to direct state funds for roadways, mass transit, school construction, and other projects toward existing areas in order to "save taxpayers from the high cost of building infrastructure to serve development that has spread far from our traditional population centers." (The state's former governor Parris Glendenning coined the term *smart growth.*)

Smart public investments can help guide future development toward existing areas and undeveloped areas that have been planned for future growth. Some states and local communities have designated specific locations as *priority funding areas* that are eligible to receive special funding for infrastructure and public service projects that strengthen existing communities. Many governmental jurisdictions also carry out *development impact studies* or *cost-benefit studies* that help determine if public investments will be cost-effective and whether they'll encourage sprawling land use and development patterns.

Local Solutions: What Cities and Suburbs Can Do

A growing number of communities are "thinking regionally and acting locally" to plan and encourage the development of places that help their region grow and change in ways that curb sprawl and contribute to the regional quality of life. Local planning, regulation, and development programs play an especially valuable role in promoting sustainable regional development because local policies typically determine how much development takes place, what kinds of development occur, where development happens, and whether development is well designed.

Designing communities with compact land use patterns

Creating spaces within the community that utilize compact land use patterns not only conserves the amount of land needed for essential functions, such as housing and workplaces, but typically also requires that less area be used for supportive infrastructure and services, such as roadways and parking lots.

Here are some approaches to compact development at the local level:

✔ **Encourage transit-oriented development.** Transit-oriented development allows for the creation of more compact land use patterns by clustering mixed-use development in walkable areas that are accessible by public transportation. The transit-oriented development approach not only supports land use patterns that are more compact at the local level, but also can provide areas that contribute to greater use of public transportation at the regional level.

✔ **Promote mixed-use areas.** Areas that feature a mix of land uses provide the opportunity to locate different features and services closer together. This often enables planners, developers, and designers to come up with more compact building arrangements and decrease the amount of space that is needed for transportation between places.

✔ **Build at appropriate densities.** The alternative to "building out" is "building up," and many communities are embracing development strategies that use land more efficiently by increasing density patterns. But there's no absolute rule for "how dense is too dense" — in some communities, new mid-rise apartment buildings may fit well into the local landscape, while in other places a decrease in the average lot size of single-family homes from one-half acre to one-third acre may represent a reasonable change.

✔ **Involve stakeholders.** Some local officials are reluctant to plan and implement measures to promote denser, more compact development because they're concerned about negative reactions from community members. Getting opinions and input from the community on future development patterns can help local officials and urban planners better understand what types of development will be embraced by the community.

Many communities fail to develop compact development patterns due to zoning codes and land use regulations that allow for sprawling low-density development. But there are a variety of ways to better understand how local regulations help shape the community. Some communities have conducted *build-out analyses* that use maps to show what the community's land use pattern would look like if every parcel of land were developed according to prevailing zoning and land use regulation. Maps of potential build-out patterns often demonstrate that local regulations may permit far more development than is necessary to meet local demand and in places that are unconnected to the existing pattern of development.

Extreme makeover, suburban edition

Many suburban areas are places that people love and offer a great quality of life, but some aren't. Some suburban areas have experienced years of decline, while others are generally stable but offer little in the way of enjoyable amenities to the community. In their book, *Retrofitting Suburbia: Urban Design Solution for Redesigning Suburbs,* Ellen Dunham-Jones and June Williamson look into three ways to remake suburbs, including re-inhabitation, redevelopment, and regreening:

✔ **Re-inhabitation:** Jones and Williamson suggest that some abandoned suburban buildings can be re-inhabited in ways that can stimulate social interaction in the community, such as the conversion of former big-box stores or industrial warehouses into up-to-date educational facilities or recreation centers.

✔ **Redevelopment:** Redevelopment can be used to replace existing buildings and vulnerable areas — such as surface parking lots — with new development that emphasizes public space and is connected to the rest of the community by public transportation, walking paths, or bicycle routes.

✔ **Regreening:** If new uses for obsolete buildings are hard to come by, regreening tactics can be used to demolish unneeded structures and refit the land as an ecological asset, such as a community garden, small habitat area, or artificial wetland.

Over the long run, every community goes through a process of change and requires periodic maintenance and upkeep. Suburban retrofitting can help many older suburbs renew themselves in ways that strengthen the community, attract a new generation of residents, and help curb urban sprawl by making good use of existing resources.

Staying put: Building communities for the long term

Creating communities with enduring qualities that people will enjoy for decades and generations can help curtail urban sprawl by giving people a reason to stay put, instead of continually moving into areas farther and farther away from the edges of metropolitan areas.

Here are some strategies that communities can use to maintain their viability over the long term:

- **Plan for maintenance and re-investment.** Cities, towns, and suburbs need to plan ahead for the ongoing maintenance of their infrastructure and public utilities. Well-maintained communities often are at an advantage in retaining their businesses and residents, as well as being magnets for continued private investment in homes and businesses.

- **Support diverse housing.** A diverse housing stock can encourage the long-term use and reuse of the community by people of different ages and backgrounds. For example, if a community has a blend of large and small homes, apartments, and condominiums, it allows people to remain in the community at different stages of their lives. A stock of well-maintained apartments can help communities retain empty nesters who decide to downsize from houses to apartments.

- **Accommodate a diversity of land uses and building types.** Land use plans, zoning codes, and other land use regulations that allow for diverse land uses and allow for changes in land use to occur naturally over time can help a community grow and change gracefully. For example, the recent application of *form-based codes* in urban design emphasizes building form over building use in ways that allow a single building to have many different uses over its lifetime.

- **Create a sense of place.** People will choose to stay in communities that feel like home. Providing the community with amenities and services such as attractive public spaces and recreational activities can reinforce a sense of community.

Community-building strategies can be worked into many components of a local comprehensive plan. For example, a strategy to provide diverse housing can be addressed not only in the housing goals of a plan, but also through land use, infrastructure, and transportation goals that support the location, maintenance, and accessibility of the housing stock.

Chapter 14

Healing the City: Planning and Disasters

. . . .

In This Chapter

▶ Identifying types of disasters

▶ Planning an effective response when disaster strikes

▶ Recovering, rebuilding, and replanning after a disaster

. . . .

*N*ew York City. New Orleans. Port-au-Prince, Haiti. Fukushima, Japan. These places have become synonymous with the disasters that they've endured: terrorist attacks, hurricanes, earthquakes, and tsunamis and nuclear meltdown. Today's cities and towns are more aware than ever of the potential for disaster to strike — whether it's a natural occurrence or a manmade event — and urban plans are increasingly addressing ways for communities to minimize their risks and be prepared in the event that a disaster occurs.

In this chapter, I look into how communities can rise to the challenge of planning for hazards and disasters by doing the following:

✔ Developing preventive plans that identify and address potential risks and hazards

✔ Preparing plans for emergency response in the event of a disaster

✔ Planning for short-term and long-term disaster recovery

In recent years, many communities have adopted *disaster resilience* as a goal of their local planning efforts. This approach recognizes that every community, regardless of past history, bears some risk of disaster occurrence and that careful planning of the community's land use and development patterns can help minimize the consequences of a disaster.

Recognizing Risks in a Changing World

An increasing number of communities are acting on the old adage that "an ounce of prevention is worth a pound of cure." Many places are developing local plans that take into account the potential for disasters to have a broad impact on the community, including both immediate impacts — such as loss of life, personal injuries, and damage to property — and far-ranging economic, social, and environmental impacts. In this section, I talk about the types of disasters that are being addressed in local plans and who's involved in planning for disaster prevention and recovery efforts.

Cities at risk: Types of hazards

Cities and towns face many types of hazards, both natural and manmade. Some disastrous events occur because of the interaction between natural conditions and human behaviors. For example, the extent of the damage associated with Hurricane Katrina in New Orleans in 2005 is described by many researchers as a product of both severe weather conditions and the failure of the manmade system of levees intended to protect the city from flooding.

Natural hazards

Natural hazards are events and conditions that exist due to the characteristics of the physical environment, such as extreme weather events or earthquakes. The U.S. Federal Emergency Management Agency (FEMA) uses five broad classifications to describe natural hazards:

- **Atmospheric hazards:** Atmospheric hazards include a wide range of extreme weather conditions, such as hurricanes, tornadoes, hailstorms, severe heat or cold, and lightning. Weather-related hazards can trigger or complicate other types of hazards, such as a wildfire that is ignited by a lightning strike.

- **Seismic hazards:** Seismic hazards have to do with the shifting conditions of the earth's crust. Seismic shifts are the cause of earthquakes and tsunamis.

- **Hydrologic hazards:** These hazards are associated with the presence and movement of water, such as floods, droughts, and storm surges.

- **Geologic hazards:** Geologic hazards are related to the underlying dynamics of the soils, minerals, and other materials that shape the surface of the earth. Common geological hazards include landslides, soil erosion, and sinkholes. These hazards often are triggered by natural events, such as weather conditions, and by human actions, such as mining or construction.

✔ **Other hazards:** People, property, and the environment are threatened by a wide range of idiosyncratic natural hazards, such as wildfires and volcanic activity.

The geographic extent of hazardous conditions can vary widely, and every community has its own range of hazards. For example, an extreme weather event such as a hurricane typically threatens very large geographic areas. In contrast, some hazards may be very localized, such as small areas within a community that are susceptible to landslides or sinkholes.

Manmade hazards

A wide range of recent events has brought attention to disasters resulting from human actions and manmade hazards, including the 9/11 terrorist attacks on New York City and Washington, D.C., and the failure of flood levees in New Orleans during Hurricane Katrina. Manmade hazards are broad in scope and generally include the following:

✔ **Technological hazards:** FEMA describes technological hazards as accidental or unintentional hazards arising from the human use of hazardous materials, such as explosives, toxic substances, infectious materials, nuclear and radioactive materials, and flammable or corrosive substances.

✔ **Terrorism:** Specific hazards arising from terrorist acts are not well defined and have typically involved unpredictable human behaviors to deliberately cause harm to people, property, and the environment, including the use of biological, chemical, and explosive materials, as well as armed attacks and *cyber* (computer-based) disruption of essential activities.

✔ **Structural hazards:** Many hazards are brought on by the poor condition or failure of building structures and infrastructure, such as dam failures, underground pipe leaks, and bridge collapses.

Federal, state, and local agencies are increasingly using a *multi-hazards approach* to identifying risks, which recognizes that local areas may be vulnerable to several different types of hazards and that some types of hazards may interact with each other.

For example, the 2011 nuclear disaster in Fukushima, Japan, was caused by an offshore earthquake that also triggered a powerful tsunami, which, in turn, caused severe damage in cities and towns along the coastline and further complicated the response to the nuclear disaster.

Who helps?

A wide range of government agencies and other community stakeholders typically are involved in making pre-disaster and post-disaster plans, as well as assisting in the response to and recovery from the occurrence of a disaster.

This section provides an overview of the different parties that usually are involved and the role that each plays.

Urban planning agencies

Local planning departments are involved in preparing pre-disaster and post-disaster plans. They're often essential to disaster relief efforts by providing maps and information about the community, including resources related to housing, transportation, infrastructure, land use, and environmental features.

Local agencies and departments

Police, fire, and emergency services departments are deeply involved in preparing disaster-related plans and serve as first-responders in the event of a disaster. Many other branches of local government, such as transportation agencies and public works departments, also are involved in planning and disaster-response efforts.

Local officials and community stakeholders

Elected officials, residents, and other stakeholders play an important role in helping to plan for potential disasters by identifying community concerns and priorities. In the event of a disaster, local officials help make decisions about the course of disaster response and recovery, and provide information and resources to help residents respond and recover from disasters.

Utility companies and other businesses

Utility providers and local businesses play a key role in identifying important elements of the community that may be particularly vulnerable to disasters, such as chemical factories or power generation facilities. These parties are often critical to disaster response and recovery efforts because they supply resources that are necessary for the effective operation of the community, such as water, power, mechanical equipment, and food supplies.

For example, Walmart utilized its extensive transportation and warehousing resources to provide food and emergency supplies to residents of New Orleans in the aftermath of Hurricane Katrina, reaching some areas with food and emergency supplies before government agencies and other disaster relief organizations did.

Other local agencies and nonprofit organizations

A wide variety of healthcare and human service agencies typically are involved in disaster planning and recovery. For example, local Red Cross chapters provide emergency supplies and shelters, local hospitals maintain contingency plans in the event of a disaster, and local school districts often use school buildings as shelters and community centers during a disaster.

State and federal agencies

A wide range of state and federal agencies are involved in pre-disaster planning and disaster recovery. Several federal agencies — including FEMA and the Army Corps of Engineers — provide assistance to state and local governments in the preparation of pre-disaster plans.

In the event of a disaster, federal and state agencies provide assistance to local communities in areas ranging from the provision of equipment and temporary housing to the assignment of National Guard troops to assist in disaster response and recovery. Residents and businesses in areas that have experienced a disaster often are assisted by state and federal post-disaster programs.

Planning for Disaster-Resistant Communities

A pre-disaster plan helps the community understand the risks that it faces and outlines a program of policies and actions that can be undertaken in order to reduce those risks. Urban planners refer to this as *hazard-mitigation planning.* Planning for hazard mitigation can be addressed in both the community's official comprehensive plan and in specialized plans:

- **Local comprehensive plans:** Due to a rising awareness of the human and financial costs of disasters, an increasing number of communities are addressing hazard mitigation in their local comprehensive plans, and some states are mandating that local plans specifically address hazard mitigation.

   According to the American Planning Association and the Insurance Institute for Business & Home Safety, 11 states require local comprehensive plans to address hazard mitigation issues. For example, the state of Oregon's statewide planning regulations require that "local governments shall adopt comprehensive plans to reduce risk to people and property from natural hazards."

✔ **Specialized plans:** Many communities also maintain specialized plans addressing hazard mitigation concerns. In some cases, local areas are required to prepare specialized plans in order to be eligible for state and federal funding programs. A variety of federal programs and policies promote local planning for hazard mitigation, including the federal Disaster Mitigation Act and National Flood Insurance Program, as well as programs related to earthquake and wildfire preparedness.

For example, the *Seattle All-Hazards Mitigation Plan* (`http://1.usa.gov/rSicx6`) addresses potential hazards faced by the city of Seattle — ranging from earthquakes and floods to landslides and snowstorms — and outlines potential mitigation measures, including upgrading the city's water supply facilities and updating the city's building regulations.

Whether it's part of a specialized plan or a comprehensive plan, local planning for hazard mitigation emphasizes two major issues:

✔ The identification of potential risks and hazards

✔ Steps that can be taken to *mitigate* (reduce) hazards prior to the occurrence of a disaster

Assessing community risks

The first step toward hazard mitigation is to determine the hazards that currently exist within the community. The hazard identification process not only creates a greater awareness of the risks faced by the community, but also allows the community to prioritize how it will allocate resources to address hazards and the order in which to address threatening conditions.

A community's hazard mitigation strategies may need to be updated on a regular basis, because the risks faced by a community can change over time. For example, housing development that occurs in or near forested areas can increase the community's overall risk of damage due to the spread of wildfires. Regular updates of the community's risk assessment can help adjust to changing circumstances and further protect the community.

Identifying hazards

There are many ways for a community to identify its risks and hazards. Information about some hazardous features is readily available from governmental agencies, such as reports of seismic activity, wildfire risk estimates, or permitting records for the use of hazardous chemicals.

The use of standardized risk assessment procedures — such as those promoted by FEMA and state emergency management agencies — can be especially useful for identifying hazards at the local level because some communities may not be aware of the full range of possible threats present in the community. Maps showing the location or impact of likely hazards often are prepared at the local level and can help local planners coordinate hazard mitigation efforts with the community's comprehensive plan.

Setting priorities

In addition to identifying potential risks, many communities also try to estimate the potential impacts of disaster occurrences. For example:

- ✔ How many acres of urbanized land are vulnerable to wildfires?
- ✔ How many lives could be lost?
- ✔ How many people could be injured?
- ✔ What would the financial cost be?

Assessing the potential impact of hazards can help the community raise, prioritize, and allocate the resources to address the situations that pose the greatest risk to the community.

Reducing potential hazards: The enemy you know

Although eliminating every risk that endangers a community isn't possible, hazard mitigation plans aim to reduce the occurrence and severity of potential disasters in ways that help save lives and reduce injuries, minimize damage to buildings and infrastructure, prevent severe economic losses, and help the community maintain its essential services during and after a disaster. The costs and complexities of hazard mitigation can range from relatively simple steps, such as creating an evacuation plan, to expensive long-term projects, such as reinforcing seawalls and flood barriers.

Mitigating existing hazards

Hazard mitigation is the process of reducing risks posed by existing threats. There are two general approaches to making a community more resistant to potential hazards:

- ✔ Directly dealing with the source of the hazards
- ✔ Providing the community with greater protection from the hazards

Hazard mitigation efforts often rely on extensive cooperation between different governmental agencies, as well as the involvement of residents and businesses. It may be possible to carry out some hazard mitigation efforts in a short period of time, while more complicated hazard mitigation efforts — such as the reinforcement of a major bridge — may take years to complete.

Directly dealing with the source of the hazards

Efforts to deal directly with a hazard typically aim to eliminate or manage the hazard:

- ✔ **Reducing the hazard:** Sometimes called *hazard abatement,* this approach aims to directly eliminate or reduce the extent of hazards. For example, many wildfires are fed by ground-level vegetation, so the clearing of ground-level vegetation can be an effective way of preventing or limiting the severity of a wildfire.

- ✔ **Containing the hazard:** Eliminating some hazards may not be possible, but it may be possible to isolate or contain a hazard in ways that reduce its impact. For example, cleared buffer zones between forested and residential areas can help isolate the impact of a wildfire and prevent it from spreading to nearby homes.

- ✔ **Preparing for a hazard:** Effectively containing or eliminating a hazard may not be possible; some known hazards — such as nuclear power generation — are calculated risks. However, advance preparations for potential disasters — such as monitoring systems, emergency notification procedures, and evacuation plans — can help reduce the impact and severity in the event that a disaster occurs due to a known risk.

Providing the community with greater protection from the hazards

Other approaches to reducing the risk of local hazards emphasize protecting the community from a potential disaster. It may be possible to provide the community with additional protection from a known hazard, such as retrofitting buildings to make them more resistant to earthquakes or improving flood control barriers to protect highly prone areas.

In some cases, putting some distance between some features of the community and a known hazard may be desirable. For example, many communities have regulations that mandate minimum distances between residential areas and factories that use hazardous materials.

Growing safe

The way in which a community grows and changes may introduce it to new risks. Planning for development that avoids potential risks enhances the security of the community. The American Planning Association defines *safe growth* as an approach to development that builds "environments that are safe for current and future generations of people" and protects the community's buildings, infrastructure, and environment.

A variety of approaches can be used to promote safer growth:

✔ **Develop in safe locations.** Local plans can improve the safety of the community by promoting future development in areas with the least hazardous conditions. Providing infrastructure and services in ways that help direct growth away from hazardous areas also can help reduce the community's vulnerability.

✔ **Design hazard resistant facilities.** Urban design guidelines and up-to-date building regulations can help communities avoid development that may be overly susceptible to hazards.

✔ **Assess risks on a case-by-case basis.** Land development projects typically require numerous reviews and approvals for everything from architectural design to parking requirements. Reviewing development proposals for specific risks can help identify issues and safety concerns that can be resolved prior to development.

Urban planners Jim Schwab and David Godschalk have developed a method called a *safe-growth audit* that communities can use to improve local plans. A safe-growth audit assesses how well a local plan promotes safe growth by asking questions such as the following:

✔ Is transportation policy used to guide growth to safe areas?

✔ Does the future land use map clearly identify natural hazard areas?

You can learn more about safe growth from the American Planning Association's Hazards Planning Research Center online at www.planning. org/nationalcenters/hazards.

Recovering from Disasters: Rebuilding Cities and Restoring Communities

A major disaster can strike in an instant, but the ways in which a community recovers from a disaster often happen in successive stages over days, months, and years. The most immediate reaction to a disaster is to provide immediate relief while the disaster is occurring and in the hours and days after.

After the situation is stabilized, post-disaster recovery moves on to dealing with short-term and long-term issues, from providing temporary shelter for displaced residents to rebuilding damaged infrastructure. Getting to the "new normal" can be a challenge for every community that experiences a disaster. A good pre-disaster plan can help a community begin its recovery in ways that are more organized and less stressful.

Disaster preparedness and emergency response: Helping in a hurry

Due to federal and state regulations, nearly every community in the United States has some sort of plan for dealing with the immediate consequences of a disaster. These plans, sometimes called *emergency operations plans,* identify who does what in the event of a disaster, including the role of emergency service providers, other governmental agencies, businesses, and people in the community.

The scope and complexity of emergency operations plans vary from one community to the next, but they typically address three main elements:

- ✔ **Ending the problem:** Stopping the damaging impacts of a disaster — such as putting out fires brought on by an earthquake or halting a flood by erecting sandbag barriers — is a high priority of an emergency plan. Not every type of disaster can be foreseen, but many local emergency plans address ways that resources can be quickly mobilized in the event of a disaster.

- ✔ **Providing aid and relief:** Helping those impacted by disasters is an immediate concern of an emergency plan and can involve ways to carry out a wide range of supportive actions, from organizing evacuations and designating shelter areas to providing medical care, food, and water.

- ✔ **Restoring operations:** Most major disasters interrupt the normal functions of the community, causing power outages, the loss of water supplies, or the closure of roads and bridges. Plans to restore operations help with the overall process of disaster recovery and are essential to long-term rebuilding efforts.

The incorporation of emergency operations concerns into the community's comprehensive plan can strengthen the ability of local emergency services to respond to disasters. Many of the resources that may be called upon during a disaster — such as evacuation routes or buildings to serve as emergency shelters — can be identified during the comprehensive planning process and can help ensure that adequate resources are available should they be necessary.

Post-disaster re-planning and rebuilding

Post-disaster recovery can take place over both the short term and the long term, although both of these time frames are relative to the needs of the community. In some cases, it may take just a few weeks for some communities to resume the normal pace of life, whereas in other communities the process may take much longer.

Prepared for the worst in Panama City

Panama City is a community of more than 35,000 people in the Florida panhandle, best known by many people as a vacation destination for college students who pack the area during spring break. Although some residents may consider the annual throng of spring-breakers to be a hazardous situation, the city has had the good fortune of being narrowly spared from some of the worst weather disasters that have struck the Gulf Coast region, including Hurricane Opal in 1995 and Hurricane Ivan in 2004.

But if disaster strikes, the city has a plan. In 2008, the city of Panama City completed its *Post-Disaster Redevelopment Plan* (http://bit.ly/w3q7on). The plan is a comprehensive guide that "identifies policies, operational strategies, and roles and responsibilities for implementation that will guide decisions that affect community long-term recovery and redevelopment after a disaster." The plan provides the community with a framework for integrating local redevelopment efforts with resources from federal, state, and county emergency management agencies.

The *Post-Disaster Redevelopment Plan* addresses a wide range of issues that would be critical to the redevelopment of the community in the event of a major disaster, including providing long-term housing for displaced residents, streamlining the redevelopment process to encourage rebuilding, providing financial assistance to local businesses, repairing infrastructure and public facilities, and restoring the environment. Panama City's disaster contingency plan outlines many steps that will be taken to improve the community's disaster readiness, including "meet[ing] with local hotels and condo owners in the city and surrounding areas to determine which can be used for temporary housing" and "encourag[ing] businesses to seek insurance that could cover business interruptions from disasters and/or set aside emergency funds for use after a disaster."

The state of Florida's Post-Disaster Redevelopment Planning program is working with communities across the state to prepare local plans similar to Panama City's. You can check out *Post-Disaster Redevelopment Planning: A Guide for Florida Communities* at http://bit.ly/rCCSO7. For more on Florida's Post-Disaster Redevelopment Planning project, go to http://bit.ly/tthnDf.

In 2011, New York City recognized the tenth anniversary of the 9/11 terrorist attack on the city with the opening of the National September 11 Memorial & Museum (www.911memorial.org). The Freedom Tower skyscraper at the World Trade Center site is expected to be completed by 2013.

Short-term recovery

Short-term recovery measures are used both to continue the immediate response to a disaster and to work toward long-term recovery. These measures address the consequences of the disaster, enable the community to function in a more regular manner, and begin to put resources in place for long-term recovery.

Short-term recovery efforts are a bridge to long-term reconstruction. Some of the "temporary" features that are instituted during the short-term recovery phase deliberately or inadvertently become long-term features of the community.

For example, FEMA provided thousands of trailer homes as temporary housing for Gulf Coast residents after Hurricane Katrina and some residents remained in the temporary trailers for more than four years after the disaster.

Assessing the damage

Determining the extent of damage caused to buildings, property, and the environment is a key task of short-term recovery. Damage assessment is used to identify buildings that may need to be demolished, structures that can be repaired, and areas that are safe for people to reoccupy. Some communities institute a moratorium on new building projects during the short-term period after a disaster in order to determine if proposed projects can be built safely.

Providing temporary sites

A community may need to provide a wide range of activities on a temporary basis, including housing, schools, or business activities. Local authorities typically work with community stakeholders and other agencies to determine what temporary activities need to be provided and where they can be sited.

Making repairs

The repair and restoration of some essential services or elements of the community — such as damaged roadways or electrical infrastructure — can take weeks or months. Repairs to essential features help the community get back to normal. Alternate arrangements — such as road detours or reduced service levels — may need to be accommodated during the repair period.

Providing assistance

In the aftermath of a disaster, people and businesses may require extensive personal and financial support. For example, short-term business loans may be used to help businesses operate until they can recover their losses. Many communities benefit from community-based counseling and mental health services that help people cope with personal and emotional impacts in the wake of a disaster.

Long-term rebuilding and replanning

Some disasters cause extensive loss of life, cause billions of dollars' worth of damage, and can have a significant impact on the environment. In these cases, the period of rebuilding and replanning can last for years, if not decades. After an extreme disaster, the long-term rebuilding needs of the community may not have been foreseen by the community's pre-disaster plans; many places have been forced to undertake extensive post-disaster replanning in order to begin the process of recovery.

The scope of a post-disaster rebuilding plan may be quite broad and address many of the same elements as a comprehensive plan:

- **Physical recovery:** Planning for the long-term physical recovery of the community typically involves the following:
    - Identifying rebuilding projects
    - Revising existing zoning and land use regulations to both encourage rebuilding and prevent rebuilding in hazard-prone areas
    - Planning for the use of financial support programs to help people and businesses rebuild structures that have been destroyed or damaged

- **Economic recovery:** A major disaster can severely interrupt the normal workings of the community's businesses. The structures housing some businesses may be damaged or destroyed, and interruptions to normal business may cause economic hardships. Long-term recovery plans look for ways to restore business operations and encourage new businesses to relocate to locations that may be less vulnerable to future disasters.

- **Environmental recovery:** Replanning after a disaster often addresses environmental issues in ways that stabilize environmental resources involved in natural disasters — such as reinforcing flood levees. In addition, the replanning of environmental features can help protect the community in the future, such as increasing the buffer zone between homes and wildfire-prone areas.

- **Social recovery:** Long-term recovery from a major disaster also involves providing supportive services to people impacted by the disaster, as well as tending to the needs of the community as a whole. Long-term recovery also may need to address community changes that have taken place as a result of the disaster.

For example, an estimated 100,000 people who evacuated the New Orleans area in 2005 during Hurricane Katrina did not return, leading to significant changes in the demographic makeup of the city. (For more information on the post-Katrina recovery of New Orleans, check out Chapter 21.)

Chapter 15

Taking Care of Business: Jobs and Economic Development

. . . .

In This Chapter

▶ Building on the strengths of the local economy

▶ Attracting new businesses to the community

▶ Providing incentives and assistance to help businesses create new jobs

. . . .

*E*very community faces a unique set of challenges when it comes to dealing with the local economy. During the 1980s and 1990s, the Fort Wayne, Indiana, metropolitan area, with a population of more than 400,000 people, fared relatively better than other places in Indiana and nearby states. During this period, the number of people and jobs in the city of Fort Wayne and the surrounding Allen County increased. But more doesn't always mean better: The area lost about 10 percent of its higher-paying jobs in the manufacturing sector from 1979 to 1999. Most of the new jobs that appeared were in lower-paying occupations in retail and service industries. The area's standard of living fell during this period as per capita income went from well above the national average to below the national average.

Looking for a solution to the area's lagging economic conditions, a task force of local officials, business leaders, and community representatives came together in 2000 to create a strategic plan to promote "quality job creation." The *Economic Development Action Plan for Fort Wayne and Northeast Indiana* (http://bit.ly/tVHw7s) set its sights on improving business and job opportunities through promoting regional cooperation, supporting business development, diversifying the local economy, improving local infrastructure, providing good locations for new businesses, and improving the skills of the local workforce.

In this chapter, I take a look at what communities can do to plan a successful local economy. I offer some details about the goals of planning for economic development and examining local economic conditions. Finally, I provide an overview of both broad approaches and specific programs that communities use to maintain and improve the health of their local economies.

Making Places That Work

The overall quality of life in every community depends on the health and productivity of its workers and local businesses. Plans for local economic development address ways to maintain and improve the performance of the local economy. A wide range of community stakeholders are involved in making plans for local economic development, and creating an effective plan requires a thorough and accurate assessment of the community's economic strengths and weaknesses.

Helping the local economy

Planning for local economic development involves coordinating economic development programs with the overall goals of the community's comprehensive plan and often involves developing strategic plans addressing short-term local economic development issues. These efforts identify the strengths and weaknesses of the local economy and help the community develop broad goals and economic development initiatives addressing concerns such as the following:

- **Creating jobs:** An increase in local employment opportunities is the most basic measure of progress for local economic development programs. Although good-paying full-time jobs are often the goal of local programs, many useful efforts also aim to create part-time jobs or entry-level jobs that can lead to better employment opportunities for local workers.

- **Improving incomes:** Not all jobs are created equal. Although every local economy requires a diversity of jobs — ranging from barbers to undertakers to CEOs — local economic development efforts typically focus on supporting the creation of jobs that pay above-average wages and contribute to income growth within the community.

- **Revitalizing industrial and commercial areas:** Local economic development efforts are closely coordinated with the community's land use plan to help encourage the revitalization of abandoned or underused industrial and commercial areas.

- **Stabilizing fiscal conditions:** Local economic development efforts also are aimed at improving governmental revenue from taxes, fees, and other charges. A healthy economy helps local government agencies fund high-quality community services, such as schools, parks, social programs, and road maintenance.

In addition to local agencies and officials, a wide variety of stakeholders are involved in developing local plans for economic development. These partners include federal and state agencies, special authorities (such as redevelopment agencies or school districts), private businesses, philanthropic and charitable organizations, and community organizations. Some strategies and implementation steps identified in local plans are carried out by local government agencies, while others may be implemented through partnerships with stakeholders.

Looking at the local economy

Making plans to improve the condition of the local economy requires a broad understanding of relevant current conditions and trends. Here's an overview of the types of information that are typically collected and analyzed in order to plan for local economic development:

- **Economic trends and conditions:** Measuring the health of the local economy can be a tricky task because several different types of information can be used to measure local economic trends and conditions:

    - **Employment and unemployment:** Data on employment and unemployment are basic measures of the health of the local economy. An increase in the unemployment rate or data showing job losses are warning signs of economic decline.

    - **Income:** Data on income and wages is a valuable measure of the overall health of the local economy. Increases in average wages or household incomes are usually a good sign for the local economy.

    - **Fiscal measures:** Keeping an eye on fiscal conditions — especially the amount of revenue taken in by local government to pay for public services — is important because decreasing tax revenue collections are a sign of problems in the local economy. For example, a decrease in local sales tax revenue is often due to job losses or declining incomes in the community.

    - **Other measures:** Plans for local economic development often utilize highly detailed information or specially produced studies about the local economy, such as reports on the number of new business startups in the community or detailed demographic characteristics of unemployed workers.

- **Structure of the local economy:** Local plans often identify the industries and specific economic activities that are most important to the local economy. As discussed in Chapter 2, many communities have lost jobs in manufacturing industries but have gained jobs in service-related industries. Understanding how specific industries are changing can help communities plan for ways to support declining industries and enhance successful industries.

- **Population characteristics:** Trends and conditions affecting the local population are also useful economic indicators. Measures such as household income, occupational characteristics, and levels of educational attainment often are used to analyze the performance of the local economy and identify areas for future improvement.

✔ **Geographic differences:** Detailed information about different geographic sub-areas within the community — such as specific neighborhoods or business districts — and maps that show the geographic distribution of economic trends and conditions often are used in plans for local economic development to identify target areas for the implementation of economic development programs and related revitalization efforts.

Accurate and timely information about the local economy is an essential element of a local plan for economic development. But these measures are sometimes difficult to interpret. For example, what's a good unemployment rate? 2 percent? 10 percent? 20 percent? There's certainly a big difference between a 2 percent unemployment rate and a 20 percent unemployment rate, but there's no correct answer.

One way to effectively interpret the meaning of local measures is to compare them to statewide or national trends. This helps answer the question of whether the local community is "falling behind" or "keeping up" with the competition. A growing local economy may be falling behind if it's growing more slowly than the statewide economy, and a local area that experiences a small drop in employment may actually be performing relatively well if there's an even larger decline in statewide employment conditions.

Planning for Local Economic Development

There are many approaches to planning for the improvement of the local economy, from attracting businesses to the community, to educating workers for better jobs, to promoting scientific innovation within the community. In this section, I cover some of the most common ways in which communities make plans to strengthen their local economies.

Strengthening the community's economic base

The *economic base* of the community consists of economic activities that draw economic resources into the area and help recirculate income within the local economy. For example, industrial factories are a valuable component of the local economic base because they typically produce items that are sold nationally or globally and bring outside investment into the community.

In the following sections, I cover some of the ways that communities are trying to enhance their economic bases.

Targeting specific industries

Many communities have developed economic development strategies that focus on building up specific industries that can bring new income into the community and provide good employment opportunities.

For example, several cities — including Cleveland, Detroit, and Pittsburgh — have recently established local initiatives to support film and television productions, which can provide a boost to local hotels, restaurants, caterers, technical support workers, and transportation providers.

Targeting industry clusters

In addition to targeting specific industries, many plans for local economic development target so-called *industry clusters* (groups of related industries that may share common resources, such as similarly skilled workers or specific types of infrastructure). For example, a cluster of biomedical industries may include local hospitals and equipment manufacturers hoping to collaborate on the development of new medical devices.

The Metro Denver Economic Development Corporation regional economic development strategy identifies seven industry clusters that are key to the health of the local economy. One of these industry clusters is "Broadcasting and Communications," which includes a variety of related businesses employing workers serving not just local consumers, but also statewide, national, and international markets in a variety of areas, including media production, electronics engineering, and telecommunications services.

Diversifying the local economy

Even places with thriving economies make plans to diversify their economic bases. Efforts to increase business activities in industries that don't have a strong presence in the local economy represent both a way to grow the local economy, as well as a way to protect the local economy from downturns in the condition of existing industries.

Buying local

Campaigns urging residents and local businesses to spend their dollars locally can help strengthen the local economy by retaining economic activity that would otherwise leave the community. Sometimes called *import substitution,* this approach involves efforts such as finding local suppliers for other local businesses and encouraging shoppers to "buy local."

The Greater Des Moines Partnership's Buy into the Circle program (www. buyintothecircle.com) helps local companies identify local vendors for office supplies production, specialized equipment, and professional services.

Developing major projects: Build it and they will come?

Many cities and towns have promoted the development of major attractions that promote tourism and help revitalize ailing areas. These efforts aim to increase outside spending in the local economy and have a positive indirect contribution. For example, when families visit Disney World in Florida, they typically not only spend money at the theme park, but also contribute to the local economy by using hotels and restaurants.

The development of new tourist attractions and revitalization projects often is carried out through *public-private partnerships* between government agencies and private businesses. These projects can involve a substantial commitment of public spending, often adding up to tens or hundreds of millions of dollars.

In the following sections, I offer some examples of major attractions that have been included in urban plans to help draw in tourists and revitalize the local economy.

Convention centers

Convention centers and meeting facilities provide local areas with an attraction to draw in tourists from national and international markets. Convention-goers typically spend money at local hotels, restaurants, and entertainment or shopping districts.

California's San Diego Convention Center hosts more than 60 annual events for national and international attendees, including the massive Comic-Con, which draws more than 120,000 people. The convention center generates more than $1.2 billion in yearly economic impacts for the region.

Professional sports facilities

Professional sports facilities have been a centerpiece of many revitalization projects in urban areas. For example, Baltimore's Oriole Park at Camden Yards was built as the new home of the Baltimore Orioles. Opened in 1992, the new ballpark helped boost attendance by nearly 40 percent and contributed to the revitalization of the city's Inner Harbor district. The ballpark was the first of the new generation of "retro-style" downtown ballparks and spawned several successors, including the Cleveland Indians' Jacobs Field (now Progressive Field) and the Detroit Tigers' Comerica Park.

Casinos and gaming

Once the exclusive turf of Atlantic City and Las Vegas, casinos and other gaming establishments now are located in a wide range of other locations and have been supported by some local communities as a means of drawing in tourists and stimulating the local economy. Although most new gaming facilities have been established in smaller towns and semirural areas, a few big cities — including Detroit and New Orleans — have developed downtown casinos in conjunction with overall redevelopment plans that include hotel, resort, and entertainment complexes.

Chasing smokestacks: Attracting businesses to your community

Efforts to attract new businesses to a community can pay off with the addition of new jobs and tax revenue for the local economy. Some areas have demographic or economic features that are attractive to new businesses — such as skilled workers or wealthy consumers — and local communities also use economic development plans and programs to provide incentives and assistance. Business startups, expansions, and relocations all can play a role in growing the local economy.

In many cases, the events leading up to business location decisions — sometimes called *site selection* — are invisible to the public, but typically a great deal of planning goes into determining where to locate a business. Local areas often have plans and programs in place to attract businesses and offer a wide range of incentives to businesses that are considering locating in the community, including technical advice and financial support.

Startups

Startup companies bring new ideas and new jobs into the community. Startups often are attracted to areas with a reasonable cost of doing business, good access to markets for their goods and services, and a well-trained labor force. Bloomberg's *Businessweek* magazine publishes an annual ranking of the best cities for startup companies. Boston and Seattle often make the grade as good places for startups due to their well-trained workforces, proximity to national and international markets, and ability to attract financing and venture capital — everything a young company needs.

Expansions

Business expansions are new activities in the community that are related to business operations in another place, such as a branch factory of an industrial manufacturer or a new location of a chain restaurant. In many cases, local areas compete against each other as the location for business expansions.

For example, in the summer of 2006, the automobile manufacturer Honda announced that it had chosen Greensburg, Indiana, over locations in Ohio and Illinois as the site for a new auto assembly plant expected to employ more than 1,000 workers.

How much help is too much?

In the world of economic development incentives, the days of "Brother, can you spare a dime?" are long gone. Since the 1980s and 1990s, governmental incentives for economic development programs have become increasingly controversial as the value of some aid packages soared into millions and millions of dollars.

In the age of mega-deals, some have asked, "How much is too much?" when it comes to helping businesses. One of the more controversial economic development deals occurred in 2005 when the auto manufacturer Nissan announced that it would move its North American headquarters from Southern California to a suburb of Nashville, Tennessee. The company's move was aided by nearly $200 million in assistance from state, county, and local authorities. The new headquarters were expected to bring about 1,300 jobs to the area,

giving the deal an average cost per job of about $150,000 — in other words, it was costing government authorities that much money for each new job that would be created by the move.

Some critics of the deal described it as "corporate welfare." Tennessee's governor called it a "good business decision" and officials in California called the move a "blow" to the Los Angeles economy. Others noted that the move was part of a "zero-sum game" for the national economy that just moved workers from one state to another.

There's lots of disagreement over the fairness and effectiveness of these sorts of mega-deals for economic development projects, but many communities clearly are willing to go to extremes to bring in new jobs — and the age of mega-deals isn't going to end anytime soon.

Relocations

Sometimes businesses are attracted to move from one place to another. These moves can be a boom for one place, while being a bust for another.

For example, in 2001, the aerospace manufacturer Boeing moved its corporate headquarters from Seattle to Chicago in order to gain better access to other companies in the aerospace and travel industries. The move involved about 500 workers in corporate positions and was seen as a coup for Chicago, while local leaders in Seattle took the move as a snub of a city that had proudly supported the company for decades. (For another relocation story, check out the sidebar "How much help is too much?")

Eds, meds, and feds: Looking at the role of education, medicine, and government

Major institutions such as universities, research hospitals, and government facilities can play an important role in supporting economic growth in the local economy. Labor economists Timothy Bartik and George Erickcek of the Upjohn Institute for Employment Research have observed that "eds and meds" can help jumpstart the local economy, and other researchers have found that governmental programs — especially federal-level programs — can help stimulate local innovation and serve as magnets for new businesses.

Colleges and universities

Higher education institutions — especially large universities — can give a big boost to the local economy. Not only can colleges and universities serve as major employers and draw lots of students into the area, but they also can help attract new businesses looking to access a trained labor force and the latest research.

For example, more than 100 companies have partnered with the University of Utah in Salt Lake City to commercialize their research and create more than 6,000 new jobs.

Hospitals and medical research institutions

Hospitals and medical research institutions can play a key role in helping a region develop new businesses related to biomedical industries and are also major purchasers of goods and services from local suppliers.

In Houston, Texas, the world-renowned MD Anderson Cancer Center serves more than 80,000 cancer patients every year and generates more than $13.5 billion in yearly economic benefits for the greater Houston economy.

Federal and state government facilities

Federal and state government facilities — ranging from jails to courthouses to research laboratories — often play a key role in the local economy. Government facilities related to research and development often stimulate the local economy and help draw in new businesses.

NASA's Jet Propulsion Laboratory in Pasadena, California, is one of several research and development facilities in the state that have helped build the state's space-related industries, which contribute nearly $80 billion annually to the California economy.

Helping at home: Supporting local entrepreneurs and businesses

Support for local entrepreneurs and existing local businesses often represents an effective way to build the local economy. And small and medium-size local businesses are a key source of employment growth for local communities. According to data from the Edward Lowe Foundation, jobs in locally managed businesses with fewer than 100 employees account for roughly 60 percent of all U.S. employment. (You can check out the data and reports on small businesses at www.youreconomy.org.)

In the following sections, I cover some approaches to supporting and expanding local businesses.

Supporting startups and new entrepreneurs

Programs to encourage entrepreneurship and startup businesses can bring new vitality and growth to the local economy.

For example, a number of cities and towns in Georgia have partnered with the state's Entrepreneur Friendly Communities program (http://bit.ly/16isTy) to help local leaders identify residents interested in starting new businesses and match them with local resources (such as local banks or training programs) that can help them start their businesses.

Helping small and medium-size businesses expand

Many communities have come to believe that "small is beautiful." Although many small businesses eventually fail, many others can bloom into viable enterprises when supported with small financial incentives and technical assistance in areas such as business management and marketing.

Since 1989, the city of Littleton, Colorado, has been using an approach called *economic gardening,* which they describe as "an entrepreneurial approach to economic development." This approach involves identifying local assets that can be used by small business (such as vacant buildings), helping businesses with market research, and providing opportunities for mentoring, training, and networking. Through this approach, some small businesses in Littleton have built local, national, and global markets for products ranging from handmade wooden furniture to gourmet food products.

Helping larger businesses expand

Larger businesses may have different needs for expansion assistance than small businesses. For example, a manufacturing facility aiming to expand from 100 employees to 200 employees may require assistance with obtaining permits to expand its building facilities, help with planning new truck routes, or finding new ways to reduce waste and pollution.

Retaining local businesses

Hanging on to existing businesses in the community is another way to promote local economic development. Some businesses may need assistance maintaining their profitability, while others may have plans to relocate away from the area. *Business retention programs* aim to help local businesses in ways that help them stay open in the community.

For example, Virginia's Fairfax County Economic Development Authority offers a business retention program that helps existing businesses identify new markets for their products, provide business coaching, and helps connect businesses to potential sources of venture capital and government contracts.

People power: Preparing workers for good jobs

Workforce development programs aim to strengthen the local economy by enabling people to participate more effectively in the labor force. These efforts typically go beyond educational and training programs offered in secondary and post-secondary education (high schools, colleges, and trade schools) by connecting the needs of local businesses to the skills of the workforce and helping to remove barriers to employment for potential workers.

Local efforts to prepare workers for good jobs are incorporated into local plans in a variety of ways, from identifying the needs of local employers to understanding the educational, economic, and social issues faced by the local workforce. Plans for effective workforce development programs often bring together a wide range of representatives from businesses, community organizations, and other institutions that help identify gaps between the existing workforce and the present and future needs of local businesses.

Matching workers to occupations and industries

Many communities have implemented workforce development programs that aim to provide workers with skills needed by specific industries and occupations.

For example, Hard Hatted Women (www.hardhattedwomen.org), a nonprofit organization in Cleveland, Ohio, provides training and placement assistance for women in jobs in traditionally male occupational trade and technical fields, including construction and industrial manufacturing.

Improving workforce readiness

Many potential workers face barriers to employment other than having the right skills and background for a job. For example, some parents may be unable to work (or have their choice of work) due to a lack of adequate access to affordable childcare. Workforce readiness programs aim to remove these barriers.

For example, local agencies in Milwaukee and Madison have teamed up with the state of Wisconsin's Employment Transportation Assistance Program to help "connect low-income workers with jobs through enhanced local transportation services." The program funds local programs for low-income workers that provide financial assistance for public transportation, carpools, shuttles, and vehicle purchase and repair loans.

Free for all: Kalamazoo's promise

In the spring of 2005, the Kalamazoo Public Schools in Kalamazoo, Michigan, announced the creation of the Kalamazoo Promise (www.kalamazoopromise.com), a new charitable program that would pay up to 100 percent of the tuition costs for in-state public colleges or universities for future graduates of the public school system. Funded by a group of anonymous private donors, the program held the promise of providing an outstanding educational opportunity for the school district's more than 10,000 students, as well as the potential to strengthen the local economy. The announcement of the program was described in the local newspaper as an "unprecedented boon to business and economic development" by providing the local economy with a new generation of skilled workers.

In the spring of 2010, President Barack Obama was the keynote speaker at Kalamazoo Central High School's graduation ceremony. He called the Kalamazoo Promise an opportunity for the school's graduating class "not just to enrich your own lives, but the lives of others and the life of the nation." During its first five years, the Kalamazoo Promise supported more than 1,500 students with nearly $17 million in funding.

Since the announcement of the Kalamazoo Promise, several other communities have tried to form similar initiatives. In 2008, the Pittsburgh Promise (www.pittsburghpromise.org) began providing yearly scholarships of up to $20,000 for qualified graduates of the Pittsburgh Public Schools, and representatives from more than two dozen communities have participated in annual PromiseNet conferences aimed at finding ways to spread the approach to other places that want to connect education to the future of their local economies.

Economic Development Programs and Policies

There are many different programs and policies that are used to stimulate local economic development, ranging from providing nonlocal companies with information about the community to multi-million-dollar incentives for companies to relocate into the community. Successful economic development initiatives often involve a complex combination of several different strategies, as well as high levels of cooperation between local officials, potential business partners, federal and state agencies, and nonprofit organizations.

Marketing the community

Letting potential businesses and customers from outside the community know what's great about your community is a valuable tool for economic development. Cities and towns are involved in promoting their communities and making themselves more business friendly in a variety of ways.

Promotional campaigns

Promotional campaigns for economic development are aimed at letting businesses know what your community has to offer as a potential location for their business. These campaigns often involve advertisements in mass media and trade publications, professional networking events, and sending local representatives to other locations to spread the word.

But getting the word out isn't always a polite affair. In 2011, the state of Illinois passed a substantial tax increase on business and some of the adjacent states made not-so-subtle advances toward Illinois businesses, urging them to relocate. The state of Indiana's Economic Development Corporation launched a website and highway billboard campaign using the slogan "Illinnoyed By Higher Taxes?" to encourage business moves across the border to the Hoosier State.

One-stop centers

One-stop centers offer potential businesses a single point of contact that can provide comprehensive information about the community and its economic development programs.

For example, Oakland County, Michigan's One-Stop Shop (www.oakgov.com/oss) is a county agency that helps businesses that are interested in locating in the county by providing them with marketing data about the region and providing businesses with technical assistance in the areas of market research, location scouting, and financial incentives and assistance.

Business improvement districts

A *business improvement district* (BID) is a government agency or nonprofit organization that carries out a variety of tasks aimed at making a specific area more user friendly to both businesses and consumers. BIDs often provide special services to their district — such as enhanced cleaning, maintenance, and security services — and help market the district to consumers.

For example, the city of Pittsburgh's Oakland district includes two major universities, a world-class hospital, several museums, and a wide range of restaurants and other businesses. The Oakland Business Improvement District (www.onlyinoakland.com) works with local businesses and institutions to provide additional security and maintenance services for the area, organizes special events and festivals, and carries out marketing campaigns aimed at both out-of-state tourists and residents of the metropolitan area.

Using financial incentives

Some local economic development programs provide new and existing businesses with financial incentives to expand or maintain their local operations. There are several different types of financial incentives for local economic development, ranging from cash subsidies to complex tax incentives. Many local economic development projects utilize more than one type of financial incentive.

Here's an overview of some the most commonly used types of financial incentives for local economic development:

- ✔ **Cash and in-kind subsidies:** In some cases, local economic development programs offer cash and in-kind subsidies as incentives. Cash subsidies often are tied to specific program goals, such as a cash payment for every new worker hired or cash payments to a company intended to defray its costs of building a new facility. In-kind subsidies include offering goods and services to a company without full payment, such as providing a company with low-cost space in an industrial park or providing a company with low-cost electricity from a public power plant.

- ✔ **Tax incentives:** Many local areas offer tax incentives to encourage local economic development. For example, many local governments offer *property tax abatements* (which provide a temporary reduction in the amount of property taxes to be paid) for the purpose of local economic development.

- ✔ **Employment-based incentives:** Some financial incentive programs are employment based and provide incentives when businesses hire additional workers or provide certain types of training to their workers.

For example, the city of Philadelphia's Reentry Employment Program (http://1.usa.gov/tLuWy2) provides tax write-offs to businesses that hire former criminal offenders.

- ✔ **Financing:** Assistance with financing for local economic development takes many forms, ranging from local venture capital funds to special bonds issued by local governments to help leverage investments by private businesses.

For example, the Milwaukee Economic Development Corporation's Capital Access Program (http://bit.ly/vm3Hg1) partners with local banks to provide loans to small companies and startup businesses that may not otherwise be able to obtain bank financing.

- ✔ **Geographic targeting:** Some local financial incentive programs require businesses to locate in specific geographic areas and are intended to both assist businesses and contribute to the revitalization of specific districts and neighborhoods.

In Virginia, the city of Roanoke's City Enterprise Zones program (http://1.usa.gov/vhDdhB) offers incentives including building improvement grants, a partial reduction in real-estate taxes, and rebates on costs associated with water and sewer services to businesses that locate in specific areas of the city.

Financial incentives for local economic development can be controversial with the public because they involve providing governmental support to private businesses. Of course, not every business venture is successful and some financial incentives fail to produce their expected benefits. Many communities include *clawback provisions* in their incentives that allow them to reclaim monies from businesses that don't live up to their end of the bargain, such as companies that accept money to train workers and fail to do so.

Coordinating economic development with land use

The provision of adequate space and supporting services for local businesses can be achieved by coordinating local economic development efforts with land use planning. Many local land use plans identify specific areas to be used for commercial and industrial activities, as well as programs to help provide services related to land development.

Here's an overview of some approaches to stimulating commercial and industrial activity that have been used successfully in many U.S. cities:

- ✔ **Zoning for future development:** One of the key functions of the land use component of an urban plan is to provide a sufficient amount of land zoned for commercial and industrial uses to meet the economic development goals of the plan. Some communities have adopted specific types of zoning and land use regulation intended to ease the process of developing new sites for commercial and industrial businesses.

    For example, land use regulations adopted by the city of Chicago identify specific areas as *planned manufacturing districts*. These districts can help prevent the loss of areas for industrial use due to the conversion of industrial land to residential or commercial uses.

- ✔ **Land assembly:** Many governmental agencies and nonprofit organizations support local economic development by identifying or providing potential locations for business development. Known as *land assembly,* this approach promotes economic development by helping businesses access "shovel-ready" sites. In some cases, local governments and other agencies that own land that could be redeveloped have programs that provide land at a subsidized rate to new businesses.

    For example, the city of Cleveland, Ohio, has an Industrial-Commercial Land Bank program (`http://bit.ly/uBpIpz`) that helps convert abandoned commercial and industrial locations into "ready-to-build land for expanding or new businesses."

- ✔ **Assistance with infrastructure and utilities:** Local government agencies and private utility companies work closely with prospective businesses to provide good access to local infrastructure and utilities. In some cases, the costs of infrastructure and utility services are subsidized by local economic development programs in order to reduce business costs and encourage new businesses to locate or expand in the community.

✔ **Industrial parks and business incubators:** Locations for industrial parks and business incubators are sometimes built or financially supported by local economic development programs in order to provide move-in-ready locations for new businesses. Industrial parks provide businesses with business-friendly locations that typically are close to needed services, such as highway access or railroad connections. So-called *business incubators* are places where small companies can receive discounted office or research space; they help promote the take-off of small companies in the local economy.

For example, the SPARK East Business Incubator (http://bit.ly/sXo4u0) in Ypsilanti, Michigan, provides selected small businesses in the areas of healthcare, life sciences, and biotechnology with low-cost work-ready office spaces.

In addition to coordinating economic development with general land use issues, many urban plans also help to coordinate the relationship between economic development and other plan components, such as housing and transportation. For example, the housing component of the plan may look into possible residential locations for workers in new businesses to make sure that the supply of local housing can keep up with demand; the transportation component of the plan may help make sure that there are adequate transportation routes between future workplaces and the rest of the community.

Chapter 16

Global Urban Planning: Answering the Challenges of Growth and Development

. . . .

In This Chapter

▶ Looking at world urbanization trends and megacities

▶ Planning for rapid urban growth in Asian, African, and Latin American cities

▶ Finding solutions to environmental problems in fast-growing cities

. . . .

*T*he world's population is bigger than ever. And it's expected to get even bigger. In 2011, the world's population crossed the 7 billion mark and did so in record time! In the year 1900, world population stood at about 1.6 billion people and increased to 5 billion by 1987. The sixth and seventh billions were each added in just 12 years. But as the world's population continues to grow — perhaps pushing past 9 billion people by the year 2050 — cities are becoming increasingly important (because a majority of the world's population now lives in urban areas).

In this chapter, I take you on a tour through Africa, Asia, and Latin America to look at urban planning where most of the world's population growth is expected to take place. These regions are facing a wide range of planning challenges, including keeping up with rapid population growth, coping with high levels of poverty, and managing their impacts on the environment. But cities in these areas are also at the forefront of efforts to improve the quality of life for the world's ever-growing population.

Finding a Place for the Next Three Billion People

By the year 2050, the world's population is expected to reach 9 billion people, with two-thirds of the world's population living in cities. Due to both rapid population growth and increasing levels of urbanization, nearly all the world's population growth — an additional 3 billion people by 2050 — is expected to take place in cities in poorer, developing countries in Africa, Asia, and South America. This trajectory poses an unprecedented challenge for urban planners around the world who are helping to plan a sustainable future.

Global urbanization trends

Between 2010 and 2050, the total number of people in cities is expected to rise by nearly 80 percent, from 3.5 billion to 6.4 billion people. The most urban growth is expected to occur in the cities of Asia, where the urban population will rise by more than 90 percent to 3.4 billion people. Africa is expected to post some of the most rapid rates of growth through the year 2050, with the region's urban population rising nearly 200 percent to 1.2 billion people. Urban populations in Latin America are anticipated to increase nearly 40 percent to 640 million people by the year 2050.

Not only is the world's urban population increasing, but so is the size of cities themselves. The world of the future is likely to be one with more and bigger cities. In 1950, there were just two urban areas with populations of 10 million or more people: New York City and Tokyo. In 2009, there were 21 *megacities* (cities with populations of more than 10 million people) across the globe. Figure 16-1 shows megacity locations on a world map; as you can see, nearly half are located somewhere in Asia, including Tokyo (Japan), Manila (Philippines), and Karachi (Pakistan).

Global urban planning challenges

The world's rising population is increasingly taking urban planning into uncharted territory, as more and more people live in different types of cities around the globe. Creating the next generation of sustainable cities to house another 3 billion city dwellers in Africa, Asia, and Latin America will require us to overcome many challenges and address a broad range of social, economic, and environmental issues:

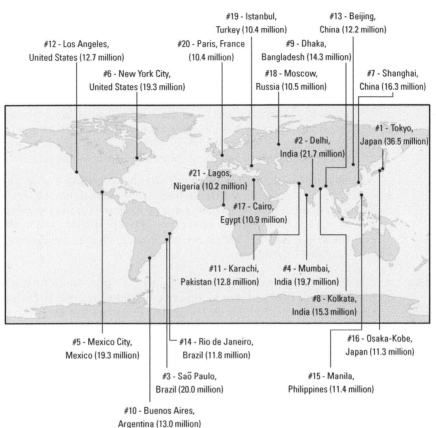

#19 - Istanbul, Turkey (10.4 million)

#13 - Beijing, China (12.2 million)

#12 - Los Angeles, United States (12.7 million)

#20 - Paris, France (10.4 million)

#9 - Dhaka, Bangladesh (14.3 million)

#6 - New York City, United States (19.3 million)

#18 - Moscow, Russia (10.5 million)

#7 - Shanghai, China (16.3 million)

#1 - Tokyo, Japan (36.5 million)

#2 - Delhi, India (21.7 million)

#21 - Lagos, Nigeria (10.2 million)

#17 - Cairo, Egypt (10.9 million)

#11 - Karachi, Pakistan (12.8 million)

#4 - Mumbai, India (19.7 million)

#8 - Kolkata, India (15.3 million)

#5 - Mexico City, Mexico (19.3 million)

#14 - Rio de Janeiro, Brazil (11.8 million)

#16 - Osaka-Kobe, Japan (11.3 million)

#3 - Saõ Paulo, Brazil (20.0 million)

#15 - Manila, Philippines (11.4 million)

#10 - Buenos Aires, Argentina (13.0 million)

Figure 16-1: The world's megacities (as of 2009).

✔ **Managing size and rapid growth:** In the coming decades, there will be more large cities than ever before. Planning for the megacities of the future will require balancing rapid population growth with efforts to prevent harmful environmental impacts and providing adequate resources for billions of new city dwellers.

✔ **Providing urban services:** Adding billions of people to cities in poorer, developing countries presents the challenge of providing basic urban services — such as clean water, good housing, and safe roadways — in areas with limited economic resources.

✔ **Reducing poverty and improving slums:** Most of the world's urban growth will take place in poorer countries where substantial numbers of people live in overcrowded urban slums that have poor-quality housing and lack adequate access to clean water or sanitation services. According to the United Nations, more than 800 million people in developing countries — 30 percent of the urban population — lived in slums in 2010.

✓ **Making cities healthy and environmentally friendly:** The world's booming population presents a variety of environmental problems, especially the degradation of air, land, and water in fast-growing urban areas. And many urban environmental problems — such as greenhouse gas emissions — may have global impacts as well.

✓ **Solving traffic and transportation problems:** Many of the fast-growing cities of Africa, Asia, and Latin America lack adequate transportation infrastructure, which limits their economic productivity and forces many residents to spend time fighting traffic. The growing use of automobiles in fast-growing cities is also a significant environmental concern.

✓ **Supporting social development:** The rapid growth of cities in poorer countries presents a dual challenge of building sustainable places while also helping people. Urban planning in developing areas often places social issues — such as education, gender equality, and healthcare — on an even footing with more traditional urban planning issues such as planning for land use.

Effective urban planning in many of the world's poorest areas, such as Bangladesh or the Democratic Republic of Congo, is likely to be especially challenging due to their limited financial resources. But as the saying goes, "necessity is the mother of invention," and the new planning approaches being pioneered in Africa, Asia, and Latin America may prove to be globally valuable.

Cities of Asia: Roaring into a New Century

Asia is the most populous world region and is home to about 4.2 billion people. Although many of the world's largest cities are located in the region, it's still more rural than urban, with just over 40 percent of the Asian population living in cities. About half of all urban dwellers in Asia live in cities of 500,000 people or fewer, while about 30 percent live in cities with between 1 million and 5 million people, and 10 percent live in megacities with populations of 10 million people or more.

Table 16-1 lists the 12 largest cities in Asia, 6 of which may have populations exceeding 20 million people by 2025. Asia's urban population is expected to increase to more than 3.4 billion people by 2050, with two-thirds of Asia's population living in cities due to a combination of overall population growth and people moving from rural to urban areas.

Table 16-1	The 12 Largest Cities in Asia			
	Population (Millions of People)			*Percent Growth, 2010–2025*
	1990	*2010*	*2025*	
Tokyo, Japan	32.5	36.7	37.1	1%
Delhi, India	9.7	22.2	28.6	29%
Mumbai (Bombay), India	12.3	20.0	25.8	29%
Shanghai, China	7.8	16.6	20.0	21%
Kolkata (Calcutta), India	10.9	15.6	20.1	29%
Dhaka, Bangladesh	6.6	14.6	20.9	43%
Karachi, Pakistan	7.1	13.1	18.7	43%
Beijing, China	6.8	12.4	15.0	21%
Manila, Philippines	8.0	11.6	14.9	28%
Osaka-Kobe, Japan	11.0	11.3	11.4	0%
Istanbul, Turkey	6.5	10.5	12.1	15%
Seoul, Republic of Korea	10.5	9.8	9.8	0%

Source: United Nations, World Urbanization Prospects (2009)

Shanghai: The "head of the dragon"

Shanghai is a rising global commercial center and is sometimes referred to as the "head of the dragon" because of the city's growing importance as China's gateway to the global economy. The economic growth of the city accelerated in the 1980s and 1990s when the city was designated by the Chinese government as an "open city" for foreign investment. The city's economic importance now rivals that of Tokyo or Hong Kong, and Shanghai's population of 17 million people is expected to push past 20 million within a few years.

Shanghai's transformation into a globally important city can be seen across the landscape of the city:

> ✔ **A center for business and technology:** Shanghai has quickly become a worldwide center for business activity. The city now boasts regional headquarters for many global corporations and is home to an increasingly important stock exchange. The city also has become a national and global media center, and the city's Oriental Pearl Tower building has become a visual icon of the city's importance.

✔ **A rising skyline:** Shanghai's growing skyline is a sign of its economic importance and growing wealth. The city boasts 8 of the world's 100 tallest buildings (only Dubai and Hong Kong have more super-tall buildings). The city's fast-rising Pudong district has become a centerpiece of the modern city. The district was merely a vacant grasslands until the 1990s, but it has seen the equivalent of billions of dollars in private investment since it was designated as a "special economic zone" by the national government. And Pudong's fairy-tale story is likely to continue in the future — plans to build a Shanghai Disneyland were announced in 2010.

✔ **A growing middle class:** Although not everyone is sharing in the city's growing economy, Shanghai is home to an increasingly sizable middle class — and everything that goes with it, such as suburban housing, new shopping centers, and an increasing number of automobiles. Controlling rapid growth in the city's outlying areas — sometimes referred to as "American-style sprawl" — has become a key challenge in this expanding metropolis.

Although Shanghai has quickly become a center of affluence and projects a modern image, the city has its share of challenges. The city faces significant environmental problems, and many areas of the city are home to slum housing and impoverished residents. Unlike most other megacities, urban planning for Shanghai is a joint undertaking involving both the national and local governments, and providing the "head of the dragon" with opportunities for success is likely to remain a national priority.

Mumbai: Big and getting bigger

Mumbai (formerly known as Bombay) is located along the western coast of India and juts into the Arabian Sea. For more than 200 years, it served as the most important British colonial outpost in south Asia, and today the city is a bustling commercial center. Home to the largest port in south Asia, nearly 40 percent of the country's international trade moves through the city, and the city's film industry (known as Bollywood) extends the city's cultural influence across India and its neighboring countries.

Already a megacity of more than 20 million people, the city continues to grow and is likely to add another 5 million to 10 million residents by the year 2025. Mumbai is one of the densest urban areas in the world, with an average population density of about 27,000 people per square kilometer. The city's Ward C neighborhood has a population density equivalent to more than 100,000 people per square kilometer.

As Mumbai's population grows, it faces a wide range of challenges:

- ✔ **Improving slums:** More than half of greater Mumbai's population lives in slum housing, and it's estimated that the majority of all housing in the area lacks adequate plumbing. Efforts to reduce the number of people living in slum conditions include initiatives to not only improve the physical quality of available housing, but also provide residents with better economic opportunities that may allow them to seek out better housing in non-slum areas.

- ✔ **Managing growth:** A growing population will challenge the ways that the city uses its land. Due to its population density, Mumbai has been growing in a relatively compact manner, but the city may have to expand into new areas in order to reduce population densities and avoid the continued overcrowding of residential areas.

- ✔ **Getting along:** Modern Mumbai is a mosaic of different people and customs. Roughly two-thirds of the area's population practices the Hindu religion, and it's estimated that only half of Mumbai's population speaks the local Marathi dialect. The city is home to migrants from across India and, increasingly, to international migrants. Mumbai has aims to improve conditions for all its residents, but moving the city forward will require finding common ground among a diverse population.

In the time it took you to read these last few paragraphs, Mumbai's population probably grew by a few more people — the city's population grows at the rate of nearly one person every minute! Although Mumbai is not the fastest growing city in the world, it is one of the largest, and the city's 2 percent growth rate adds up quickly. Moving ahead, the greater Mumbai region faces the daunting challenge of both addressing existing problems and planning ahead for the next millions of people who will call the city home.

Cities of Africa: Overcoming Poverty and Improving Lives

Africa is the least urbanized region of the world — but that's changing. As of 2010, the region was home to about 1 billion people, only 40 percent of whom lived in cities. By 2050, it's anticipated that the number of people living in African cities will triple to more than 1.2 billion people, with over 60 percent of the entire population living in cities.

Table 16-2 shows the 12 largest cities in Africa. As of 2010, the region was home to just two megacities: Cairo, Egypt, and Lagos, Nigeria. Compared to Asia or Latin America, a smaller proportion of the population in Africa lives in large cities. About 60 percent of the region's urban population lives in cities with fewer than 500,000 people, and only 30 percent lives in cities with more than 1 million people.

Table 16-2	The 12 Largest Cities in Africa			
	Population (Millions of People)			*Percent Growth, 2010–2025*
	1990	*2010*	*2025*	
Cairo, Egypt	9.1	11.0	13.5	23%
Lagos, Nigeria	4.8	10.6	15.8	49%
Kinshasa, Democratic Republic of the Congo	3.6	8.8	15.0	72%
Khartoum, Sudan	2.4	5.2	8.0	54%
Luanda, Angola	1.6	4.8	8.1	69%
Alexandria, Egypt	3.1	4.4	5.6	29%
Abidjan, Côte d'Ivoire	2.1	4.1	6.3	53%
Johannesburg, South Africa	1.9	3.7	4.1	12%
Nairobi, Kenya	1.4	3.5	6.2	77%
Cape Town, South Africa	2.2	3.4	3.8	12%
Kano, Nigeria	2.1	3.4	5.1	49%
Dar es Salaam, Tanzania	1.3	3.3	6.2	85%

Source: United Nations, World Urbanization Prospects (2009)

Along with the challenges of population growth and urbanization, the region is also the poorest in the world. In the Middle East and North Africa, the average per capita gross national income (GNI) is the equivalent of roughly $8,000 per year, while the average per capita GNI in sub-Saharan Africa is just $2,000 per year (or, less than $6 per day). The combination of rapid population growth and widespread poverty is a tremendous challenge for urban planning because local plans must address both physical change and social development.

Johannesburg: Laying the foundation for prosperity

The Johannesburg metropolitan area is home to more than 3.5 million people and is situated in northeastern South Africa. Sometimes called the "City of Gold," Johannesburg was originally settled by white Europeans looking for gold in the 1880s. Native Africans were formally banned from living in the city during the late 1800s and early 1900s. During the country's apartheid era, from the 1940s to the 1990s, the city was planned and developed in ways that forced black residents to live in specific areas of the city and its outlying townships.

Since the end of apartheid in 1994, change has come rapidly to Johannesburg. Johannesburg and the surrounding Gauteng Province region have become an important commercial center for all of sub-Saharan Africa, although the city continues to struggle with its apartheid legacy. The city of Johannesburg's *Joburg 2030* urban development plan presents a hopeful future for the city and lays out an ambitious vision statement:

> In 2030, Johannesburg will be a world-class city with service deliverables and efficiencies that meet world best practice. Its economy and labor force will specialize in the service sector and will be strongly outward oriented such that the city economy operates on a global scale.

> The result of this competitive economic behavior will be strong economic growth that will drive up city tax revenues, private sector profits, and individual disposable income levels such that the standard of living and quality of life of all the city's inhabitants will increase in a sustainable manner.

Joburg 2030 (`http://bit.ly/ss22LW`) identifies several key programs that will be undertaken to improve the city:

- ✔ **Transportation improvements:** The centerpiece of the city's transportation improvements is the Gautrain passenger railway, a multi-billion-dollar project linking Johannesburg to Pretoria and the region's international airport that began service in 2011. In 2009, the city's Rea Vaya bus rapid transit (BRT) service began operations; it links downtown Johannesburg to the apartheid-era township of Soweto.

- ✔ **Education and the economy:** The plan proposes a City Skills Program that would provide new and improved workforce training in order to provide businesses with a skilled workforce and capitalize on the region's growing role as an economic hub on the African continent.

- ✔ **Improving housing and land use:** Improving the "spatial planning" of the city and its region is one of the key goals of the plan, including connecting areas of the city that are currently isolated, improving the quality of housing, and directing future growth into new well-planned areas of the city.

The city of Johannesburg began the process of updating its plan in 2011. Known as the *Joburg 2040 Growth and Development Strategy,* you can find out more about it online at `http://bit.ly/sZkbeG` and even follow them on Twitter at `www.twitter.com/GDS2040`.

Cairo: Bringing modern changes to an ancient city

Sitting at the crossroads of Africa, Asia, and Europe, Cairo has been one of the world's most important cities for thousands of years. Already a city of more than 2 million people in the 1950s, the population of the greater Cairo region has more than quadrupled in size. Today's Cairo is the capital of Egypt and a sprawling megacity that is home to nearly a quarter of the country's population.

The city's modern development occurred in an unplanned and haphazard fashion that has created many problems. A majority of Cairo's housing was built in informal settlements that lack adequate public services, and the provision of infrastructure has not kept up with rapid growth. The region's environmental quality has suffered as a result of unplanned growth, leading to an increase in pollution and respiratory diseases. Cairo's traffic is notoriously congested, and many of Cairo's neighborhoods and settlements are poorly connected to the rest of the region.

The most recent effort to create a plan for the city is known as *Cairo Vision 2050: The Strategic Urban Development Plan of Greater Cairo Region* (http://bit.ly/sGohL7) and was led by the Egyptian Ministry of Housing, Utilities, and Urban Development. The plan was partially funded by the United Nations and aspires to shape the future of greater Cairo in ways that are "global, green, and connected":

- ✔ **A global region:** The new plan for Cairo envisions the city as a global gateway between Africa and the Middle East whose strategic location and unique past can serve as a stimulus for increased trade and tourism.

- ✔ **A green region:** Upgrading the region's informally developed and squatter settlements so that they provide a basic level of decent housing and access to healthy public services is a key goal of the new plan. The plan also aims for new public parks, natural conservation areas, and public plazas to help green the city.

- ✔ **A connected region:** Improving roads and expanding the public transportation system are seen as ways to reduce pollution, help businesses conduct trade, and allow people to move more easily between residential and commercial areas of the city.

The recent revolution in Egypt may complicate Cairo's plans for the future. Egypt's "Arab Spring" protests of 2011 led to the ouster of the country's longtime leader, Hosni Mubarek, and the formation of a provisional government led by the military. As of this writing, the country's political future is unclear, but it seems inevitable that Cairo will continue to grow, planned or not.

Cities of Latin America: Searching for Stability

Latin America is the most urbanized region of the world. Nearly 80 percent of the region's total population lives in cities. About 50 percent of the urban population lives in cities of fewer than 500,000 residents, while another 40 percent lives in cities with more than 1 million people, including one of the region's four megacities: São Paulo (Brazil), Mexico City, Buenos Aires (Argentina), and Rio de Janeiro (Brazil). Check out Table 16-3 for a list of Latin America's 12 largest cities.

Table 16-3	The 12 Largest Cities in Latin America			
	Population (Millions of People)			Percent Growth, 2010-2025
	1990	2010	2025	
São Paulo, Brazil	14.8	20.3	21.7	7%
Mexico City, Mexico	15.3	19.5	20.7	6%
Buenos Aires, Argentina	10.5	13.1	13.7	5%
Rio de Janeiro, Brazil	9.6	11.9	12.7	6%
Lima, Peru	5.8	8.9	10.5	18%
Bogotá, Colombia	4.7	8.5	10.5	24%
Santiago, Chile	4.6	6.0	6.5	9%
Belo Horizonte, Brazil	3.5	5.9	6.5	10%
Guadalajara, Mexico	3.0	4.4	4.9	11%
Pôrto Alegre, Brazil	2.9	4.1	4.5	9%
Salvador, Brazil	2.3	3.9	4.4	13%
Brasília, Brazil	1.9	3.9	4.5	15%

Source: United Nations, World Urbanization Prospects (2009)

Between 2010 and 2050, the cities of Latin America are expected to grow more slowly than those in Africa and Asia will, with an annual growth rate averaging just 0.5 percent. But that still adds up to another 140 million people. The region's urban population is expected to rise to 730 million people, with 90 percent of the total population living in cities. The region's economy is also growing. But economic prosperity has not reached everyone, and many of the region's cities are a study in contrasts, where gleaming skyscrapers overshadow impoverished neighborhoods.

Mexico City: Planning for growth and sustainability

Mexico City proudly hosted the 1968 Summer Olympics and was until recently the largest city in Latin America (that title passed to São Paulo in the 1990s). Today the metropolitan area is home to more than 20 million people and ranks among the world's five largest urban areas. Mexico City is also the heart of a nation, serving as the capital of Mexico and accounting for up to half of the country's commercial and industrial activity.

In addition to its sheer size, successful planning for Mexico City has to overcome several other complicating factors, including the city's location in an area that is prone to earthquakes and flooding. Nearly 10,000 people were killed in a 1985 earthquake. The city is located in a valley, which traps the city's polluted air. In recent years, some portions of the city have begun to sink deeper into the earth as underground water has been pumped from below and weakened the ground beneath.

Efforts to plan for the growth and development of the city address a wide range of social, economic, and environmental challenges:

- **Upgrading housing:** Many steps are being taken to improve the city's residential conditions. The city's general plan, *Programa General de Desarrollo del Distrito Federal,* aims to improve conditions in poor neighborhoods, provide financial assistance for housing to poor households, reduce the amount of housing in areas with risks of flooding and earthquakes, and identify new areas that are suitable for building new housing.

- **Improving transportation options:** Mexico City is well known for its Metro subway system, which is the largest in Latin America and provides nearly 5 million trips per day. But the city also is home to roughly 4 million cars that clog the highways and contribute to the smog that pervades the metropolitan area. Efforts to improve transportation and reduce pollution include the MetroBus bus-rapid-transit service (known as BRT), which began operation in 2005, as well as the replacement of aging taxis and buses and expansion of the Metro system.

- **"¡Reverdece tu ciudad!":** "Make your city green" is the message of Mexico City's campaign to clean up the environment and encourage sustainable development. The centerpiece of the campaign is the *Plan Verde (Green Plan),* which proposes a wide range of projects to help green the city, including building more urban gardens, limiting greenhouse gas emissions, promoting bicycle-sharing programs, and improving greenbelts along the major freeways. Several of Mexico's most popular entertainers are helping to promote the plan. You can check it out online at www.planverde.org.

Mexico City is a pride of the nation and enjoys a special status as the home of the national capital. The planning and development of greater Mexico City is carried out by a combination of federal, state, and local authorities. Although the city's leadership is taking steps to move in a more sustainable direction, these efforts are frequently overshadowed by the nation's economic challenges in the wake of the U.S.-led recession that started in 2008 and a wave of narcotics-related crime that began to grip the country in the late 2000s.

São Paulo: The challenges of hyper-urbanization

São Paulo was founded in the mid 1500s and became the center of Brazil's lucrative coffee industry in the late 1800s. By the 1950s, São Paulo had moved beyond its agricultural past to become the nation's most important industrial center, producing everything from textiles to automobiles.

Today São Paulo is the third-largest city in the world, a teeming megacity of more than 20 million people. Combined with the neighboring metropolis of Rio de Janeiro and surrounding areas, the two megacities form a region of nearly 45 million people, a quarter of the national population; the area makes up one-third of Brazil's economy.

Although the city is one of the most economically productive and wealthy in both Brazil and Latin America, it's also a study in contrasts. The city is home to both the very wealthy and the extremely poor. It's a city where modern shopping malls, luxurious high-rise apartment towers, and office parks are located alongside the city's numerous downtrodden residential areas, known as *favelas* and *cortiços*. In addition to social inequality, environmental issues have become increasingly important to the sustainability of the São Paulo region, especially concerns over widespread pollution and a lack of adequate infrastructure in many areas.

In 2002, the municipal government of São Paulo adopted a strategic master plan. The plan concerns the core city — home to more than 11 million residents — and addresses the city's most critical issues:

- ✔ **Raising the quality of life:** The municipality's plan aims to improve the overall quality of life through public and private efforts addressing health, education, housing conditions, and the completion of numerous projects to improve infrastructure and public services.

- ✔ **Reducing inequalities:** The municipality hopes to bridge the gap between the city's rich and poor by reducing social and economic inequalities between wealthy and poor households, as well as between rich and poor areas of the city.

✔ **Promoting sustainable development:** In a city coping with the consequences of rapid growth and environmental degradation, the municipal plan aims to encourage the sustainable development of the city's ecological resources and the protection of its historic and cultural features.

✔ **Making the city healthier:** The plan aims to improve the health of the city's residents — especially the poorest — by improving air and water quality, cleaning up chemical contamination in slum areas, and providing more green and open spaces.

São Paulo's municipal plan addresses a wide range of important issues. But what actually happens in the future will depend on more than the priorities and actions of the municipal government. To make a difference, the plan also will have to influence the decisions of millions of people and businesses as to how and where they want to live, work, and invest their resources.

Part IV

Getting Involved and Going Further

Part IV

Getting Involved

and Going Further

In this part . . .

There's a role for everyone in urban planning, whether you're a resident looking to get more involved in your community or a college student thinking about urban planning as career. This part explores opportunities for community involvement and professional development in urban planning.

Chapter 17 opens the door to getting more involved in urban planning in your community, whether as a concerned resident, a helpful volunteer, a community activist, or a social entrepreneur. Chapter 18 is a guide to becoming a professional urban planner; it talks about what planners do, what skills they use, and what kind of training is needed to become a professional urban planner.

Chapter 17

Getting Involved in Your Community

. . . .

In This Chapter

▶ Finding out more about urban planning in your community

▶ Participating in the planning process

▶ Joining your local planning commission

. . . .

*G*etting involved in urban planning in your community can make the difference between a plan *for* the community and a plan *by* the community. Taking an active role in the planning process makes for a better plan and leads to improvements in your community in a variety of ways:

- ✔ **Volunteering your time and knowledge to improve your community's plan can lead to more successful results and implementation.** Nobody knows a community better than its residents and stakeholders.

- ✔ **Getting involved in the planning process helps the community make better decisions, such as figuring out which goals are most important and which development projects will be most beneficial.** Without community involvement, urban planners may not be able to accurately judge which decisions will best serve the community.

- ✔ **Participating in urban planning efforts brings your unique experience and abilities into the mix.** Each person's interests and resources are important community assets, and everyone has a valuable role to play in contributing to the future of his or her community.

Although professional urban planners play an important role in creating successful communities, a community's residents and stakeholders are the ones who are directly impacted by plans and community change. Getting involved in your community's plan is a wise investment in the future, and there are many opportunities for getting involved, from participating in public meetings to becoming a local planning official.

Getting More Information on Local Planning Issues

Even a small community can be a complicated place. Finding useful and accurate information about urban planning in your community often can present a considerable challenge. Here are some ways you can find out more about what's happening in your community.

Finding information about local planning

Perhaps you want to know more about your community's local plan or whether there are other plans that impact your community. The first place to start is your local government. The planning agency for your local government — often called a *planning department* or a *community development department* — is the best source for information on local plans. Planning departments often post their plans and related documents on their city's website. You may want to call the planning department directly to ask whether there are any ongoing planning initiatives or updates.

Your community may be part of specialized or regional plans other than those of your local government. For example, planning for highways in your community also may be addressed in the plan of statewide or regional transportation agencies, known as *metropolitan planning organizations* and *councils of governments* (see Chapter 3). Your local planning agency will probably have information on plans by other agencies and organizations.

Getting information about development projects, zoning decisions, permits, and other land use issues

Perhaps you've driven by a construction site and you want to know what's being built. Or you've heard that a real-estate development company wants to build a new shopping center in your neighborhood, and you're concerned about how it may impact the community.

The most useful first step is to contact your local government. Most decisions about land use issues involve either your city's planning department or its building department. You may want to contact the political representative for your community, such as a mayor or city council member, to help figure out which departments deal with different planning and development issues.

Some major development projects — like casinos, nuclear power plants, or certain types of factories — are regulated by state and federal authorities. Getting information on the approval process for these types of developments can be much more difficult. Your local planning department is likely to have information on these types of developments. Local news reports also may offer some information on which nonlocal government agencies are involved in the approval process.

Learning more about your community

The desire to keep current with information on how your community is changing is natural. Here's an overview of some useful resources (turn to the appendix for more):

- **The U.S. Census:** The U.S. Census (www.census.gov) is the most comprehensive source for information on population and housing trends in your community. The 2010 U.S. Census and the American Community Survey provide up-to-date data on a wide variety of community topics. Your local planning department also may have reports or "fact sheets" based on U.S. Census data that can give you a quick overview of major trends in your community.

- **Your local library:** Local libraries are usually good resources for planning-related information about the communities they serve. Libraries often have access to U.S. Census data, as well as copies of reports, planning documents, and news or reference items that help keep track of how the community is changing.

- **Local government and community organizations:** Your city's planning department and other agencies probably have reports and online information about general community issues. Other community organizations such as chambers of commerce, convention and visitors bureaus, and local colleges or universities, also may have reports and other up-to-date information about trends and changes in your community.

Getting Your Point Across: Attending Public Meetings and Hearings

Government agencies use public meetings and hearings to get input and opinion from community residents and other stakeholders during the planning process. Planning agencies typically conduct numerous public meetings to gather stakeholder input on the plan and hold official hearings prior to the formal approval of the plan. Other local government agencies also conduct hearings on matters related to local planning and development, such as city council hearings on budgetary matters.

Although the two terms often are used interchangeably, public meetings and public hearings have some significant differences:

✔ **Public meetings:** As part of a planning process, public meetings are informal events where the city's planners make a presentation to a public audience, respond to audience questions, and often ask for feedback or other input from participants. Urban planners may hold public meetings on various topics throughout the planning process, ranging from meetings about the possible goals of a plan to meetings about plan implementation strategies.

✔ **Public hearings:** During the planning process, there is typically a legal requirement that a plan be given a public hearing by the government agency in charge of preparing the plan prior to its final adoption. At a public hearing, residents and other stakeholders are given a chance to make verbal comments on the plan, sometimes under a set time limit (such as two or three minutes). Written comments usually also are accepted — they're a way for you to provide more extensive input.

Public meetings and public hearings help urban planners and other local officials get a better understanding of which specific issues and planning approaches are preferred or disliked by the community. Communicating effectively at meetings and hearings will help you get your point across and make sure that your perspective is considered. Here are some tips for participating in public meetings and hearings:

✔ **Give your perspective.** Meetings and hearings are an important opportunity for community members to present new ideas and different points of view. Talking about how you see things and how you would solve problems provides important input for the overall plan:

 • What are your most favorite and least favorite things about your community? Why?

 • What do you think can be done to improve your community?

 • How would you be personally affected by the implementation of the plan?

✔ **Ask specific questions.** If there's an opportunity to ask questions, make sure your questions are as specific as possible. For example, instead of asking how a plan is going to "solve housing problems," you may gain more information by asking, "How can this plan help make housing more affordable?" or "What can be done to repair houses that are in poor condition?" A specific question helps pinpoint issues of concern and helps identify issues that may need further research.

✔ **Be prepared.** Speaking in public is a challenge for many people, especially when it's in front of a large crowd or if there's a strict time limit. Writing an outline or an actual script of what you want to say can be a big help.

✔ **Be open to new ideas and other points of view.** Successful urban plans are the result of reaching consensus and making compromises. Listening to others is a good way to learn about the community and understand how your own point of view fits into the bigger picture.

Being a Part of the Solution: Participating in Planning

In addition to public meetings, there are many other opportunities for public participation in the planning process. Although a public meeting is an easy way to quickly share information or give your opinion, other activities may allow you to learn more about your community and get involved in coming up with new ideas and solutions.

Here are some examples of public participation opportunities that are frequently used in urban planning:

✔ **Focus groups:** These small meetings allow residents and other community stakeholders to provide their opinions on issues such as community conditions, planning strategies, or potential planning goals.

For example, when the city of Fort Collins, Colorado, began its latest comprehensive plan in 2010, more than 200 people participated in focus groups to help develop planning goals in a wide range of areas, including options for new housing and infrastructure funding issues.

✔ **Planning charrettes:** In a *planning charrette* (also called a *design charrette*), community volunteers work closely over a few days with professional urban planners and architects to develop a preliminary urban design plan for a specific project or small area. This gives residents and other stakeholders the opportunity to work directly alongside architects and urban planners on ideas that will help shape their communities. (You can find more information about charrettes in Chapter 8.)

✔ **Planning workshops:** In a planning workshop, urban planners work hands-on with community stakeholders to review community information and come up with possible goals and solutions. A workshop may last just one afternoon or take place over several days or weeks.

In Oakland, California, urban planners and residents used a mapping exercise to help plan for the city's waterfront Central Estuary. In this workshop, small groups were given poster-size maps of the waterfront area and asked to draw in their ideas for which areas they would like to see used for pedestrian trail access and as natural preservation areas.

✔ **Advisory committees:** Many urban planning efforts use *advisory commit-tees* (also called *steering committees*) to get residents and other stake-holders involved in the planning process. Advisory committees help put a reality check on the planning process by providing real-world advice and helping to make sure that the plan addresses issues of broad con-cern to the community.

In Austin, Texas, the city's Imagine Austin Comprehensive Plan included a Citizens Advisory Task Force consisting of more than 30 residents who reviewed the progress of the plan and helped the city's urban planners in community outreach efforts.

Taking a greater interest in urban planning and volunteering in planning efforts is a great way to contribute to your community. Whether you're able to share just an afternoon or you can commit a greater amount of time and energy, participating in the planning process can be an enjoyable way to learn more about your community and improve its plans for the future.

Don't let time constraints stop you: You may be able to participate online by responding to surveys or contributing to discussion boards.

Taking Action! Opportunities for Volunteering, Activism, and Social Entrepreneurship

The planning process provides many opportunities for making change happen, including creating new goals for the community and working toward new development strategies. There are lots of ways to take action in the plan-ning process, whether you're interested in helping to prepare a successful plan or you want to work more deeply on issues raised by the plan.

Here are some ways you can play a role in the planning process:

✔ **Volunteer.** There are lots of ways to support a successful planning pro-cess, ranging from general volunteering to helping with specific projects. You may be able to set up a coffee station at a public meeting or hand out flyers about a community event. Many planning efforts have oppor-tunities for deeper involvement, such as participating in committees or workshops (see "Being a Part of the Solution: Participating in Planning," earlier in this chapter).

If you have technical skills, you may be able to help support the profes-sional urban planners and consultants working on the plan. For example, an architect may volunteer to help with site drawings or someone expe-rienced in online social media may volunteer to help promote outreach events to the community.

✔ **Be an activist.** The planning process represents an opportunity to champion an issue and have it addressed as part of the overall development of the community. For example, maybe you'd like to see more opportunities for bicycling in your community. By getting involved in the planning process, you may be able to have specific issues addressed and have new initiatives included in the plan, such as the creation of dedicated bicycle lanes or new incentives for bike-to-work programs. As the old saying goes, the squeaky wheel gets the grease!

✔ **Be a social entrepreneur.** The planning process often creates new opportunities for social entrepreneurship for enterprising individuals and nonprofit organizations. Plans often identify new community needs and new approaches to solving problems, but there may not be existing efforts addressing these issues. For example, suppose a newly adopted community plan identifies some local strategies for addressing climate change, such as promoting car-sharing services in order to reduce greenhouse gases from automobile emissions. A social entrepreneur might see this as an opportunity to establish a new enterprise that would contribute to the health of the community and may be especially able to attract support from charitable funding sources or investors because it's been identified as a community planning priority.

For more information on social entrepreneurship, check out *Social Entrepreneurship For Dummies,* by Mark B. Durieux, PhD, and Robert A. Stebbins, PhD (Wiley).

The planning process, from conception to implementation, has many functions. One of the important functions of the planning process is to provide a coordinated process for managing all the complex components of a city, such as land use and transportation systems. But one of the other important functions of the planning process is to inspire people to get involved and take action in tackling new issues, new problems, and new solutions.

Making It Official: Joining a Planning Commission

If you're interested in helping your community make important decisions about its future, then joining your local government's planning commission may be for you. A *planning commission* (sometimes also called a *planning board*) is the part of local government that is involved in making comprehensive and specialized plans, as well as sometimes making official decisions on land use and zoning issues.

Local urban planning depends on regular people to serve as elected and appointed planning officials on planning commissions and other boards. Being a planning official is similar to being a city council member — both have official duties in local government, but planning officials are usually appointed rather than elected.

In some cases, a planning commission makes legal decisions on land use issues, such as requests from property owners for zoning variances. (A *zoning variance* is permission from the local government allowing a property owner to do something with his property that would otherwise not be permitted by the city's zoning laws.) Sometimes these decisions are made by planning commissions, but some local governments have a separate body known as a *board of zoning appeals,* which deals with local land use regulations. Boards of zoning appeals also rely on appointed and elected citizen volunteers.

The local government representing your community may have several different opportunities to serve as an appointed or elected planning official, depending on what commissions or boards are present in your community. If you're interested in serving as a planning official, here are some things to expect:

- ✔ **Attending meetings:** Planning commissions and boards are representative public bodies, like city councils. They typically meet in public at the local city hall on a regular basis, usually once or twice a month.

- ✔ **Working with staff and consultants:** Planning officials often work closely with professional urban planners and consultants who provide information and recommendations on planning issues being considered by the commission or board.

- ✔ **Participating in planning:** Planning officials usually are very involved in the planning process when the planning commission is making or updating its comprehensive or specialized plans. This may include working with your city's professional urban planners to organize the planning process or attending additional meetings and community events that are part of the plan-making and community outreach process.

- ✔ **Doing some homework:** Planning officials often have to do a little homework to prepare for regularly scheduled meetings, such as reviewing planning reports for upcoming meetings or getting a briefing on a specific issue from the professional urban planners who work with the commission.

- ✔ **Making decisions:** Many planning commissions and boards make legally binding decisions on the adoption of urban plans and decisions related to zoning and other land use regulations. Some of these decisions are eventually challenged through lawsuits and often can raise strong emotions from property owners and community members. Prospective planning officials should be prepared to take criticism and understand that their decisions may not be popular with everyone in the community.

Becoming a planning official is a great way to get involved in your community and play a leadership role in planning for its future. One way to learn more about what's involved in being a planning official in your community is to talk with current or past planning officials. Many communities also provide some introductory training in urban planning and local government procedures to help their new planning officials learn the ropes (see the sidebar "Becoming a citizen planner" for some examples).

Becoming a citizen planner

Good urban planning uses the time and talents of many different people, not just professional urban planners. Cities and towns rely on their residents to become elected or appointed planning officials on planning commissions or to participate as volunteers in planning and development projects. In recent years, a variety of universities, professional associations, and government agencies have started programs to help prepare "citizen planners" to serve as volunteers and planning officials.

Since 2002, the Michigan Citizen Planner program at Michigan State University (www.citizenplanner.org) has trained more than 3,000 local planning officials throughout the state. These officials help lead the planning process and make decisions on planning and land development issues, but many don't have a background in urban planning and aren't well prepared to make informed decisions. This program helps citizen planners better understand the roles and responsibilities of local planning officials and provides training on specific planning issues and techniques. By working directly with citizen planners, this effort aims to help residents create "more livable communities" and make "better overall land use decisions throughout Michigan."

Philadelphia's Citizen's Planning Institute (www.citizensplanninginstitute.org) prepares neighborhood residents who are "interested in playing a more informed and active role in shaping the future of their communities" to participate in the city's planning process and volunteer with community organizations. The city's training programs provide online, classroom, and hands-on training in areas ranging from land use and zoning to business district development and transportation planning. Overall, this effort is helping the city to make better planning decisions and to help improve struggling neighborhoods by giving its citizen planners "the know-how to address change head-on and create a vision for their community's future."

Chapter 18

Becoming a Professional Urban Planner

. . . .

In This Chapter

▶ Defining the job of an urban planner

▶ Finding out the skills required

▶ Acquiring education, training, and credentials in urban planning

. . . .

*P*rofessional urban planners are rarely bored. Each day brings new, hands-on challenges in a wide range of areas. Plus, urban planners have the opportunity to help improve cities and the lives of their residents. In this chapter, I talk about career opportunities in urban planning and how to prepare for them.

I describe the main elements of what urban planners actually do in their day-to-day jobs and the kinds of organizations that employ urban planners. I fill you in on the professional skills used by urban planners and professional specialties within urban planning. And I give you an overview of training and educational opportunities in urban planning and guide you to some useful resources.

The field of urban planning is growing and offers some unique career opportunities. The U.S. Department of Labor estimates that the number of jobs for urban planners in the United States will grow by nearly 20 percent over the next decade and that jobs in urban planning are a good fit for people with diverse interests who want to work in ways that are investigative, enterprising, and artistic. If this sounds like fun and fulfilling work, then maybe you should consider a career in urban planning!

What Do Urban Planners Do?

In 2009, 2010, and 2011, *US News & World Report* listed urban planning as one of the best careers for the coming years. In 2009, the magazine described urban planning as "a multifaceted job for a multitalented person." This is an accurate description, because the typical urban planner is called upon to do many different things on the job.

Preparing urban plans

Preparing urban plans is the most important function of urban planners and local planning agencies. This task includes developing comprehensive plans and specialized plans, such as a plan for a specific neighborhood or a plan for a specific topic (see Chapter 3 for more on the various types of urban plans).

A planning department for a small community may work on its city's official comprehensive plan only every few years. But a planning department for a major city may have staffers who work full-time year-round producing comprehensive and specialized plans.

Preparing an urban plan requires planners to engage in a wide range of tasks and duties:

- **Working with the public:** Urban planners work with local officials, residents, business owners, and other community stakeholders in all phases of the planning process. Planners use a variety of techniques to work with the public, including holding public meetings and workshops, conducting surveys and focus groups, and using social media, like Facebook and Twitter, to stimulate community interest and participation.

- **Collecting and using information:** Urban planners gather and analyze information that will be used in their plans. This includes items such as research reports on specific issues, land use surveys, or results of community surveys. Urban planners often use maps and statistical techniques to analyze information. Urban planners also must be able to communicate their research effectively to broad audiences, not just to other urban planners.

- **Using urban planning techniques to solve problems:** Urban planners may need to research or develop a wide range of planning methods and techniques to help solve problems and meet goals identified throughout the planning process. For example, if reducing traffic congestion is identified as one of the goals of a plan, then urban planners will need to do some research to identify a variety of possible solutions and their likely outcomes. Coming up with workable strategies and recommendations for implementing the plan is a key task of urban planners.

✔ **Coordinating the production of the planning document and its distribution:** Whether distributed in print form or as an online document, urban planners are responsible for producing the final planning document that will be submitted for approval by local officials. Urban plans often consist of hundreds of pages of material, using maps, graphics, data tables, and technical appendix material. Pulling all the material together and making it available to the public is both necessary and time-consuming.

Carrying out development projects

Many urban planners who work for government agencies, nonprofit organizations, and private businesses are directly involved in carrying out development projects. These types of urban planners are typically called *community development planners* or *economic development planners,* and they tend to work primarily on project development and management tasks like the following:

✔ **Managing projects:** Community and economic development planners manage the implementation of specific projects, such as the rehabilitation of buildings in a historic district or the implementation of an economic development program intended to increase the number of small businesses in a community.

✔ **Writing and administering grants:** Raising funds and generating new resources is a key task of community and economic development planners. This includes preparing grant applications and development proposals for funding from a wide range of sources, such as banks, government agencies, and philanthropic foundations. These planners also must keep track of the resources used in their projects and provide reports on the use and status of such projects.

✔ **Working with the public:** Community and economic development planners work directly with the public. For example, a development planner working on small business promotion issues would probably meet regularly with local business owners and try to find people interested in starting their own businesses.

Handling day-to-day operations

Most urban planners either work for or work closely with local government in a planning department or agency (see "Employment opportunities in urban planning," later in this chapter). These agencies provide day-to-day services to the public and handle many administrative tasks, including the following:

✔ **Working with local officials and the public:** Urban planners work on a daily basis with a variety of public officials, whether it's providing information to the mayor's office or reviewing planning documents for the next meeting of the planning commission. Urban planners also are typically called on to work directly with the public on official matters, such as providing follow-up answers to questions raised by residents at public meetings.

✔ **Administering the zoning code and other development regulations:** Many local government planning agencies are responsible for the day-to-day operation of the city's land use regulations, especially the zoning code. The urban planners who manage these regulations work regularly with residents and property owners on matters related to land development, such as reviewing development plans for compliance with local regulations.

✔ **Working with other agencies and community organizations:** Urban planners often provide support to other government agencies and community organizations. For example, urban planners from a local planning agency often participate in broader planning efforts, such as state or regional transportation improvement planning. Many planning agencies also provide technical assistance to community organizations, such as social service agencies and neighborhood associations, by providing them with useful maps and data or helping to research ideas for new programs and strategies.

The Skills You Need to Be an Urban Planner

Urban planners use a broad range of skills. They carry out tasks that are technical in nature, such as analyzing data or creating maps. But many urban planning tasks also require a strong ability to work well with people, such as facilitating community meetings. Being an effective urban planner requires a balanced combination of "hard" and "soft" skills.

The ability to understand and identify patterns of community change

Urban planners are trained to understand and identify patterns of community change related to demographic, economic, social, and environmental issues. This may include analyzing demographic data to determine if a community is gaining or losing population, or monitoring environmental trends to see how industrial pollution is impacting recreational areas. By understanding how and why communities are changing, urban planners are able to assist the community in developing new approaches to solve problems and enhance the quality of life in the community.

The ability to manage the entire planning process

Whether working on a long-range comprehensive plan for a large city or a specialized plan for a small township, urban planners need to know how to manage the planning process from start to finish. Managing the planning process involves many different tasks, ranging from working directly with residents to working with complex data to preparing final reports and plans.

Most planning efforts follow a predefined step-by-step process, but urban planners also have to be able to customize the planning process in ways that are appropriate for the community and know when to change the process to fit a changing situation.

The ability to digest lots of information

Urban planners work with lots of information, ranging from data that is part of a comprehensive plan to current reports on community conditions. Local government planning agencies also are frequently called upon to provide information and analysis in response to requests from local officials. Being familiar with a wide range of data sources and analytical techniques is essential to being an effective urban planner who can collect, analyze, and disseminate useful information to a broad audience.

Technical skills

Urban planners are trained in a wide range of technical skills, such as computer-aided mapping, spreadsheet and database software programs, and computer-aided urban design programs. Urban planners who work in specialty areas have a deeper knowledge of specific technical skills, such as how to manage geographic information systems or create technical drawings used to rehabilitate historic buildings. (For more information on specific skills, check out the "Urban planning specialties" section, later in this chapter.)

Communication skills

Urban planners work with many diverse segments of the community, and planners need to be able to communicate in many different ways. Planners produce a wide variety of written documents, from flyers advertising neighborhood meetings to complex technical reports. Written planning documents also use graphical elements, such as maps, charts, and other illustrations, to help convey important information.

Planners engage in many oral and in-person types of communication, ranging from presentations to large crowds at public meetings to speaking with colleagues in staff meetings. Electronic communication through websites, e-mail, and social media has become an increasingly useful way for planners to reach out to a larger and more diverse audience.

A Growing Field: Careers in Urban Planning

Urban planning is a relatively new profession, but it has experienced rapid growth in recent years. One of the first milestones for professional urban planning was the 1909 National Conference on City Planning, recognized as the first professional meeting of urban planners. In 1923, Harvard University became the first university to offer advanced training in urban planning, and the field quickly gained acceptance as a profession on par with architecture, law, or engineering. Although the jobs carried out by today's urban planners are very different from those of decades past, urban planning has continued to grow as a profession by continually adjusting to the ever-changing challenges faced by communities and their residents.

Education and training in urban planning

Professional urban planners typically complete a specialized college degree, often at the master's level, and have a professional certification in urban planning. Advanced training and professional certification help to ensure that professional urban planners have a strong understanding of basic urban planning issues and have up-to-date skills and knowledge. Professional training and experience in urban planning may lead to careers in related fields, such as real-estate development or public administration.

Getting a degree in urban planning

Most career-track professional positions in urban planning require a master's degree in urban planning. More than 65 colleges and universities in the

United States and Canada offer accredited degree programs in urban planning, including Harvard, Ohio State, Cornell, Columbia, UCLA, UC Berkeley, the University of North Carolina, and the University of Toronto.

Universities that offer accredited degree programs have had their programs reviewed and approved by the Planning Accreditation Board, an independent organization recognized by the Council for Higher Education Accreditation, to ensure that they provide the following:

- ✔ Knowledge of urban development processes, including social, economic, environmental, geographic, and political issues

- ✔ Knowledge of professional standards and practices in urban planning, including professional ethics

- ✔ Training in planning-related skills and techniques, such as mapping, computer-aided design, quantitative analysis, or project management

- ✔ Training in specialized areas of urban planning, such as urban design or environmental planning

- ✔ Pre-professional experience in urban planning through internships and workshop projects

More than a dozen universities — including Arizona State, the University of Illinois, and the University of Virginia — offer undergraduate degrees recognized by the Planning Accreditation Board and provide entry-level training in planning. Many graduates of these programs eventually return to school to complete graduate-level training, although graduate degree programs in planning typically don't require an undergraduate degree in urban planning as a prerequisite. Many aspiring urban planners complete undergraduate degrees in related areas — such as political science, urban studies, economics, or environmental studies — prior to entering a graduate program in urban planning.

One of the main professional benefits of completing a degree at an accredited institution is that it allows for professional credentials to be earned more quickly (see "Obtaining a professional credential in urban planning," later in this chapter). Many universities offer non-accredited degrees in urban planning and degree programs in other fields, such as geography or political science, that focus on urban planning.

The Association of Collegiate Schools of Planning (www.acsp.org) publishes the *Guide to Undergraduate and Graduate Education in Urban and Regional Planning*, which you can view or download at http://bit.ly/uvjPUN. Another good source for information and opinion is Planetizen's *Guide to Graduate Urban Planning Programs* (http://bit.ly/mH3eEO), which includes profiles of more than a hundred American and Canadian planning programs with rankings of top programs by region and specialty.

For information on planning degree programs worldwide, the website of the Global Planning Education Association Network (www.gpean.org) has links to schools around the world.

Obtaining a professional credential in urban planning

Urban planning is a technical profession, similar to law, architecture, or engineering. However, practicing urban planning typically doesn't require a government-issued license. Only one U.S. state, New Jersey, requires that professional urban planners pass a licensing exam.

The leading U.S. professional credential in the field of urban planning is certification by the American Institute of Certified Planners (www.planning.org/aicp). To earn AICP certification, you need *one* of the following combinations of experience and education:

- ✔ Two years of professional experience in urban planning and an accredited graduate degree in urban planning

- ✔ Three years of professional experience and either an accredited undergraduate degree in planning or a non-accredited graduate degree in planning

- ✔ Four years of professional experience and any graduate or undergraduate college degree

- ✔ Eight years of professional experience without a college degree

Membership as an AICP-certified urban planner carries a continuing education requirement that must be completed every two years. Certified planners also must adhere to a Code of Ethics and Professional Conduct that addresses issues such as conflicts of interest and professional responsibilities. In 2011, the AICP began offering advanced specialty certifications in transportation planning and environmental planning to help identify professionals with special skills in these areas.

In some cases, professionals who work in fields closely related to urban planning, such as architects, lawyers, or engineers, may have substantial experience in planning and be eligible for AICP certification.

Some urban planners hold additional credentials from other professional organizations in a variety of specialty areas, including:

- ✔ **LEED credentials:** The Green Building Certification Institute (www.gbci.org) offers several training programs and professional credentials related to environmental design and sustainable development, including the LEED Green Associate credential.

✔ **GIS Professional (GISP):** The GISP certification is offered by the GIS Certification Institute (www.gisci.org) for professionals who specialize in mapping and the use of geographic information systems.

✔ **Certified Economic Developer (CeCD):** The CeCD credential is offered by the International Economic Development Council (www.iedcon line.org) for professionals with expertise and experience in economic development.

Many other countries, including Canada, Australia, and the United Kingdom, have urban planning organizations that offer professional certification programs. The website of the Global Planners Network (www.globalplanners network.org) has links to organizations around the world that support professional urban planning and offer credentialing programs.

Urban planning specialties

Professional urban planners work in a wide range of areas and activities that are different from place to place. Some urban planners have to engage in a broad range of issues and tasks on a regular basis, while others deal mostly with specialized areas.

Here are some common areas of specialization within the field of urban planning:

✔ **Urban planner or general planner:** Works on a wide range of issues, especially those related to preparing comprehensive and specialized plans. May also have day-to-day responsibilities such as working with planning commissioners and reviewing planning-related proposals and applications. This job title is probably the most common in local government planning agencies for entry-level and career-track positions.

✔ **Planning director or manager:** Works as the leader of a public agency or private firm as an administrator of other urban planners and is mostly involved in administrative or bureaucratic issues, such as agency budgeting or finding new clients. Provides leadership for major planning projects and reviews the work of other planners.

✔ **Land use planner:** Deals primarily with land use planning issues related to comprehensive and specialized plans. May be responsible for collecting and analyzing a wide range of data sources, including demographic data, citizen input, and environmental surveys.

✔ **Transportation planner:** Specializes in planning for the transportation system and its users, including the provision of infrastructure and routes for motorized transportation, as well as routes and facilities for nonmotorized transportation, such as bicycles and pedestrian paths.

- ✔ **Environmental planner:** Deals with issues related to air, water, and land, as well as the areas of planning for energy, biodiversity, and hazardous materials. Involved in comprehensive and specialized planning, as well as in day-to-day operations, such as monitoring specific natural areas or reviewing development permit applications for compliance with local plans and regulations.

- ✔ **Geographic Information Systems (GIS) specialist:** Manages information and creates maps. May be involved in comprehensive and specialized planning efforts, as well as day-to-day tasks such as the collection of new information and maintaining online data and mapping resources.

- ✔ **Economic development planner:** Works on issues related to job creation, business development, and land development, including preparing specialized plans and working on day-to-day tasks such as seeking financing for development projects or overseeing construction of development projects.

- ✔ **Community development planner:** Works on issues related to neighborhood development, especially in low-income or distressed areas. Involved in the preparation of area-specific plans and may deal with a range of day-to-day issues including public safety concerns, housing improvement projects, and neighborhood beautification efforts. Also known as a *neighborhood planner*.

- ✔ **Urban designer:** Prepares urban design plans for inclusion in comprehensive and specialized plans. May be responsible for collecting and analyzing information on design and architectural features, as well as working day-to-day with building owners, community residents, and other professionals on development projects.

- ✔ **Historic preservation planner:** Works on maintaining and preserving areas with historic importance. Contributes architectural and neighborhood surveys to short-range and long-range plans, and may work on day-to-day issues including surveys of historic areas and supervising the renovation of historic buildings.

- ✔ **Housing planner:** Works on issues related to housing, especially housing for low-income and at-risk populations, and for areas with physically deteriorating housing. Involved in comprehensive planning and may have day-to-day tasks such as handling federal grants for local housing programs and developing housing improvement programs.

- ✔ **International development planner:** Works on plans and projects outside the United States, typically in cities and towns of developing countries. Often employed by nongovernmental organizations, these planners work on a wide range of issues, such as improving conditions in urban slums or building infrastructure in poor regions. (Chapter 16 has more details on international development.)

Searching for a job in urban planning

Many people use the Internet to find job opportunities in urban planning. There are two general options for starting your search. The first is to use websites that cater specifically to jobs in urban planning and closely related areas. The second is to look for jobs in urban planning (or related areas) on general job search websites.

Here are three of the most popular urban planning websites that carry job postings:

✔ **American Planning Association (APA):** The APA's website (`www.planning.org/jobs`) is probably the most popular site for employment listings in urban planning. APA members can gain access to some additional job hunting features on the site, but all postings are open to the public and can be searched by region, experience level, and specialty.

✔ **Planetizen:** This website (`www.planetizen.com/jobs`) features all sorts of news and information about urban planning, including a section for employment advertisements.

✔ **Cyburbia:** This website hosts a wide variety of interactive online discussion forums on topics related to urban planning, including a job board (`http://bit.ly/d3hzjt`).

You also can search for urban planning jobs on general job search websites such as CareerBuilder.com or Monster (`www.monster.com`) or job search aggregator websites, like Indeed (`www.indeed.com`). But it can be tricky to find relevant jobs in urban planning on these sites because many jobs in urban planning don't come with the exact job title of "urban planner." Searching for keywords related to urban planning skills and specialties may turn up a larger number of positions. Try searching for keywords related to your skills and interests, such as *zoning, urban design, economic development, demographic analysis, GIS, land use,* or *environmental planning.* Using keyword searches on general job search websites may return a sizeable number of irrelevant listings that you have to comb through, but you may find that needle in the haystack that's just right for you!

Employment opportunities in urban planning

Many different employment opportunities are available to people with training and experience in urban planning. Here are some of the main areas where urban planners are employed.

Local government

According to the U.S. Department of Labor, roughly two-thirds of urban planners work in local government. A planning department in a large city may employ several or dozens of urban planners who have specialized job duties focusing on specific areas, such as urban design or housing. In a small town planning agency, the planning staff may be just two or three people dealing with a wide range of planning issues (including getting their own coffee!).

Private consulting firms

Planners at private consulting firms typically provide services to local government agencies, as well as private businesses like real-estate development companies. Large firms may work across a wide variety of urban planning specialties and have an interdisciplinary staff that includes architects, landscape architects, and engineers. Smaller firms often focus on general planning issues or specialize in providing a specific kind of service, such as demographic analysis or land use surveys.

Nonprofit organizations

Many nonprofit organizations employ people with experience or training in urban planning, such as community development organizations that work in low-income neighborhoods or organizations that research and promote environmental conservation.

Other employers

People with a background in urban planning are desirable to a wide range of other employers that do work related to urban development, such as state and federal government agencies, real-estate developers, architecture and engineering firms, financial institutions, or utility companies. These types of employers often appreciate the technical skills, organizational skills, and knowledge areas that are familiar to urban planners.

Part V
The Part of Tens

The 5th Wave   By Rich Tennant

In this part . . .

Every *For Dummies* book has a Part of Tens, and this one has some fun with cities and urban planning by presenting you with facts, figures, and oddities about places around the globe, with some useful tips along the way.

Chapter 19 is a checklist of ten ways to use urban planning techniques to improve your community. Chapter 20 talks about ten great cities that all are outstanding examples of successful urban planning. The book's grand finale, Chapter 21, presents ten urban plans you can find online that may just give you some new ideas for how urban planning can be used to improve your community.

Chapter 19

Ten Ways to Make Your Community a Better Place to Live, Work, and Play

In This Chapter
▶ Figuring out what's already great about where you live
▶ Taking a look at ways to improve your community
▶ Planning for places that people will love

*T*his chapter is all about ways that urban planning can be used to improve your community, ranging from simple steps to big projects. Here I give you some quick tips on things like making places greener, making it easier for people to get where they're going, and getting to know your neighbors.

Each of the ten ideas in this chapter includes descriptions of specific planning approaches. These descriptions aren't meant to be complete lists of everything that you can do for every idea, but they are a smorgasbord of tips worth trying.

Make Public Places That People Will Love

One of the ways to make your community a better place to live is to create public places that people will love — places where residents can meet other people, relax, shop, and more. The key is that people need to enjoy the places enough to make leaving behind the comforts of home worth their while.

Here are a few ways you can put some love into your community:

- ✔ **Find out what people want.** Ask residents and other stakeholders what they want the community to offer. For example, maybe they'd like to see improvements to public parks, a wider variety of shops and stores, or more walking trails.

- ✔ **Plan great neighborhoods.** A great neighborhood is one that puts everything that people need within easy reach and where using a car isn't always necessary. This means mixing parks, recreation, retail, services, and places to work into places where people live. Your community can encourage the development of mixed-use areas by revising zoning codes and other land use regulations to allow mixed-use development.

- ✔ **Provide public space.** Making room for different kinds of public spaces — such as parks, pedestrian malls, or community gardens — gives people places to gather and helps build social relationships that strengthen the community.

- ✔ **Preserve the past.** Hanging on to what people already love about the community is a smart move. Historic preservation of special buildings and districts can celebrate the past while looking toward the future.

Help People Get Where They're Going

A good transportation system serves everyone in the community and all areas of the community. Helping people get where they're going can help reduce pollution, allow for better coordination between land use and transportation, and make it easier for people to get to work or shopping places.

Here are some ways to make transportation easier for everyone:

- ✔ **Plan for many kinds of transportation.** Coordinating how people use roads, cars, and mass transit with walking and bicycling can help more people get where they're going.

- ✔ **Connect people and places.** Routes for non-motorized transportation, like bikeways and walking trails, help people use and see more of their community. Connect people to shared transportation with ride sharing or bike rental programs (sometimes called *bike sharing*).

- ✔ **Plan for transit-oriented development.** Look for opportunities to develop and redevelop neighborhoods and districts that can be served by public transportation. Not only is public transit good for the environment, but easy access to public transportation makes getting around easier for people without cars.

Pay Attention to Design Details

Using good urban design techniques makes places more attractive and easier to use. Places within the community that are loved and well used are important to a community's overall quality of life.

Here are some ways to use design approaches in your community:

- **Look at what already works.** Take a look at your community and make note of features that already work pretty well, such as streets that have lots of walking activity. Ask people what they like about the design of the community, such as their favorite buildings.

- **Create a distinct look and feel.** Good urban design helps make places that are attractive and have an interesting appearance that supports a wide range of uses, from shopping to relaxation. Design and architectural standards often can be incorporated into your community's zoning code or other land regulations.

- **Don't forget the small stuff.** Good urban design adds amenities to the places that people use every day. Public art, small gardens, fountains, and attractive signage for businesses are great finishing touches that enrich the community.

Make Room for Nature

Green is good! Making room for nature in the city protects the environment, encourages people to live healthy lifestyles, and helps make places more attractive.

Here are some ways to bring nature closer to your community:

- **Make a green inventory.** Figure out what's green in your community, like open space, water resources, and animal habitats. Knowing what's there can help your community make plans for environmental protection and conservation.

- **Add green paths, small parks, and community gardens.** Sometimes it's the little things that can make a big difference. Small features that are near homes can help make nature accessible to lots of people.

- **Plant trees.** Tree species that are appropriate for your community can help reduce energy costs and pollution (by providing shade and natural cooling), support animal habitats, help clean the air, and make for an attractive addition to yards, streets, and parks.

✔ **Green up houses and buildings.** Everything from bird feeders to solar panels can be added to existing houses and buildings. Environmentally friendly add-ons can help support a city's natural elements, conserve resources, and reduce pollution.

✔ **Connect farms to cities.** Farmers' markets are a way to bring local agriculture products into the city. This helps preserve rural areas near cities by creating new markets for local products and supports healthy lifestyles by bringing good food into cities and towns.

Include Different Types of Housing

Planning for a diverse housing stock helps to ensure that everyone has a good place to live and that housing contributes to the overall health and vitality of the community.

Here are some ways that communities can plan for housing:

✔ **Assess the need for housing.** Figuring out your community's future housing needs is a good place to start and helps the community plan for the right amount and types of housing.

✔ **Plan for a mix of housing types.** A mix of housing types — such as apartments, small homes, and large homes — helps ensure that everyone will have a good place to live. Plans can help set goals for how much affordable housing and other special types of housing will help meet the needs of the community.

✔ **Provide housing close to workplaces.** Housing that's located near where people work helps reduce automobile traffic and can provide more opportunities for people to walk, bike, or use mass transit to get to work. Shortening the distance between home and work is less expensive for workers and better for the environment.

✔ **Add housing to mixed-use development.** Combining housing with other uses, such as shops and stores, helps create lively "all-in-one" areas where people don't need to go very far to find what they need. Plus, local residents provide built-in customers for local businesses.

Provide Places for Recreation

Making room for recreation helps communities in many ways. Not only does it help people stay active and healthy, but good recreational opportunities contribute to the overall quality of life in a community and can help improve environmental quality by maintaining open space and green areas.

Here are some tips for planning approaches that may work in your community:

✔ **See what you have and how well it works.** Take an inventory of your community's recreational opportunities, how much they're used, and how well they're liked. This inventory can help identify what's working and help point out possible changes and improvements.

✔ **Give everyone a chance to play.** Recreational areas should serve the whole community. Specialized opportunities may be needed to help the elderly or disabled get in on the action.

✔ **Provide lots of options.** Recreational areas can take lots of different shapes and require different kinds of planning, ranging from neighborhood parks with plenty of playground equipment to nature preserves with quiet walking paths.

✔ **Make every place near a recreation space.** Neighborhoods and districts that provide good routes for walking and bicycling and small parks or plazas help make active spaces and build recreation into everyday lives.

Build a Sense of Community

The writer Gertrude Stein famously said of her hometown that "there is no there there" — in other words, the city didn't feel like a special place with a unique sense of community.

Here are some ways to help your community make itself a special place:

✔ **Plan for gathering places.** Whether it's a grand town square or small parks in neighborhoods, places where people can see and be seen help create a sense of community and generate activity that makes places lively and entertaining.

✔ **Use events and activities to make it lively.** Places that offer room for arts, music, and other lively activities help people enjoy the community and encourage the use of public spaces.

✔ **Learn from history and recognize diversity.** Events and elements — such as festivals, monuments, or wall murals — that celebrate local history and culture give places a unique feel that's valued by residents and tourists alike.

Revitalize Neighborhoods

Revitalizing existing urban and suburban neighborhoods helps improve the lives of existing residents and also helps to make good use of existing community resources that provide an alternative to urban sprawl.

Here are a few approaches that are being used in communities across the country:

- ✔ **Use resources strategically.** Unfortunately, there are many struggling neighborhoods in cities and suburbs around the country and too few resources to rescue them all at once. Targeting specific locations and specific priorities, such as improving housing or reducing crime, can help create the critical mass needed for successful revitalization.

- ✔ **Put shopping where people need it.** Many urban and suburban neighborhoods don't have enough shops and stores — especially grocery stores — where people can easily buy basic goods, and many residents lack cars or other transportation to get around.

- ✔ **Find ways to reuse vacant land.** Many neighborhoods have vacant land that can be reused for a wide range of purposes, including new homes and buildings, small parks, or community gardens.

Grow Smart

Change is good! The smart growth approach to managing the growth of urban and suburban areas (see Chapter 13) can help your community grow and change in positive ways that are less costly to state and local governments — and their taxpayers!

Here are some ideas that may work in your community:

- ✔ **Rate your community.** Use a community scorecard to help figure out if your community has plans in place that will help it grow smart. You can find examples of smart growth scorecards at `http://1.usa.gov/unDH1M`.

- ✔ **Plan regionally and cooperatively.** Regional plans that allow cities and towns to coordinate their future development help to conserve land and other natural resources, avoid duplication of expensive services and infrastructure, and plan for regional priorities, such as housing and transportation.

- ✔ **Make plans for compact and efficient places.** Communities can save precious tax dollars by planning for compact land use patterns where places to live, work, and play are located close to each other. This strategy minimizes the costs of transportation improvements and other expensive infrastructure projects.

- ✔ **Focus on existing areas.** Smart growth planning uses public resources effectively by concentrating spending on schools, roads, sewers, and other services in areas that are already developed. Updating older neighborhoods is usually less costly in the long run than building new neighborhoods.

For more on smart growth, check out the great online resources at the Smart Growth America website (www.smartgrowthamerica.org).

Make the First Move

Making your community a great place is everyone's business, but sometimes it takes just one special person to get the ball rolling — and you can be that person!

Here are some steps you can take to get started:

- ✔ **Look for what works.** You can find lots of examples of great urban planning in this book, but be on the lookout for more. Places that you've visited and enjoyed may serve as inspiration for approaches that could work in your community. And if you've read or heard about some great ideas in other places, you may want to take a trip and check it out for yourself (even if it's just in the next town over).

- ✔ **Get help.** If your community lacks the financial resources to make a plan, you may be able to take advantage of low-cost or free assistance from professional associations or educational institutions that conduct outreach programs. The following are great places to start:

    - American Planning Association: www.planning.org

    - Association of Collegiate Schools of Planning: www.acsp.org

    - The American Institute of Architects: www.aia.org

- ✔ **Find funding.** Do you have an idea for a project to improve your community, such as starting a community garden or helping disabled homeowners maintain their houses? You may be able to raise funds for community projects from community members, foundations, charities, and private businesses. Check out *Fundraising For Dummies,* 3rd Edition, by John Mutz and Katherine Murray, or *Social Entrepreneurship For Dummies,* by Mark B. Durieux, PhD, and Robert A. Stebbins, PhD (both published by Wiley), for great step-by-step how-to guides that show you how to look for the resources you need to get started.

- ✔ **Be a leader.** Sometimes you have to get your own hands a little dirty. Ask yourself, "If I don't do this, who will?" One way to get started is to see if other people share your concerns. Talk to friends and neighbors about planning issues in your community, write a letter to your local newspaper, or blog about how to plan and improve your community.

Chapter 20

Ten Great Cities with Great Plans

In This Chapter

▶ Taking a trip around the world to see some great cities

▶ Discovering old and new ideas about urban planning

*P*eople and their cities have faced countless challenges over thousands of years. Over this long history, advances in how people plan their cities have not only solved current problems, but also been passed down through the ages from city to city across the globe.

Every place has its own unique history and story. This chapter visits ten places around the world that are interesting examples of urban planning and development. At each stop, I fill you in on what's unique about each city and how each city has been shaped by different urban planning techniques.

Rome

For more than 2,000 years, Rome has been a center for great ideas on everything from art and science to philosophy, music, and architecture. One of Rome's most influential contributions to urban planning came relatively recently, during the Renaissance. In the 1580s, a new plan for Rome, guided by Pope Sixtus V, put in place many new ideas that would shape the city for centuries to come, including the following:

✔ **Streets:** Several main streets were planned to be longer and wider than previous streets, allowing for easier transportation and commerce. Plazas and monuments were placed at key intersections or at the ends of streets.

✔ **Plazas:** Plazas were inserted into the form of the city and served several purposes — they were central gathering places, transportation centers, and areas for commerce.

✓ **Landscapes:** The drawings for Rome's Renaissance plans used techniques from art and theater set design to envision vistas and landscapes of the city that would be seen from different vantage points.

These techniques were added to the repertoire of urban design for cities in Europe and throughout the world. The streets and plazas laid out under Pope Sixtus V have endured for centuries, and so has the very plan itself, parts of which are included in wall murals that adorn the chambers of the Vatican Library.

Amsterdam

Today, Amsterdam is a favorite destination among tourists because of its rich artistic and cultural heritage. Founded around the 12th century, Amsterdam eventually became a center for trade and grew wealthy. The oldest portions of Amsterdam reflect centuries of urban growth and features that are similar to other European cities of the era, including the following:

✓ **A dense core:** The core of the city takes up a relatively small space and is densely packed with buildings of all kinds, ranging from houses to businesses to museums. Built long before cars ruled the roads, the distance between places was small by necessity, and dense cities allowed for a jumble of different uses to be tightly packed together side-by-side.

✓ **Walkability:** The city's core street pattern is organized around a hub of streets that arc away from the central port district and cross over a system of canals that also give form to the city. These routes make the city a true walking city.

When Dutch explorers headed off to the "new world" across the Atlantic Ocean during the age of exploration, they took a vision of their homeland with them. The form of the classic European town can be found deep in the roots of many cities in the Americas, including a Dutch colony once known as New Amsterdam that was seized by the British and eventually renamed New York. (Yes, that New York.)

Savannah

Savannah, Georgia, was established by English settlers in 1733 and has become one of the best-loved historic cities in the United States. The original plan for the city, laid out by General James Oglethorpe, organized the city around two important features that lend Savannah a unique feeling:

- **Wards:** The original lot and street pattern of the city was laid out in a series of four neat rectangles, each of which had its own central square. This helps create a sense of community within each ward but still allows each ward to be part of the larger city.

- **Open squares:** Open squares within each ward helped create a further sense of community. They took on many roles, as gathering places for residents, as marketplaces, and as places for monuments and public events.

The regularity of Savannah's wards and squares allowed it to expand in an orderly way by adding new wards that were similar to the existing areas. Over more than a hundred years, the city grew from its four original wards of 1733 to include an area of 24 wards in 1856, while still maintaining the essential character of the city. Over the years, the residents of Savannah have proudly preserved their city, and much of old Savannah appears today as it did hundreds of years ago.

Washington, D.C.

If Thomas Jefferson had had his way, Washington, D.C., would be a very different place. In 1790, the brand-new U.S. Congress authorized President George Washington to establish a district to serve as the headquarters of the federal government. Jefferson is known to have presented several sketches for the new city to Washington, but the job of designing the new capital instead fell to a surveyor named Pierre Charles L'Enfant.

L'Enfant presented Washington with "a grand plan" for the capital. He proposed a unique design for the new city that emphasized civic virtue and its status as the center of a newly independent democracy. Key features of the plan included the following:

- **Streets and squares:** The plan combined a regular street grid with a series of irregular avenues that connected 15 plaza squares, one for each state.

- **Civic beauty:** The plan envisioned major streets as grand avenues featuring fountains and gardens intended to add beauty to the city.

- **Public space:** One of the most important features of the plan was the prominence of public space and plans for the city to hold numerous civic institutions, including churches, colleges, monuments, and government buildings.

The original plan for Washington, D.C., took a bold approach. The scale of the plan was unprecedented in the young United States. The plan laid out enough space for at least 15,000 houses, larger than any existing city in the country at the time. Although the city has grown and changed over the years, the capital retains much of its original form and remains a national symbol of civic inspiration.

New York City

New York City has been the largest city in the United States ever since the first U.S. Census was taken in 1790 — although that may not be saying very much, because the city was home to a mere 33,000 people at the time. New York City has been home to many innovations in urban planning over the years, many of which were required to keep up with the city's pace of growth and its growing size. Some key moments in New York City's evolution include the following:

- **The street grid took over.** In 1810, about 100,000 people were living in Manhattan, mostly on its southern tip near where the city was originally settled. But the city was growing rapidly, and, in 1811, the city's commissioners approved a plan to create a regular grid of streets that carved the island of Manhattan into nearly 2,000 blocks that were mostly uniform in size.

- **Central Park was built.** By 1850, more than 500,000 people lived on Manhattan, which was becoming increasingly overcrowded and dirty. In 1858, the city's leaders selected a plan by Frederick Law Olmsted and Calvert Vaux that created Central Park. The grand park brought nature back into the city and was so successful that it led many other cities to adopt similar plans.

- **A zoning code was adopted.** In 1898, the five boroughs formally merged as one city and had a combined population of more than 3.5 million people. In 1916, the city enacted the nation's first zoning code. This new set of laws was intended to create a safer and healthier pattern for the city's rapid development. Despite legal challenges, cities around the country quickly adopted similar laws based on the example set by New York.

The Garden Cities of England

In 1900, London was the largest city in the world and home to more than five million people. For some, it was a great place to live. For many others, life in the city was an unpleasant combination of poverty and pollution. One person with a solution to London's "urban problem" was a London court reporter named Ebenezer Howard.

Howard's 1898 book, *Garden Cities of To-morrow,* proposed the creation of new garden cities instead of simply adding more people to an already crowded London. The book explained how future population growth could be directed to newly built "slumless smokeless cities" of 30,000 to 60,000 people. These garden cities would have a number of innovative features:

- ✔ **Keeping land uses separate:** Unlike London's mishmash of dirty factories and tenement homes, Howard proposed separate districts for different types of activities. He envisioned a central core of civic and commercial buildings, surrounded by outlying rings of residential districts, with factories at the edge of the city where they would be least harmful.

- ✔ **Conserving open space:** Howard believed that his garden cities would be an ideal balance of urban and rural. He proposed that each garden city be surrounded by forests and agricultural areas that would provide not just food and resources for the city, but also a nearby place to which residents could take retreats.

- ✔ **Making the city fair:** Howard's garden cities represented a breakthrough not only in the design of cities, but also in how they would benefit their residents. Howard proposed that the garden city itself would be owned by the members of the community, giving each resident a permanent home and a lasting stake in the city's success.

Although Howard had no formal training in town planning (as it was called in Britain), his ideas rank as some of the most influential of the 20th century. Some of his concepts were applied in the development of two new British towns, Letchworth and Welwyn, and even influenced plans to build new towns in the United States as part of the New Deal in the 1930s. More generally, Howard is credited with popularizing suburbs as an alternative to life in the big city.

Canberra

In 1908, Canberra was selected as the new capital of Australia, and, in 1912, a plan for the new city was chosen in a design competition. The winning design was prepared by two Americans from Chicago, Walter Burley Griffin and Marion Mahony Griffin. Both had worked with Frank Lloyd Wright and were in Chicago during the years that Daniel Burnham worked on Chicago's World's Fair and his 1909 *Plan of Chicago.*

The plan for Canberra resulted in one of the grandest national capitals of the era. Some key features of the plan include the following:

- ✔ **A grand scale:** The plan is often described as having features similar to Ebenezer Howard's idea of the garden city, except on a grander scale. The plan featured a set of connected districts that would make up the city's areas for governmental, residential, commercial, and manufacturing districts.

- ✔ **Using the landscape:** Canberra's plan was spread across a challenging topography of hills and water elements. Instead of avoiding these challenges, the plan incorporated them as important elements. The plan placed major political, commercial, and military centers at the highest points of the city, literally elevating their status, and fully integrated the city's waterways into a series of parks.

In addition to the grand city envisioned in the plan, the plan itself is considered a work of art, featuring lavish drawings by Marion Mahony Griffin. The original plans are held by the National Archives of Australia and were considered lost for many years before being restored and displayed in an exhibition in 2002.

Chandigarh

Chandigarh is a city of nearly a million people in India's northern state of Punjab, 170 miles east of Lahore, Pakistan. After gaining independence from Britain in 1947, the national government designated the city as a regional capital and set about creating a new planned city that would reflect the nation's independence and modernization. After some initial fits and starts, the Swiss architect known as Le Corbusier (his real name was Charles-Édouard Jeanneret) was named to develop a plan for the city.

By this time, Le Corbusier was already a well-known architect, having been a central figure in the International Congresses of Modern Architecture that were held in Europe starting in 1928. Le Corbusier was best known for plans featuring sleek architecture and mammoth skyscrapers arranged in blocks on large-scale street grids.

In Chandigarh, Le Corbusier was given the chance to work mostly from scratch and with leaders who shared his vision. The plan and resulting city includes Le Corbusier's signature designs for avant-garde architecture and groups of street blocks organized around tall buildings surrounded by open spaces. Over the years, Le Corbusier's work in Chandigarh has been preserved, and an "architectural tourism" program has been developed to promote the city.

Vancouver

Vancouver frequently appears near the top of lists of the world's most sustainable and livable cities. Blessed with a stunning location, the city juts into the waters of the Strait of Georgia and is surrounded by snowcapped mountains. Beyond its natural beauty, Vancouver has a distinctive urban pattern:

- **High-rise living:** More than 5 percent of the city's total land use is made up of apartment and condominium buildings, many of which are high-rises in the city's downtown peninsula.

- **Lots of green space:** In addition to its scenic beauty and nearby land preserves, the city is dotted with small parks that make up nearly 10 percent of all the land in the city.

- **Population density:** Compared to other major cities, Vancouver has a higher population density, which keeps people closer to where they work and play. This allows the city to offer a greater range of mass transit services and helps create a more walkable city.

Vancouver's plans for the future envision a city that values its diversity, inclusiveness, sustainability, and livability. The city faces many challenges, from managing the environmental impacts of population growth to providing more affordable housing, but Vancouver's future may just show the world that even a big city can be a green city.

Celebration

Celebration is known to some people as "the town that Disney built." Just minutes from Walt Disney World, near Orlando, Florida, the town was conceived by the Walt Disney Company in the 1990s and is now a community of about 11,000 residents. It's become one of the best known examples of the movement in architecture and urban planning known as New Urbanism (see Chapter 8).

The collaborative team that prepared the master plan for the new community featured several leading architects, including Robert A. M. Stern and Andrés Duany. Three of the most important elements of Celebration and its plan are

- **An emphasis on community:** The plan organizes all the essential elements in a community — from homes to shops to workplaces — into areas that are well connected by walking paths and have public spaces that allow people to interact with each other.

✔ **Mixed-use development:** The plan features mixed-use development areas where shops and homes are located near each other or within the same buildings.

✔ **Architectural patterns:** Buildings in Celebration are designed using a pattern book, which provides a range of architectural options and helps maintain a consistent look and feel for the community.

In addition to the overall plan for the community, the city's town center also features a number of specific buildings by "starchitects," including Robert A. M. Stern, Michael Graves, Philip Johnson, Robert Venturi and Denise Scott Brown, and César Pelli. The Walt Disney Company sold off its stake in Celebration several years ago, but to many people, Celebration is still the town where a vacation never has to end.

Chapter 21

Ten Urban Plans You Can Find Online

In This Chapter

▶ Looking at real-world urban plans

▶ Asking questions to find out what a plan is all about

▶ Finding new ideas to use in your community

Whoever wrote *Golf For Dummies* had it easy. Everyone knows what that is — it's golf. And, even if you didn't know what golf was, that problem could be easily solved by showing you a few pictures or steering you to the Golf Channel on TV.

Urban planning is a bit trickier. There's no Urban Planning Channel (at least not yet), and I don't have enough room in this book to show you an entire urban plan. Real-world urban plans are often hundreds of pages long, with numerous maps and drawings. But lots of good urban plans are out there for you to look at, and that's where the Internet comes in!

This chapter is my guide to ten urban plans you can find online. Here, I give you a bit of background information on each plan and answer several basic questions about each plan.

I've read through literally hundreds of urban plans, and I've found that asking a few basic questions can help you understand what a plan is all about. Here are the questions I ask when I'm reading an urban plan:

- ✔ What geographic area does the plan address?

- ✔ How far into the future does the plan look? Is the community planning for short-term or long-term changes (or both)?

- ✔ What topics does the plan address?

- ✔ Why was the plan prepared?

- ✔ Who was involved in making the plan?

> ✔ What does the plan say about the community's strengths and weaknesses?
>
> ✔ What are the plan's most important goals and objectives?
>
> ✔ What are the plan's most important recommendations?
>
> ✔ How will the plan be implemented?

You can always search the Internet for more urban plans and use them to discover new ideas.

A Recovery Plan for New Orleans's Lower Ninth Ward

New Orleans's Lower Ninth Ward was devastated by Hurricane Katrina in the fall of 2005. Lives were lost, homes were destroyed, and thousands of people evacuated the neighborhood. In 2007, a citywide initiative known as the Unified New Orleans Plan completed a plan titled *A Framework for Sustainable Resilience in the Lower Ninth Ward* (http://bit.ly/uM2RUc).

The plan takes a comprehensive approach to understanding both the immediate recovery needs of the neighborhood, as well as its long-term reconstruction and development over the next 10 to 20 years. The plan looks at issues including housing, economic recovery, restoration of infrastructure and utilities, hurricane and flood protection, transportation, community services, and historic preservation.

A Framework for Sustainable Resilience in the Lower Ninth Ward was adopted by both New Orleans's city council and the state redevelopment agency, which are working with other government agencies, businesses, and charitable organizations to carry out the plan. Overall, the plan seeks to empower residents and rebuild a sustainable and diverse community by implementing a wide range of specific programs, including providing financial incentives to housing reconstructions and redeveloping the neighborhood business areas. The post-disaster recovery of the Lower Ninth Ward is no small challenge, and this plan is just the first step of what will be a long journey.

A Regional Plan for Chicago

The Chicago metropolitan area is the third largest in the United States. More than 2.5 million people live in the city of Chicago, but millions more live in the surrounding suburbs and towns. In fact, the metropolitan area stretches across seven counties and includes 284 cities and towns, along with nearly a thousand other units of government, such as school districts.

The Chicago Metropolitan Agency for Planning was recently authorized by the state of Illinois to serve as a regional planning agency for the greater Chicago area. In 2010, the agency completed *GO TO 2040* (http://1.usa.gov/9FTVCC), a regional comprehensive plan to coordinate the long-term development of the region.

The plan was produced using extensive public participation, including residents and community stakeholders, as well as representatives from the city and county governments in the region. The plan argues that a regional agenda for sustainable prosperity, community collaboration, and long-range planning is necessary for the future health of the region and that no one city can survive without the others.

The plan addresses four broad themes:

✔ Creating livable communities

✔ Improving human capital

✔ Establishing more efficient government practices

✔ Enhancing the regional transportation system

The plan develops a series of goals for each theme, including supporting economic innovation and improving public transit. The plan identifies many specific actions that can be taken to implement the plan, but it's up to the region's cities and towns to take the lead on projects such as increasing local food production and coordinating local land use with regional transportation improvements. The most important element of this plan is coordination and the hope that the region can work together to ensure a brighter future.

Planning for Health and Wellness in California

Richmond, California, is a city of about 100,000 people located about 9 miles north of Oakland in the San Francisco Bay Area. The city's official comprehensive plan is called the *Richmond General Plan 2030* (www.cityofrichmondgeneralplan.org). The plan aims for Richmond to "be an inclusive city where the built environment is functional and accessible to all residents, development impacts are shared equitably, and new development is sensitive to a diverse array of social, cultural and environmental contexts."

The plan addresses a wide range of topics, such as housing, economic development, and transportation. It also deals specifically with the health and wellness of the community, a growing concern not just in Richmond, but in communities throughout the country. The plan states that a "disproportionate number of Richmond residents are at high risk of developing poor health conditions," especially the city's low-income residents and people of color.

The *Richmond General Plan 2030* examines a variety of issues related to the health of the population, including pollution levels in residential neighborhoods; access to grocery stores and healthy foods; availability of medical services; and opportunities for walking, bicycling, and other exercise. The plan sets goals for the future health and wellness of the community and makes many specific proposals, including providing incentives to healthy food stores, developing safe routes for children to walk to school, encouraging more green businesses, and monitoring air quality in at-risk neighborhoods.

Some people say that "you are what you eat," and urban planners are increasingly saying that "you are where you live." Richmond's plan recognizes that the health and wellness of the community can be improved with both good choices made by individuals and good places to live.

New York City: Bigger and Greener by 2030

New York City's mayor, Michael Bloomberg, unveiled an ambitious new plan for the city on Earth Day in 2007. Called *PlaNYC: A Greener, Greater New York* (http://on.nyc.gov/v9IU7K), the plan is a long-range strategic plan that outlines the challenges facing the city and looks for ways to make the city a more environmentally sustainable place while still accommodating future growth and improving quality of life. But the plan doesn't just "think local"; it's also thinking global and looking for ways to reduce the city's impact on global climate change.

PlaNYC focuses on three key challenges facing the city:

✔ Keeping up with population and employment growth

✔ Updating the city's aging infrastructure

✔ Reducing the city's impact on the environment

The plan sets big goals for several areas, including good housing for another million residents, improving the city's smaller parks, cleaning up contaminated land, reducing traffic congestion, using cleaner energy sources, and reducing the city's greenhouse gas emissions.

PlaNYC lays out more than a hundred initiatives that the city will use to meet the goals of the plan. These range from common-sense ideas — like reducing engine idling by trucks and taxis — to making multi-billion-dollar investments in new transportation and water infrastructure to using breakthrough technologies, such as green buildings that absorb greenhouse gases instead of producing them. Once again, New York is looking for ways to lead the world, not just in quantity, but in quality.

Boulder's Plan for Transit-Oriented Development

In 2007, the city of Boulder, Colorado, adopted a small-area comprehensive plan for the development and redevelopment of a 160-acre area known as Boulder Junction. Focusing on the core of the city, the *Transit Village Area Plan* (http://1.usa.gov/sl1xsw) is a long-range development guide for Boulder Junction that envisions the area as "a lively, mixed-use, pedestrian-oriented place where people will live, work, shop, and access regional transit" that could become an important employment center and home to several thousand new residents.

The *Transit Village Area Plan* is an example of transit-oriented development planning that coordinates the area's future land use pattern with a variety of transportation options. The plan proposes high-density residential areas that include affordable housing, mixed-use areas (with buildings that combine apartments with offices or shops), and streets that are safe for walking and bicycling. The plan locates everything close to public transportation and hopes to create a new community where, even if you have a car, you may not need to use it very often.

Tulsa's Community Vision

In Tulsa, Oklahoma, it's all about the vision. City planners asked the community to think about what the community could be in the future, and their responses are the cornerstone of Tulsa's official comprehensive plan, *PLANiTULSA: The Tulsa Comprehensive Plan* (www.planitulsa.org).

PLANiTULSA is an example of community visioning that involved the participation of thousands of people in activities such as community surveys, public meetings, brainstorming workshops, and other hands-on exercises that gave the public a chance to suggest new ideas. In one workshop, hundreds of people were given simple maps of the city and asked to draw what they thought the city should look like in the future.

Through the visioning process, Tulsans said that the city should have a dynamic economy, be attractive to young workers, have good transportation, provide a variety of housing choices, protect the environment, and promote a sustainable future. This input was used to create a conceptual land use map that illustrates the community's vision and depicts its key elements, including future growth areas, reinvestment in older neighborhoods, improvements and additions to parks and open spaces, and downtown revitalization.

But a vision isn't the same as results. The plan calls the community vision-ing process "the easy part" and says that carrying out the plan will ask even more of the community, including "leadership, dedication, hard work, and above all, cooperation among people with different perspectives, opinions, and expertise."

Grand Rapids's Blueprint for the Future

In 2000, the mayor of Grand Rapids, Michigan, appointed a 31-member steer-ing committee to guide the creation of a new official comprehensive plan for the city that would replace the city's previous plan from 1963. At the time, there was no legal requirement for the city to update its master plan. But Mayor John Logie (and many others) felt that a new plan would help energize the community to take on its challenges, including creating new jobs in health-care and high-tech industries to replace once-plentiful factory jobs. The result was the *City of Grand Rapids 2002 Master Plan* (http://bit.ly/tDcjG2).

Thousands of people were involved in creating the plan (most of whom are thanked individually in very small type in the plan itself), and the plan's goals look ahead to a city that provides great neighborhoods, high-quality business districts, transportation options for everyone, a strong economy, and a city in balance with nature.

The plan calls itself a "vision, blueprint, and strategy" for the future of the community. It provides a framework for future "local and regional coopera-tion and public and private partnerships" to get the community involved in carrying out the plan. The *City of Grand Rapids 2002 Master Plan* includes a detailed implementation matrix that shows how the plan can be carried out, not just by the local government but by the community as a whole. Grand Rapids's plan recognizes not only that cities are changing places, but also that a community's people and institutions may need to change and cooper-ate if they're going to make their community a better place.

Planning the Suburbs in Ohio

The city of Dublin, Ohio, is located about 20 miles north of Columbus, and it hasn't always been a city. Founded more than 200 years ago, it was once a vil-lage, then a small town, before eventually becoming an attractive and upscale suburb in the 1970s. Today, the city is home to more than 35,000 people, and its official comprehensive plan, *2007 Dublin Community Plan* (http://bit.ly/sDsDTo), aims to manage continued growth, while protecting the city's historic character and environmental resources.

This long-range plan addresses a wide range of topics, including land use, transportation, community facilities, budgetary issues, infrastructure, natural resources, community character, and historic preservation.

The plan considers a variety of possible scenarios for future growth and how different areas may be used to accommodate new housing, offices, and retail development. The plan aims to coordinate transportation improvements with the development of new residential areas, provide more mixed-use districts that combine housing with office or retail uses, and maintaining the city's historic downtown village as the center of the community.

The city of Dublin intends to implement the plan through its own development programs and enforcement of land use regulations. The plan says that it serves as a framework for development by private businesses and that proposals for future development should be consistent with the comprehensive plan. By adopting general goals and specific regulations for future development, Dublin hopes to build on its long and successful history.

Planning for America's Megaregions

Most cities and towns have their own comprehensive plans. Some metropolitan areas, like Chicago, have comprehensive plans. But what about plans for even larger areas? A nonprofit organization called America 2050 (`www.america2050.org`) thinks that we should be planning for the future of our "megaregions." America 2050 outlines its goals in *America 2050: A Prospectus* (`http://bit.ly/tFdLJC`).

More of a report than an actual plan, the prospectus observes that most of the U.S. population lives and works in megaregions that are connected by their environment, infrastructure, economies, land use patterns, and shared histories. Here are two examples of places that this interesting report defines as megaregions:

- **The Northeast Megaregion:** Stretching from Boston through New York, Philadelphia, and Baltimore, to Washington, D.C., this megaregion includes 18 percent of the U.S. population and is expected to grow 20 percent by the year 2025.

- **The Piedmont Atlantic Megaregion:** This megaregion runs through several southern states, connecting Atlanta, Charlotte (North Carolina), and Birmingham (Alabama). The population of this megaregion is expected to grow by 40 percent by 2025.

America 2050 thinks that planning for megaregions can help the United States solve both local and national problems, including becoming more competitive in the global economy and protecting environmental resources. America 2050 also suggests that the nation and its cities can use megaregional planning to make better decisions about costly transportation and infrastructure investments, such as investing in high-speed rail systems to connect cities within megaregions. By 2050, the U.S. population is expected to grow by more than 100 million people, and planning for megaregions may be one way to help deal with the big changes ahead.

Designing the Future in Fayetteville

Fayetteville is a midsize city in central Arkansas, home to about 75,000 people and the University of Arkansas. The city has been growing in recent years, and its official comprehensive plan, *City Plan 2025* (http://bit.ly/rKWeBq), is a great example of how urban design can be used to shape urban growth in ways that are both attractive and functional.

The plan identifies several challenges for the community, including promoting the redevelopment of existing urban areas, making room for new growth in ways that strengthen the community, and protecting rural and undeveloped areas from urban sprawl.

Fayetteville's plan uses many techniques from the New Urbanism approach to urban design (see Chapter 8). The plan's land use concept map identifies new areas that can be developed as neighborhoods, mixed-use districts, and corridors. The plan states that new development should be "compact, complete, and connected," meaning that future development should minimize land use, include mixed land uses, and be connected to the transportation network in multiple ways (not just by car).

One of the plan's innovative aspects is that it proposes that the city adopt a form-based code, rather than traditional zoning, to regulate future land use. In particular, a form-based code will be used to guide the development of mixed-use districts, streets that encourage pedestrian and bicycle usage, and residential areas that provide a mix of different housing types and styles. This plan uses lots of great maps and drawings that show the city's path to a well-designed future.

Appendix

Resources

· ·

*U*rban planning is a broad field that draws on ideas and information from a wide range of resources. The practice of urban planning also changes on a frequent basis in order to incorporate new concepts, address changing conditions, and experiment with new urban planning techniques. The resources in this appendix will help you learn more about urban planning and keep you up to date on the latest information and ideas that you can use to help plan your community.

Professional and Educational Organizations

American Institute of Architects (www.aia.org): The American Institute of Architects (AIA) website provides news and information about architecture, design, and planning. The AIA's Community by Design program to encourage "healthy, safe, and sustainable" local communities is featured on its website and contains many downloadable publications with ideas for improving the design of cities and towns.

American Planning Association (www.planning.org): The American Planning Association (APA) is the leading professional organization in the United States representing urban planners and their communities. The APA website has information on current events in urban planning, articles from *Planning Magazine,* links to state and local chapters, and information about APA conference and awards programs. Information about the American Institute of Certified Planners, the APA's program for professional credentials for urban planning, also can be found on this website.

American Society of Landscape Architects (www.asla.org): The American Society of Landscape Architects (ASLA) website contains lots of useful information about local planning, including sections on livable communities and local advocacy efforts. There are also links to state licensing agencies for landscape architecture, information about state chapters, and selections from the ASLA's magazine, *Landscape Architecture.*

Association of Collegiate Schools of Planning (www.acsp.org): The Association of Collegiate Schools of Planning (ACSP) is a consortium representing most American and Canadian colleges and universities that offer training and degree programs in urban planning. The website features a downloadable version of its Guide to Undergraduate and Graduate Education in Planning and links to ACSP member programs.

Canadian Institute of Planners (www.cip-icu.ca): Also known as Institut Canadien des Urbanistes (ICU), the Canadian Institute of Planners (CIP) is a professional association representing the "voice of Canada's planning community." The CIP website includes information about local affiliates, Canadian urban planning conferences, news about urban planning in Canada, and information on Canadian employment opportunities in urban planning.

Planners Network (www.plannersnetwork.org): Planners Network is a U.S.-based international association that advocates progressive urban planning, including social, economic, and environmental justice. Its website includes information on local chapters, resources for online networking, discussion forums, and a Student Disorientation Guide with advice for college students interested in urban planning and social change.

News and Blogs

Cyburbia (www.cyburbia.org): This website bills itself as "a place for planners, planning students, architects, urbanists, and others interested or involved in shaping the built environment." It features news, blogs, and free-wheeling forums for discussions about urban planning.

New Urban Network (www.newurbannetwork.com): This is the website of the *New Urban News,* a printed publication that goes out eight times per year. The website features news and discussions that focus on new urbanism and sustainable design.

Planetizen (www.planetizen.com): Planetizen features up-to-date news and blogs related to every aspect of urban planning. The site also contains urban planning job listings and online professional training courses.

Planning Commissioners Journal (www.plannersweb.com): This is a companion website to the printed publication. The website features news and in-depth articles about urban planning that are geared toward nonprofessional planning commissioners who serve on local planning and zoning boards.

Streetsblog (www.streetsblog.org): This website is a great source for information and conversation about the growing importance of alternative transportation, especially walking and bicycling. Its companion site, Streetfilms (www.streetfilms.org), has dozens of videos on how to improve local streets.

Urban Design and Historic Preservation

Congress for New Urbanism (www.cnu.org): This 20-year-old nonprofit organization promotes walkable, mixed-use neighborhood development, sustainable communities, and healthier living conditions. Its website provides information on state chapters and initiatives for legislative reform to support new urbanism, as well as updates on its conferences and many free downloadable publications.

National Trust for Historic Preservation (www.preservationnation.org): This organization was founded through an act of the U.S. Congress and advocates for the nation's historic places and buildings. Its website has details about the organization's programs and services, as well as informative how-to resources on local historic preservation and articles from its magazine, *Preservation.*

Project for Public Spaces (www.pps.org): The Project for Public Spaces (PPS) is a nonprofit planning, design, and educational organization dedicated to helping people create and sustain public spaces that build stronger communities. Its website has a wealth of informative materials, as well as a "Hall of Shame," which features poorly designed urban spaces.

Regional Planning and Sustainable Development

American Farmland Trust (www.farmland.org): This organization is dedicated to preserving ranchland and farmland. Its website provides studies and reports on farmland preservation, as well as an "action center" where you can learn more about national and local efforts to preserve farmland.

The Nature Conservancy (www.nature.org): This million-member nonprofit organization works to preserve natural lands and is active in all 50 U.S. states and in 30 other countries. Its website is a comprehensive source for information on land conservation and features the Development by Design initiative, which promotes sustainable urban and rural development.

Smart Growth America (www.smartgrowthamerica.org): Smart Growth America is a national coalition of organizations that advocate the smart growth approach to regional development (see Chapter 13). Its website features up-to-date news about smart growth, research reports, and examples of best practices in local planning.

Trust for Public Land (www.tpl.org): This organization helps local communities develop new, publicly accessible resources for conservation and recreation. The website features information on land conservation methods, as well as articles from its magazine, *Land and People.*

U.S. Green Building Council (www.usgbc.org): The U.S. Green Building Council (USGBC) is a membership-based, nonprofit organization that is best known for the development of the Leadership in Energy and Environmental Design (LEED) standards for environmentally friendly buildings. Its website has lots of information on green neighborhood development, technical information about green buildings, and articles from its *GreenSource* magazine.

Community and Economic Development

Center for Neighborhood Technology (www.cnt.org): Founded in 1978, this organization promotes sustainable community development at the neighborhood level. Its website features downloadable reports on a wide range of topics and some cool interactive tools, like the Housing + Transportation Affordability Index, which shows customized local maps of housing, transportation, and environmental conditions.

International Economic Development Council (www.iedconline.org): This organization represents professionals involved in local and regional economic development. It offers a professional credential (Certified Economic Developer), and its website features an Economic Development Reference Guide on topics ranging from business attraction to venture capital.

NeighborWorks America (www.nw.org): This national nonprofit organization provides communities across the country with financial support and technical assistance related to affordable housing and community development. Its website has up-to-date information on housing foreclosure prevention and links to local organizations providing housing assistance programs. An affiliated website called StableCommunities.org (www.stablecommunities.org) features case studies of best practices in housing and neighborhood development from across the United States.

Transportation and Infrastructure

Institute of Transportation Engineers (www.ite.org): The Institute of Transportation Engineers (ITE) is a professional association and publisher of industry-standard studies and reference publications used in transportation planning. Its *Trip Generation* series of manuals is a standard reference source used in local plans. Its website features information on topics ranging from traffic calming to childhood obesity to pedestrian safety.

Reconnecting America (www.reconnectingamerica): This nonprofit organization works with communities across the country to promote the improvement of local transportation systems. Its website features lots of useful resources and downloadable reports. An associated program, called the Center for Transit-Oriented Development (www.ctod.org), serves as a clearinghouse for information on transit-oriented development that can be used to promote and implement local projects.

Report Card for America's Infrastructure (www.infrastructurereport card.org): This program of the American Society of Civil Engineers features a nationally recognized report card that grades the condition of the nation's bridges, highways, schools, and other infrastructure elements. An interactive map feature provides information on infrastructure conditions in states and selected local areas.

Surface Transportation Policy Partnership (www.transact.org): This nonprofit organization advocates for federal, state, and local support for transportation policies that "enhance the quality, livability, and character of communities and support revitalization without displacement." Its website includes a variety of downloadable reports of transportation topics and how-to guides that can be used to improve local transportation systems.

Transportation Research Board (www.trb.org): This organization, a division of the National Academies, provides transportation engineers and other professionals with the latest research, information, and analyses on a wide variety of transportation topics. Its website features lots of useful data on transportation and free downloadable research reports on a wide range of transportation topics, including sustainable transportation and community walkability.

U.S. Government Agencies

The federal government carries out policies and programs in a wide range of areas related to urban and regional planning. Websites for federal agencies are a great source of information on policies related to local and regional planning, as well as sources of historic and current data. The following list isn't intended to be comprehensive, but it includes information about some of the federal agencies that are most relevant to urban planning:

Census Bureau (`www.census.gov`): The Census Bureau is an invaluable source for social, demographic, and economic data about national, state, and local conditions. Its website hosts interactive database and mapping tools to access the decennial U.S. Census and the yearly American Community Survey (see the next section).

Department of Housing and Urban Development (`www.hud.gov`): The Housing and Urban Development (HUD) website features information on federal programs supporting local housing and urban planning, specialized databases on urban development and housing, and a library of resources related to homeownership, community development, and housing discrimination.

Department of Transportation (`www.dot.gov`): This website features information on the federal government's transportation programs, current and historic data on transportation use, and research reports on a wide range of national, regional, and local transportation issues.

Environmental Protection Agency (`www.epa.gov`): This website features information and data related to Environmental Protection Agency (EPA) programs, including the agency's Office of Sustainable Communities, which aims to "help communities become stronger, healthier, and more sustainable through smarter growth and green building."

Federal Emergency Management Agency (`www.fema.gov`): The Federal Emergency Management Agency (FEMA) website provides information and guides about pre-disaster planning for local communities, as well as extensive information on post-disaster management and assistance.

U.S. Army Corps of Engineers (`www.usace.army.mil`): The Army Corps of Engineers website features information about its facilities (such as dams and levees), as well as information on the use of federally protected natural resources, including wetlands and other bodies of water.

U.S. Geological Survey (`www.usgs.gov`): The U.S. Geological Survey (USGS) is a scientific agency that conducts research in many different areas of earth science. Its website features databases and mapping tools that provide customized information on topics including earthquake risks, natural habitats, and hydrologic conditions.

Research, Data, and Maps

American Community Survey (`www.census.gov/acs`): The American Community Survey provide the most up-to-date information on population and housing in the United States, with detailed data on hundreds of topics pertaining to states, metropolitan areas, cities, and neighborhoods. Unlike the U.S. Census that is collected once every ten years, this survey program conducts a small annual survey of the American public to learn about current demographic, economic, and housing conditions.

Brookings Institution's Metropolitan Policy Program (www.brookings. edu/metro.aspx): The Brookings Institution is a nonpartisan think tank based in Washington, D.C., and its Metropolitan Policy Program publishes a wide range of cutting-edge research reports on topics related to urban policy, urban economics, urban demographics, and urban planning.

Esri (www.esri.com): Esri produces the most popular software used by geographic information systems (GIS). Its website features a wide range of examples of the use of GIS and free online training courses that are used by many colleges and universities.

Google Earth (http://earth.google.com): Google Earth, along with Google SketchUp (see the next listing), are among the coolest online mapping and planning tools on the Internet. Google Earth provides detailed maps and supplemental information for places across the globe.

Google SketchUp (http://sketchup.google.com): Google SketchUp is a 3-D drawing tool that can be used independently or with Google Earth (see the preceding listing) to create virtual models of buildings.

HUDUSER (www.huduser.org): This website is a service of the U.S. Department of Housing and Urban Development and provides access to an extensive collection of professional and academic research reports on topics related to housing and urban planning.

Lincoln Institute for Land Policy (www.lincolninst.edu): This research and educational organization focuses on "issues concerning the use, regulation, and taxation of land" in the United States and abroad. Its web resources include reports, data, and online courses about land development issues.

Urban Land Institute (www.uli.org): The Urban Land Institute (ULI) is a U.S.-based nonprofit organization that promotes the "responsible use of land and . . . creating and sustaining thriving communities worldwide." Its website features data and reports related to real estate development and urban planning across a wide range of topics.

U.S. Census (www.census.gov): The Census Bureau's decennial U.S. Census provides detailed information on demographic and housing conditions in the United States and is based on a survey of the entire U.S. population. This survey is conducted every ten years and is required by the Constitution in order to apportion seats in the House of Representatives based on the population of each state.

Global Planning

United Nations (www.un.org): Several departments and divisions of the United Nations address global urban planning issues:

- ✓ **The Department of Economic and Social Affairs** publishes the *World Urbanization Prospects* report (http://esa.un.org/unpd/wup) and oversees the Division for Sustainable Development (www.un.org/esa/dsd), which promotes sustainable development programs throughout the world.

- ✓ **The United Nations Development Programme** (www.undp.org) publishes an annual *Human Development Report,* which includes data on urban development conditions around the world. The UNDP also administers the UN Millennium Development Goals program (www.un.org/millenniumgoals), which seeks to improve urban conditions in the world's poorest countries.

- ✓ **The United Nations Human Settlements Programme,** known as HABITAT (www.unhabitat.org), provides technical assistance on urban planning and development to governments and nongovernmental organizations around the world. This agency also collects and distributes a wide range of data and information on the world's cities, including regular publication of its *State of the World's Cities* and *Global Report on Human Settlements.*

The World Bank's Urban Development program (www.worldbank.org/urban): The World Bank is a multinational financial institution supported by member countries that provides financial support and technical advice to developing countries and regions. Its Urban Development program promotes "sustainable cities and towns that fulfill the promise of development for their inhabitants." The website provides data, reports, and information on programs related to urban development in developing cities and countries.

Index

• A •

access by proximity, 134, 143
ACSP (Association of Collegiate Schools of
    Planning), 318
active open space, 158
activist, becoming an, 275
adaptive reuse, 203–204
adult care, 104
advisory committees, 274
aesthetic character of community, housing
    contributing to, 98
affordable housing, 105–107, 116–117, 205
Africa, 259–262
agricultural land use, 82, 158
air freight, 127
air quality, 152
airports, 126
alternative fuels, 123, 133, 167
America 2050: A Prospectus (online urban plan),
    315–316
American Community Survey, 322–323
American Farmland Trust, 319
American Institute of Architects (AIA), 317
American Institute of Certified Planners (AICP), 286
American Planning Association (APA), 289, 299, 317
American Society of Landscape Architects
    (ASLA), 317
Amsterdam, Netherlands, 302
Anaheim, California, 88
architects, 54
architectural styles, using diverse and
    complementary, 141–142
arts and culture, 199–202
Asia, 256–259
assisted living for the elderly, 105
Association of Collegiate Schools of Planning
    (ACSP), 318
atmospheric hazards, 224
attached single-family houses, 101
Austin, Texas, 58, 59, 73, 201
automated toll-road collection, 132
automobiles
    car sharing, 134
    car-free zones, 189
    carpooling programs, 132
    dependence on, 209

green vehicles, supporting, 189
vehicle emissions, reducing, 183
Zipcar, 134

• B •

Baby Boomers, 87, 195
Baltimore, Maryland, 199
bars and liquor stores, 95
Bartik, Timothy (labor economist), 244
beaches, 156, 157
bicycling, 125
BIDs (business improvement districts), 249
big box stores, 95
bike sharing, 134, 294
biodiversity, 155–156
bio-regional plans, 194
BIXI (bike share program), 134
blocks (street), 138–140
block-style buildings, 102
Bloomberg, Michael (mayor of New York City), 312
Boston, Massachusetts
    park system, 159
    race, makeup of population by, 31–33
Boulder, Colorado, 99, 313
Brawer, Wendy (artist), 193
Brookings Institution's Metropolitan Policy
    Program, 323
brownfields, 155, 187
budget, during preliminary planning creating a, 58
building codes, 94
buildings
    accessory elements, 137
    appearance of, 137
    energy efficient, 184
    shape of, 137
Burnham, Daniel (urban planner), 1, 305
bus rapid transit (BRT), 123
bus services, 123
business districts, 139–141
business expansions, 243
business improvement districts (BIDs), 249
business incubators, 252
business retention programs, 246–247
businesses, attracting new, 19, 243–244
buying local, 185, 241

• C •

Cairo, Egypt, 262
Canadian Cohousing Network, 107
Canadian Institute of Planners (CIP), 318
Canberra, Australia, 305–306
careers in urban planning, 21, 284–290
carpooling programs, 132
cars. *See* automobiles
casinos and gaming, developing, 242–243
CDCs (community development corporations), 205
Celebration, Florida, 307–308
Census Bureau, 322
Center for Neighborhood Technology, 320
central cities, 24
Central Park (New York, New York), 159
Certified Economic Developer (CeCD)
    certification, 287
challenges for urban plans, 15–20
Chandigarh, India, 306
cheap housing, 107
Chicago, Illinois
    GO TO 2040, 310–311
    high-rise apartments in, 198
Chicago Metropolis 2020 (Commercial Club of
    Chicago), 49
children, increase in number of, 30
CIP (Canadian Institute of Planners), 318
cities and towns
    official comprehensive plans, 47
    overview, 47
    slow growth trend in, 27
    specialized plans, 47–48
    strategic plans, 48
    sub-area plans, 47
    topical plans, 48
    urban design, 140–141
citizen planners, 277
city councils, 52
City of Grand Rapids 2002 Master Plan (online
    urban plan), 314
City Plan 2025 (online urban plan), 316
civic organizations, 49, 56
civil and transportation engineers, 54
clawback provisions, 251
clean and safe, making community, 205
Clean Water Act, 154
Cleveland, Ohio, 205
climate change, 183–184
cluster development, 110–111
co-housing, 107
Cohousing Association of the United States, 107
collector streets, 121–122

colleges and universities affecting jobs and
    economic development, 245
combined sewer system, 171
commercial land use, 82, 88
commercial transportation, 125–127
commercial zones, 92
communities. *See also* improving your community
    data on, collecting and analyzing, 60–63
    demographic changes in, 61–62
    economic changes in, 62
    facilities and services, 172–174
    general background information on, 61
    involvement in, 269–277
    long-term, building communities for, 221
    needs, assessing, 175–176
    parks, 159
    risks, assessing, 228–229
    sense of, 136
    service areas, 176
    site locations, 176
    stakeholders, 55–56
    SWOT approach for analyzing information on, 62
    types of, 47–50
    understanding, 60–63
    urban sprawl causing loss of sense of, 211
community design, 144–147
community development, 204–206
community development corporations
    (CDCs), 205
community development department, 270
community development planners, 281, 288
community facilities map, 176
community indicators, 71, 193
community organizations, 56
community outreach programs, 206
commuter buses, 123
commuter rail, 124
complete streets, 139
comprehensive community development
    initiatives, 206
comprehensive plans. *See* urban plans
computerized traffic signal systems, 131
conceptual future land use map, 89, 90
Congestion Charge Zone (London, England), 133
congestion pricing, 133
Congress for New Urbanism, 136, 319
conservation and preservation of environment
    advantages of, 151
    conservation areas, 155–158
    ecological resources, 151–155
    health impacts, 161
    inventory of natural resources, taking, 161
    management of natural resources, 162
    monitoring conditions, 160–162

open space, 158–159
overview, 149–151
parks and recreation, 159–160
regulations, 150, 162
conservation areas, 155–157
conservation easements, 218
consulting services, 59
controversial land use, 94–96
convention centers, developing, 242
corridors, 191
cost-benefit studies, 219
councils of governments, 49, 270
county governments, 48–49
Cowan, Stuart (ecologist), 143
critical habitat, 162
cross-acceptance, 217
culture and arts, 199–202
Curitiba, Brazil, 190
Cyburbia (website), 289, 318

• *D* •

Dallas, Texas, 202
damage, assessing disaster, 234
data on community, collecting and analyzing, 60–63
data resources. *See* research, data, and map resources
Dayton, Ohio, 200
The Death and Life of Great American Cities (Jacobs), 107
deficient housing conditions, 115
demographers, 55
demographic trends and changes
age groups, planning for all, 29–30
children, increase in number of, 30
in community, 61–62
diverse population, planning for a, 30–33
future land use demand affected by, 86–87
infrastructure and public services affected by, 165
older people, increase in, 30
overview, 29
working-age adults, number of, 30
density, building at appropriate, 219–220
Denver, Colorado, 192, 203
Department of Economic and Social Affairs (United Nations), 324
design. *See* urban design
detached single-family houses, 100–101
Detroit, Michigan
employment trends in, 36–37
food deserts in, 185
schools, closing, 174

disaster planning
hazard-mitigation planning, 227–231
hazards, types of, 224–225
local agencies and departments involved in, 226
local officials and community stakeholders involved in, 226
manmade hazards, 225
multi-hazards approach to, 225
natural hazards, 224–225
nonprofit organizations involved in, 227
overview, 223–224
parties involved in, 226–227
post-disaster recovery, 231–235
state and federal agencies involved in, 227
urban planning agencies involved in, 226
utility companies and local businesses involved in, 226
disaster resilience, 223
diverse population, planning for a, 30–33
domestic wastewater, 170
downtown areas
attractive and distinctive downtowns, designing, 196–197
full-time use of, 197
high-rise apartments, 198
housing in, 198
lofts and industrial conversions, 198
overview, 196
range of uses for, promoting, 196
revitalizing, 196–198
urban villages, 198
downtown plans, 50
drainage facilities, 171
Duany, Andres (New Urbanist architect), 140
Dublin, Ohio, 314–315
Dunham-Jones, Ellen *(Retrofitting Suburbia: Urban Design Solution for Redesigning Suburbs)*, 220
Durieux, Mark B. *(Social Entrepreneurship For Dummies)*, 275, 299
duties of professional urban planners, 280–282

• *E* •

ecological design, 143
ecological footprint analysis, 192–193
ecological resources, 151–155
ecological restoration, 191
economic base, strengthening community's, 240–241
economic development. *See* jobs and economic development
economic development planner, 281, 288
economic gardening, 246

economic trends and changes
  in community, 62
  employment trends in 12 largest industries in
    U.S., 33–38
  future land use demand affected by, 86–87
  and housing, 116–117
  infrastructure and public services affected
    by, 165
  overview, 10
  sustainable urban development, economy as
    element of, 182
economists, 55
education and training for professional urban
    planners, 284–287
educational organizations. *See* professional and
    educational organizations
electrical generation facilities, 166–167
emergency housing, 105
employment
  access to, 211
  jobs and economic development, employment-
    based incentives for, 250
  opportunities for professional urban planners,
    289–290
  trends, 33–34, 35–38
empty nesters, 114
energy resources, 166–167, 185
energy use
  improving, 183
  national trends in, 168
environment. *See also* conservation and
    preservation of environment
  concerns about, 11
  global ecological impact, reducing, 16
  global urban planning, 256
  green, going, 16
  impact on
    housing, 117–118
    infrastructure and public services,
      165, 177–178
    transportation, 120, 129–130, 133–134
  land use, environmental factors in, 80, 85–86
  post distaster environmental recovery, 235
  sustainable urban development, environment
    as element of, 182
  trends in environmental issues, 39
  urban geographies, 39
environmental footprint, 192–193
environmental impact review, 94
environmental planner, 288
Environmental Protection Agency (EPA),
    152, 322
environmental scientists and engineers, 54

environmentally friendly. *See* green
    (environmentally friendly)
Erickcek, George (labor economist), 244
Esri, 323
examples of urban planning
  Amsterdam, Netherlands, 302
  Canberra, Australia, 305–306
  Celebration, Florida, 307–308
  Chandigarh, India, 306
  garden cities of England, 304–305
  New York, New York, 304
  Rome, Italy, 301–302
  Savannah, Georgia, 302–303
  Vancouver, Canada, 307
  Washington, D.C., 303–304
existing development, 86
existing land use, 81–84

• F •

farmland preservation, 218
fastest-growing cities, 28
Fayetteville, Arkansas, 316
Federal Emergency Management Agency
    (FEMA), 322
financial incentives for jobs and economic
    development, 249–251
First Suburbs Coalition, 212
floodplains, 156, 157
Florida, Richard *(The Rise of the Creative
    Class)*, 200
focus groups, 273
food deserts, 185
food systems, supporting local, 185
forests, 157–158
form-based codes, 147, 221
Fort Wayne, Indiana, 237
fossil fuels, 183
*A Framework for Sustainable Resilience in the
    Lower Ninth Ward* (online urban plan), 310
Freed, Eric Corey *(Green Building &
    Remodeling)*, 117
Fulton, William (urban planner), 208
Fundraising For Dummies (Mutz and Murray), 299
future land use demand
  commercial land use, 88
  demographic changes affecting, 86–87
  economic changes affecting, 86–87
  estimating, 87–88
  forecasting, 86–90
  future land use map, 89–90
  population changes affecting, 86
  residential land use, 88
  supporting land uses, 88

future land use map, 89–90, 91
Future Melbourne (comprehensive plan), 69

• *G* •

garden cities of England, 304–305
Garden Cities of To-morrow (Howard), 305
general planner, 287
general plans, 11, 44, 45, 47
Geographic Information Systems (GIS)
    specialist, 288
geographic targeting for jobs and economic
    development, 240, 250
geographic trends affecting infrastructure and
    public services, 165
geologic hazards, 224
GHG (greenhouse gases), 151, 152–153, 183–184
GIS Professional (GISP) certification, 287
Glendenning, Parris (former Maryland
    governor), 218
global climate change. *See* climate change
global ecological impact, reducing, 16
global urban planning
    for Africa, 259–262
    for Asia, 256–259
    challenges, 254–256
    environmental issues, 256
    for Latin America, 263–266
    overview, 253–254
    poverty, reducing, 255
    rapid growth, managing, 255
    resources, 324
    slums, improving, 255
    social development, supporting, 256
    traffic and transportation problems,
        solving, 256
    trends, 39, 254
    urban services, providing, 255
global urban population, 40–42
GO TO 2040 (online urban plan), 310–311
Godschalk, David (safe-growth audit), 231
Golden Triangle (Pittsburgh), 197
Google Earth, 83, 323
Google SketchUp, 323
government agencies, 53–54
government incentives for jobs and economic
    development, 244
Grand Rapids, Michigan, 314
graywater, 170
green (environmentally friendly)
    buildings, 186–187
    energy, 183
    going, 16

housing, 117–118, 188
industries, promoting green business
    practices for, 184
infrastructure, 189
maps, 193–194
transportation alternatives, 188–189
Green Building & Remodeling (Freed), 117
greenbelts, 159, 160
greenhouse gas emissions, 151, 152–153,
    183–184
greenprints, 190–192
greenways, 159, 160
Griffin, Marion Mahony (architect), 305–306
Griffin, Walter Burley (architect), 305–306
growth management planning, 17–18
Guide to Graduate Urban Planning Programs, 285
*Guide to Undergraduate and Graduate Education
    in Urban and Regional Planning,* 285

• *H* •

habitats, 155–156, 191
hazard abatement, 230
hazard-mitigation planning
    community risks, assessing, 228–229
    existing hazards, mitigating, 229–230
    identifying hazards, 228–229
    local comprehensive plans, 227
    overview, 18, 227–228
    priorities, setting, 229
    reducing potential hazards, 229–231
    safe growth, promoting, 230–231
    specialized plans, 228
hazards
    containing, 230
    housing, 117–118
    preparing for, 230
    reducing, 230
    types of, 224–225
health
    environmental issues, 39, 161
    housing contribution to health of
        community, 98
    infrastructure and public services, impact of, 164
    urban sprawl, health issues associated with, 211
heavy rail, 124
high-density multifamily housing, 103
high-rise apartments, 198
highways, 210
historic districts, 203
historic features, using, 142
historic preservation, 202–204
historic preservation planner, 288

hospitals, 174, 245
housing
  aesthetic character of community,
    contribution to, 98
  affordable, 105–107, 116–117
  age of, 114
  attached single-family houses, 101
  cheap, 107
  co-housing, 107
  costs, 114, 116–117
  current housing supply, 113
  deficient housing conditions, 115
  demand for, keeping up with, 113
  detached single-family houses, 100–101
  in downtown areas, 198
  economic trends and, 116–117
  energy conservation, 117–118
  environmental impact of, 117–118
  future housing demand, 113
  green, 117–118, 188
  hazards, health and safety, 117–118
  health and welfare of community, contribution
    to, 98, 117–118
  high-density multifamily housing, 103
  high-rise apartments, 198
  household income spent on, 106
  land use, relation to, 79, 99
  location, 115–116
  lofts and industrial conversions, 198
  low-density multifamily housing, 101–102
  maintenance, 114–115
  manufactured housing, 103–104
  medium-density multifamily housing, 102
  mixed-use development, 188
  multifamily, 188
  overview, 97–98
  owner-occupied, 114
  planning
    for diverse, 296
    for greener, 187–188
  public, 106
  public services, relation to, 99
  quality of life and, 98
  renter-occupied, 114
  residential areas, 108–112
  resource conservation, 117–118
  role of, 98–99
  Section 8 housing program, 106
  smaller houses, 188
  for special needs, 104–105
  subsidized, 106–107
  tax revenue from, 98
  types of, 99–104, 113–114
  urban villages, 198

housing planner, 288
Houston, Texas, 36–37
Howard, Ebenezer *(Garden Cities of To-morrow),*
  305
hub-and-spoke system, 126
HUD (U.S. Department of Housing and Urban
  Development), 118
Hudson Valley region (New York), 213
HUDUSER, 323
hydrologic hazards, 224

• *I* •

Imagine Austin Comprehensive Plan, 58, 59
import substitution, 185, 241
improving your community
  design techniques for, 295
  enjoyable public places, creating, 293–294
  housing, planning for diverse, 296
  nature, including, 295–296
  neighborhoods, revitalizing, 297–298
  overview, 20–21
  recreation, providing places for, 296–297
  smart growth approach for, 298–299
  special place, making community a, 297
  starting, ideas for, 299
  steps for, 299
  transportation system, creating a good, 294
incentive zoning, 93
inclusionary zoning, 93
Indianapolis, Indiana, 199, 201
industrial land use, 82, 95
industrial parks, 252
industrial wastewater, 170
industrial zones, 92
industries
  matching workers to, 247
  promoting green business practices for, 184
  targeting specific, 241
infill redevelopment, 187
informal plans, 44
infrastructure and public services
  capital improvements, costs of, 177
  changing communities, coordinating with,
    165–166
  community facilities and services, 172–174
  community needs, assessing, 175–176
  costs of, 164
  demographic trends affecting, 165
  duplication of, 211
  economic trends affecting, 165
  environmental impact, 165, 177–178
  evaluating, 175–178

future improvements, determining locations
for, 176–177
geographic trends affecting, 165
health impact of, 164
housing, relation to, 99
importance of, 164–165
land use, coordinating with, 80, 164
local government assistance with, 251–252
long-lasting nature of, 164
overview, 163–164
resources, 320–321
sustainable urban development, 189
utilities and services, 166–172
inner-ring suburbs, 212
Institute of Transportation Engineers (ITE),
320–321
intelligent transportation systems (ITS), 131–132
interaction, designing places for, 142
intercity buses, 126
intermodal transportation, 126
international development planner, 288
International Economic Development Council, 320
Internet resources
Cyburbia, 289, 318
New Urban Network, 318
Planetizen, 289, 318
Planning Commissioners Journal, 318
Streetsblog, 318

• J •

Jacobs, Jane (*The Death and Life of Great
American Cities*), 107
Jeanneret, Charles-Édouard (architect), 306
jobs and economic development
analyzing local economy, 239–240
assets, building on local, 19
business expansions, 243
business improvement districts (BIDs), 249
business incubators, 252
businesses, attracting new, 19, 243–244
buying local, 241
cash and in-kind subsidies for, 250
casinos and gaming, developing, 242–243
colleges and universities effect on, 245
convention centers, developing, 242
diversifying local economy, 241
economic base, strengthening community's,
240–241
employment-based incentives for, 250
expansion of larger businesses, 246
expansion of small and medium-sized
businesses, 246

federal and state government facilities effect
on, 245
financial incentives for, 249–251
geographic targeting for, 240, 250
goals for, 238
government incentives, 244
hospitals and medical research institutions
affecting, 245
industrial parks, 252
industries, targeting specific, 241
infrastructure and utilities, local government
assistance with, 251–252
land use, coordinating with, 251–252
major projects and attractions, developing,
242–243
one-stop centers, 249
overview, 19, 238–239
planning for, 240–247
population characteristics and, 239
professional sports facilities, developing, 242
programs and policies, 248–252
promotional campaigns for, 249
relocations, 244
retaining local businesses, 246–247
startup companies, 243, 246
supporting local businesses, 245–247
tax incentives for, 250
workforce development, 247
Johannesburg, South Africa, 260–261

• K •

Kalamazoo, Michigan, 248
Kalamazoo County, Michigan, 155–156
Kansas City, Missouri, 204
Kyoto Protocol, 183

• L •

land assembly, 251
land cover analysis, 83
land resources, 154–155
land suitability, 85
land use
aerial photography of, 83
agricultural, 82
bars and liquor stores, 95
big box stores, 95
building codes, 94
classifications, 81–82
commercial, 82
controversial, 94–96

land use *(continued)*
  coordinating with
    infrastructure and public services, 164
    jobs and economic development, 251–252
  environmental factors, 85–86
  environmental impact review, 94
  environmental resources and, 80
  existing, 81–84
  existing land use maps, 83–84
  finding information about, 270–271
  future land use demand, forecasting, 86–90
  geographic location of city's essential
    features, 78
  housing, relation to, 79, 99
  importance of, 78
  increasing land use by urban areas, 39
  industrial, 82, 95
  infrastructure and public services and, 80
  inventories, 83
  LULUs (locally unwanted land uses), 95
  mixed, 82, 142
  natural environment, impact of city on, 79
  objectionable land use, balancing community
    concern with, 95–96
  open space, 82
  overview, 78
  patterns, determining, 120
  planning, 85–90, 187
  properties, classifying, 82–83
  public, 82
  redevelopment, 187
  regionally coordinating, 217
  regulations, 94
  relationships between different elements of
    city, 79
  residential, 81
  satellite images of, 83
  sexually oriented businesses, 95
  site conditions, 85
  site plan review, 94
  special-needs housing, 95
  subdivision regulations, 94
  supply, analyzing, 85–86
  transportation and, 80
  urban design and, 80, 187
  urban development guided by, 78–79
  zoning, 90–93, 251
Land Use, Transportation, Air Quality
    (LUTRAQ), 153
land use planner, 287
Latin America, 263–266
Le Corbusier (architect), 306
leapfrog development, 208

LEED (Leadership in Energy and Environmental
    Design)
  certification, 286
  overview, 186–187
  standards, 117
legal requirements
  overview, 45–47
  updating plan to meet, 72
  zoning, 91
L'Enfant, Pierre Charles (designed Washington,
    D.C.), 303
Lermer, Jamie (former mayor of Curitiba,
    Brazil), 190
level of service (LOS) ratings, 128
Levittown, New Jersey, 107
libraries, 174
light rail, 124
Lincoln Institute for Land Policy, 323
linear parks, 160
local agencies and departments involved in
    disaster planning, 226
local buses, 123
local business and property owners, 55
local comprehensive plans, 227
local economy, supporting, 19
local government
  and community organizations as source for
    learning more about our community, 271
  employment opportunities in, 289
  planners and officials, 52–53
local policies for managing urban sprawl, 219–221
local resources, using, 184–185
local streets, 122
location-efficient land use patterns, 183
lofts and industrial conversions, 198
Logle, John (mayor of Grand Rapids,
    Michigan), 314
London, England, 133
long-term, building communities for, 221
Los Angeles, California, 202
LOS ratings, 128
lot coverage and placement, 137
low-density development, 208
low-density multifamily housing, 101–102
LULUs (locally unwanted land uses), 95
LUTRAQ (Land Use, Transportation, Air
    Quality), 153

• *M* •

major projects and attractions, developing,
    242–243
Manhattan, Kansas (Little Apple), 201

map resources. *See* research, data, and map resources
master plans, 11, 44, 45, 47
McHarg, Ian (landscape architect), 150
medium-density multifamily housing, 102
megacities, 41–42, 254, 255. *See also specific cities*
megaregions, 315–316
Melbourne, Australia, 69
metropolitan areas
  civic organizations, 49
  councils of governments, 49
  county governments, 48–49
  growth of, 24–26
  overview, 24, 48
  population, 24–26, 26–27
  regional plans for, 48–49
metropolitan planning organizations, 49, 215, 270
Mexico City, Mexico, 264–265
Michigan, 200, 277
migration, 86
minor arterial roadways, 121
mixed-use areas
  housing, 188
  overview, 82, 111–112
  promoting, 219
  zoning, 93
multifamily housing, 188
multi-hazards approach to disaster planning, 225
multi-modal transportation, 126
Mumbai (Bombay), India, 258–259
Murray, Katherine *(Fundraising For Dummies),* 299
Mutz, John *(Fundraising For Dummies),* 299

• *N* •

National Complete Streets Coalition, 139
National Trust for Historic Preservation, 319
natural areas, preserving, 218
natural environment, impact of city on, 79
natural hazards, 224–225
natural resources, 16, 149
natural systems restoration, 191
The Nature Conservancy, 319
neighborhood planner, 288
neighborhoods
  appearance of, 140
  development in, 140
  open spaces in, 140
  overview, 139–141
  parks, 159
  plans, 49, 50
  revitalizing, 297–298
  street pattern in, 140
  strengthening urban, 204–206

NeighborWorks America, 320
Nelessen, Anton Tony (urban designer), 145
neo-traditional design. *See* New Urbanism
New Orleans, Louisiana, 310
New Urban Network (website), 318
New Urbanism, 136
New York, New York
  Central Park, 159
  examples of urban planning, 304
  greenhouse gas emissions, reducing, 151
  land use inventory, 83, 84
  PlaNYC: A Greener, Greater New York, 312
  Port Authority of New York & New Jersey, 122
  Street Design Manual, 139
non-attainment areas, 152
non-motorized transportation, 125
nonprofit organizations
  in disaster planning, 227
  employment opportunities in, 290
Northeast megaregion, 315
The Not So Big House: A Blueprint for the Way We Really Live (Susanka), 188

• *O* •

objectionable land use, balancing community concern with, 95–96
official comprehensive plans, 11, 44, 45, 47
Olmstead, Frederick, Law (co-designer of Central Park), 159, 304
online urban plans
  America 2050: A Prospectus, 315–316
  City of Grand Rapids 2002 Master Plan, 314
  City Plan 2025, 316
  A Framework for Sustainable Resilience in the Lower Ninth Ward, 310
  GO TO 2040, 310–311
  PLANiTULSA: The Tulsa Comprehensive Plan, 313–314
  PlaNYC: A Greener, Greater New York, 312
  Richmond General Plan 2030, 311–312
  Transit Village Area Plan, 313
  2007 Dublin Community Plan, 314–315
open space
  active, 158
  in business districts, 140
  conserving, 217–218
  in neighborhoods, 140
  overview, 82, 149, 158–159
  passive, 158
  sustainable urban development, 191
  zoning, 93
owner-occupied housing, 114

• *P* •

Panama City, Florida, 233
paratransit services, 124
parking management, 132
parks and recreation, 159–160
passive open space, 158
pattern books, 146–147
pedestrians, roads and paths for, 125
Pendall, Rolf (urban planner), 208
performance spaces, 200–202
performance zoning, 93
Philadelphia, Pennsylvania, 203, 277
physical recovery post-disaster, 235
Piedmont Atlantic megaregion, 315
pipelines, 127
pipes, 169
Pittsburgh, Pennsylvania, 124–125, 197, 204
place attachment, 142
plan implementation matrix, 67–68
Planetizen (website), 289, 318
PLANiTULSA: The Tulsa Comprehensive Plan
    (online urban plan), 313–314
planned manufacturing districts, 251
Planners Network, 318
planning actions, 66–67
planning board, 52, 275–277
planning charrettes, 273
planning commission, 52, 275–277
Planning Commissioners Journal (website), 318
planning department, 52, 270
planning director or manager, 287
PlaNYC: A Greener, Greater New York (online
    urban plan), 312
pocket parks, 160
pollution
    environmental degradation due to, 39
    transit operations, pollution due to, 129–130
poor-quality design, 209
population
    in central cities, 24
    change, 10
    decrease, 26–27, 28
    fastest-growing cities, 28
    future land use demand affected by changes
        in, 86
    growth of, 23
    Hispanic population, 31
    jobs and economic development affected
        by, 239
    in metropolitan areas, 24–26
    overview, 23–24
    by race, 31

slow growth trend in 15 largest cities, 27
    trends in, 23–29
    urban, 40–42
population growth, 19–20
Port Authority of New York & New Jersey, 122
Portland, Oregon
    LUTRAQ (Land Use, Transportation, Air
        Quality), 153
    urban growth boundary in, 207
ports, 127
post-disaster recovery, 231–235
preliminary planning, 57–60
preservation of environment. *See* conservation
    and preservation of environment
private consulting firms, employment
    opportunities in, 290
professional and educational organizations
    American Institute of Architects (AIA), 317
    American Planning Association (APA), 317
    American Society of Landscape Architects
        (ASLA), 317
    Association of Collegiate Schools of Planning
        (ACSP), 318
    Canadian Institute of Planners (CIP), 318
    Planners Network, 318
professional credentials, obtaining, 286–287
professional urban planners
    accredited degree programs for, 284–286
    careers in urban planning, 284–290
    communication skills of, 284
    community development planner, 288
    day-to-day operations, handling, 281–282
    development projects, carrying out, 281
    duties of, 280–282
    economic development planner, 288
    education and training for, 284–287
    employment opportunities for, 289–290
    environmental planner, 288
    general planner, 287
    Geographic Information Systems (GIS)
        specialist, 288
    historic preservation planner, 288
    housing planner, 288
    information, providing and analyzing, 283
    international development planner, 288
    land use planner, 287
    local government, employment opportunities
        in, 289
    managing the planning process, 283
    nonprofit organizations, employment
        opportunities in, 290
    overview, 279–282
    patterns of community change, understanding,
        282–283

planning director or manager, 287
preparing urban plans, 280–281
private consulting firms, employment
    opportunities in, 290
professional credentials, obtaining, 286–287
skills needed by, 282–284
specialization, areas of, 287–288
technical skills of, 283
transportation planner, 287
urban designer, 288
urban planner, 287
Project for Public Spaces (PPS), 319
property tax abatements, 250
public facilities zones, 93
public hearings, attending, 271–273
public meetings, attending, 271–273
public participation
    architects, 54
    civil and transportation engineers, 54
    community, collecting and analyzing data on, 61
    community design, 144–146
    community stakeholders, 55–56
    demographers, 55
    economists, 55
    environmental scientists and engineers, 54
    federal government, 53
    feedback, 66
    government agencies, 53–54
    lawyers, 55
    local government planners and officials, 52–53
    overview, 51–52
    in planning goals, 65–66
    in planning objectives, 65–66
    real-estate development consultants, 55
    state government, 53
    tourism and marketing experts, 55
    urban planning consultants, 54
public safety, 172–173
public services. See infrastructure and public
    services
public transportation systems, 123–125

race, population by, 31
rail service, 124, 126
railroads, 127
rapid growth, managing, 255
real-estate development consultants, 55
reasons communities make urban plans, 44–47
Reconnecting America, 321
recreational areas, 149, 296–297
redevelopment, 187

A Region at Risk (Island Press), 49
regional parks and preserves, 159–160
regional plans
    for metropolitan areas, 48–49
    overview, 17–18, 48
    and sustainable development resources,
        319–320
    urban sprawl, regional plans to manage,
        214–219
regions, 140–141
regulations
    conservation and preservation of
        environment, 150, 162
    land use, 94
    subdivision, 94
relocations, 244
renter-occupied housing, 114
Report Card for America's Infrastructure, 321
research, data, and map resources
    American Community Survey, 322–323
    Brookings Institution's Metropolitan Policy
        Program, 323
    Esri, 323
    Google Earth, 323
    Google SketchUp, 323
    HUDUSER, 323
    Lincoln Institute for Land Policy, 323
    Urban Land Institute, 323
    U.S. Census, 323
residential areas
    housing, 108–112
    land use, 81, 88
    medical care facilities, 105
residential zones, 92
residents, 55
resilient communities, 18
resource conservation, 117–118
Retrofitting Suburbia: Urban Design Solution for
    Redesigning Suburbs (Dunham-Jones and
    Williamson), 220
revitalizing downtown areas, 196–198
Richmond, California, 311–312
Richmond General Plan 2030 (online urban
    plan), 311–312
The Rise of the Creative Class (Florida), 200
roadways
    collector streets, 121–122
    construction and maintenance of, 210
    local streets, 122
    minor arterial, 121
    overview, 121–122
    principal arterial, 121
    tolls, 132–133
Rome, Italy, 301–302

• S •

safe and clean, making community, 205
Safe Drinking Water Act, 154
safe growth, promoting, 230–231
San Diego, California, 213
San Francisco, California, 31–33
Sante Fe, New Mexico, 169
São Paulo, Brazil, 265–266
Savannah, Georgia, 302–303
scattered development, 208
schools, 173, 245
Schwab, Jim (safe-growth audit), 231
Seattle, Washington
    greenhouse gas emissions, reduction of, 183
    neighborhood plans, 49
Section 8 housing program, 106
seismic hazards, 224
sense of place, creating, 142–143
service areas, 176
services and amenities, improving, 206
sewer services. *See* water and sewer services
sexually oriented businesses, 95
Shanghai, China, 257–258
Shepard Davern district (St. Paul, Minnesota),
    50–51
short-term recovery, 233–234
single-use areas, 209
site conditions, 85
site locations, 176
site plan review, 94
site selection, 243
skills needed by professional urban planners,
    282–284
slow growth trend in cities, 27
slums, improving, 255
small parks, 160
smaller houses, 188
smart growth
    improving your community, smart growth
        approach for, 298–299
    overview, 212–213
    urban sprawl, smart growth approach to curb,
        212–213
Smart Growth America, 319
social and economic opportunities,
    increasing, 206
social development, supporting, 256
Social Entrepreneurship For Dummies (Durieux
    and Stebbins), 275, 299
social recovery, post-disaster, 235

social services, 174, 206
solid waste disposal and recycling, 171–172
special districts, 50
special place, making community a, 297
specialized plans
    for cities and towns, 47–48
    downtown plans, 50
    hazard-mitigation planning, 228
    to manage urban sprawl, 215
    neighborhood plans, 50
    overview, 44
    special districts, 50
specialized public transit, 124–125
special-needs housing
    adult care, 104
    assisted living for the elderly, 105
    emergency housing, 105
    group homes, 104
    housing shelters, 105
    land use for, 95
    overview, 104–105
    residential medical care facilities, 105
    transitional housing, 105
special-purpose districts, 172
sprawling cities. *See* urban sprawl
St. Paul, Minnesota, 50–51
startup companies, 243, 246
state government, 53, 245
state-to-state migration, 87
statewide plans and goals to manage urban
    sprawl, 214
Stebbins, Robert A. *(Social Entrepreneurship For
    Dummies)*, 275, 299
steering committees, 274
steps for creating and using an urban plan
    adopting plan, 70
    carrying out plan, 70
    community, understanding the, 60–63
    coordinating goals and strategies, 67–68
    evaluating plan, 69
    implementing plan, 69, 70
    monitoring progress, 71–72
    overview, 57
    planning actions, 66–67
    planning goals, 64–66
    planning objectives, 65–66
    planning strategies, 66–67
    preliminary planning, 57–60
    starting over with new plan, 73
    updating plan, 70, 72
    vision statement, creating, 63–64

Stewart, Potter (U.S. Supreme Court Justice), 145
storm water, 171
strategic plans, 48
street blocks, 138–140
Street Design Manual, 139
streets, 138–140
Streetsblog (website), 318
streetscape elements, 139
structural hazards, 225
sub-area plans, 47
subdivision regulations, 94
subsidized housing, 106–107
substations and storage, energy, 167
suburban areas
  retrofitting, 220
  subdivisions, 109–110
subways, 124
suitability analysis, 154–155
supply lines, 167
support services, deciding on, 59
Surface Transportation Policy Partnership, 321
Susanka, Sarah *(The Not So Big House: A
    Blueprint for the Way We Really Live),* 188
sustainability, 136
sustainable urban development
  bio-regional plans, 194
  buying local, 185
  climate change
    adapting to, 184
    buildings, creating more energy efficient, 184
    energy use, improving, 183
    greenhouse gas emissions, reducing, 183–184
    industry, promoting green business
      practices for, 184
    overview, 183
    vehicle emissions, reducing, 183
  community indicators and report cards, 193
  Curitiba, Brazil as model of, 190
  ecological footprint analysis, 192–193
  ecological restoration, 191
  economy as element of, 182
  encouraging, 143
  energy resources, developing alternative, 185
  environment as element of, 182
  equity (social) as element of, 182
  food systems, supporting local, 185
  green buildings, 186–187
  green maps, 193–194
  greenprints, 190–192
  habitats and corridors, 191
  housing, planning for greener, 187–188
  infrastructure, 189
  land use, planning for greener, 187
  LEED (Leadership in Energy and
    Environmental Design), 186–187
  local resources, using, 184–185
  natural systems restoration, 191
  open spaces, 191
  overview, 16, 181–182
  planning for, 182–191
  tools for, 192–194
  transportation, 188–189
  urban agriculture, 191
  urban forestry, 191
SWOT approach for analyzing information on
    community, 62

● *T* ●

Talen, Emily (urban planning professor), 140
tax incentives for jobs and economic
    development, 250
technical skills of professional urban
    planners, 283
technological hazards, 225
technological innovations, 11
telecommunications, 171
terrorism, 225
Texas Triangle, 216
topical plans, 48
Toronto, Canada, 199
tourism, promoting, 201
town plans. *See* urban plans
towns. *See* cities and towns
traditional neighborhoods, 108–109
traffic flow and layout, 138
traffic management, 131–133, 256
trail systems, 160
training for professional urban planners,
    284–287
transect planning, 140–141
transit village, 134
Transit Village Area Plan (online urban plan), 313
transitional housing, 105
transit-oriented development, 134, 189, 219
transportation
  accessibility, 128–129
  car-free zones, 189
  commercial, 125–127
  connecting places by multiple means of, 142
  environmental impact, 120, 129–130, 133–134

transportation *(continued)*
  evaluating, 127–130
  green alternatives, 188–189
  and infrastructure resources, 320–321
  intelligent transportation systems (ITS), 131–132
  intermodal, 126
  and land use, 80, 120
  local plan for, 130–131
  LOS ratings, 128
  management programs, 132–133
  multi-modal, 126
  needs of community, meeting, 128–129
  non-motorized transportation, 125
  overview, 119–121, 129–130
  pollution due to transit operations, 129–130
  promoting transportation alternatives, 188
  public transportation systems, 123–125
  reducing trips using motorized, 133–134
  roadways, 121–122
  sustainable urban development, 188–189
  system, creating a good, 294
  traffic management, 131–133
  transit-oriented development (TOD), 189
  vehicle emissions, reducing, 183
transportation planner, 287
Transportation Research Board, 321
treatment and storage facilities, 169
trucking and warehousing, 126
Trust for Public Land, 320
Tulsa, Oklahoma, 313–314
2007 Dublin Community Plan (online urban plan), 314–315

• U •

unintended consequences, updating plan as response to, 72
United Nations, 324
updating plan, 70, 72
urban agriculture, 191
urban design
  architectural styles, using diverse and complementary, 141–142
  buildings, 137
  business districts, 139–141
  cities and regions, 140–141
  community, sense of, 136
  community design, 144–147
  connecting places by multiple means of transportation, 142

districts, 146
elements of, 136–141
functionality, 136
and historic preservation resources, 319
land use
  guiding, 78–79
  mixing multiple land uses, 142
lots, 137
neighborhoods, 139–141
overview, 135–136
role of, 135–136
sense of place, creating, 142–143
street blocks, 137–138
streets, 138–139
sustainability, 136, 143
visually appealing and user-friendly, making places, 141–142
and zoning, 187
urban designer, 288
urban environment
  conservation areas, 155–158
  ecological resources, 151–155
  open space, 158–159
  parks and recreation, 159–160
urban forestry, 191
urban geographies, 38–39
urban growth boundaries, 207, 217
Urban Land Institute, 323
urban open space, 158
urban planner, 287
urban planning consultants, 54
urban plans. *See also* global urban planning
  challenges for, 15–20
  components of, 12–15
  creating, 11–12
  disasters, helping cities before and after, 18
  economic trends, 10
  environmental component of, 11, 14–15
  examples of, 302–308
  housing component of, 13
  improving your community, 20–21
  infrastructure and services component of, 15
  land use component of, 13
  local economy, supporting, 19
  older cities, renewing, 16–17
  online, 311–316
  overview, 10–11
  people, involving, 12
  population change, 10, 19–20
  reasons communities make, 44–47

sprawling cities, dealing with, 17–18
suburban areas, 10
sustainable, making cities and towns, 16
technological innovations, 11
transportation component of, 13–14
types of, 11, 43–44
urban design component of, 14
urban population
  global, 40–42
  megacities, increase in, 41–42
  by world region, 41
urban revitalization
  adaptive reuse, 203–204
  affordable housing, promoting, 205
  arts and culture, 199–202
  clean and safe, making community, 205
  community development, 204–206
  cultural amenities, 200
  downtown areas, 196–198
  historic preservation, 202–204
  neighborhoods, strengthening urban, 204–206
  new development, stimulating, 205
  overview, 16–17, 195–196
  performance spaces, 200–202
  services and amenities, improving, 206
  social and economic opportunities, increasing, 206
  social services, expanding, 206
  tourism, promoting, 201
  waterfront areas, 199
urban service areas, 177, 217
urban service boundaries, 177
urban services, providing, 255
urban sprawl
  automobiles, dependence on, 209
  characteristics of, 208–209
  community, loss of a sense of, 211
  consequences of, 209–211
  employment, access to, 211
  environmental impact of, 210
  health issues associated with, 211
  identifying where future development will and won't take place, 215
  land use, regionally coordinating, 217
  leapfrog development, 208
  local policies for managing, 219–221
  low-density development, 208
  open space, conserving, 217–218
  overview, 17–18, 38–39, 208–209
  poor-quality design, 209

priority funding areas, designating, 218–219
public resources, effect on, 210–211
public services, duplication of, 211
regional comprehensive plans to manage, 214
regional strategies used to manage, 214–219
roads and highways, construction and maintenance of, 210
single-use areas, 209
smart growth approach to curb, 212–213
social issues associated with, 211
specialized regional plans to manage, 215
statewide plans and goals to manage, 214
urban villages, 198
U.S. Army Corps of Engineers, 322
U.S. Census, 271, 323
U.S. Department of Housing and Urban Development (HUD), 118
U.S. Geological Survey (USGS), 322
U.S. government agencies, list of, 321–322
U.S. Green Building Council (USGBC), 186, 320
utilities and services
  disaster planning, involvement in, 226
  energy resources, 166–167
  overview, 166
  solid waste disposal and recycling, 171–172
  special-purpose districts, 172
  telecommunications, 171
  water and sewer services, 167–171

Van der Ryn, Sim (ecologist), 143
Vancouver, Canada, 307
Vaux, Calvert (co-designer of Central Park), 159, 304
vehicle emissions, reducing, 183
vision statement, 63–64
visually appealing and user-friendly, making places, 141–142

Walk Score (website), 115–116
walking, roads and paths for, 125
Washington, D.C., 303–304
wastewater, 170
water and sewer services
  availability of water, 170
  combined sewer system, 171

water and sewer services *(continued)*
  domestic wastewater, 170
  drainage facilities, 171
  industrial wastewater, 170
  on-site water supplies, 169
  overview, 167
  pipes, 169
  sources of water, 168
  storm water, 171
  treatment and storage facilities, 169
  wastewater, 170
water resources, 154
water use neutral, 169
waterfront areas, 199
websites. *See* Internet resources
wetlands, 156–157
Wheeler, Stephen (urban planning
  researcher), 130

wildland urban interface (WUI), 158
Williamson, June *(Retrofitting Suburbia:*
  Urban Design Solution for Redesigning
  Suburbs), 220
windshield surveys, 115
workforce development, 247
working landscapes, 158
World Bank's Urban Development program, 324
world region, urban population by, 41

● *Z* ●

Zipcar, 134
zoning, 90–93
zoning variance, 276

Printed and bound by CPI Group (UK) Ltd, Croydon, CR0 4YY

11/05/2023

03217835-0001